The Sugar Control Bible and Cookbook

The Complete Nutrition Guide to Revitalizing Your Health

The Sugar Control Bible and Cookbook

The Complete Nutrition Guide to Revitalizing Your Health

By Dr. Jacqueline Paltis, D.C., N.D.

The Sugar Control Program is intended to be used under the supervision of a TBM physician so that the Program can be tailored for individual needs. The diet presented here is not designed for anyone with kidney problems, Parkinson's Disease, for pregnant women or women trying to become pregnant, or for athletes. If you are on medication, have diabetes, high blood pressure or any cardiovascular disease or problem, or have had a heart attack in the past year, do not attempt this program without a doctor's supervision. No one should begin a diet or fitness program without consulting a physician first.

Figures 2.1 and 2.2 are used by permission of Dr. Kurt Donsbach. They originally appeared in Oral Chelation Therapy. Rosarto Beach, Baja California, Mexico: Wholistic Publishers. ©*1988.*

Dr. Jacqueline L. Paltis
New Energy Dynamics
POB 963
Greensburg PA 15601

Publisher's Cataloging-in-Publication
(Provided by Quality Books, Inc.)

Paltis, Jacqueline.
　　The sugar control bible and cookbook : the complete
nutrition guide to revitalizing your health / by Jacqueline
Paltis. -- 1 st ed.
　　p. cm.
　　Includes bibliographical references and index.

　　1. Low-carbohydrate diet. 2. Low-carbohydrate diet--
Recipes. 3. Sugar in the body. 4. Sugar-free diet--Recipes
I. Title

RM237.73.P35 1998　　　　　613.2'6
　　　　　　　　　　　　　　　QBI98-333

Published in the United States of America. 10 9 8 7 6 5

To My Husband, Sam

Contents

ABBREVIATIONS AND SYMBOLS USED IN THIS BOOK

C	8 ounce cup	lb	pound, dry
oz	ounce	qt	quart, liquid
tsp	teaspoon	T	tablespoon
[brackets]			optional ingredient/procedure

Title Case (capital letters)— a recipe included in the **Cookbook**, e.g. Chicken Broth

Acknowledgments

I gratefully acknowledge those who have been inspirational and instrumental in bringing this book from the germ of an idea to fruition.

To Drs. Victor and Diane Frank, who developed the program and then let me run with it.

To my many patients who followed the Sugar Control Program under my supervision, who shared their stories with me and their process, and who kept asking me for strategies and recipes, and who then took the recipes and tried them out.

To the anonymous Apple Performa and Microsoft Word technical support staffs, who sometimes talked to me at 2 A.M., and who sometimes had the answers and sometimes didn't.

To the Q-Link, which made me stop procrastinating after two years and write the book.

To my husband Sam Wieder, who tried the recipes as a diner and chef, who cheered me on and edited the output, who listened to my rantings and ravings, and kept cheering anyway. I love you.

❖ ⌘ ❖

INTRODUCTION

❖ ⌘ ❖

I first set my foot on the road to writing this book in 1968. I had been relatively healthy most of my life. I had the occasional case of tonsillitis and the typical childhood diseases. Then, after my first flu shot in 1968, I began to have cold after cold. I had never actually had the flu. They were just giving free flu shots and I thoughtlessly had one. Within three hours I had the flu. I became so ill, I couldn't care for myself. I had to call my family to come and get me. For the next ten days, I was semi-conscious most of the time. My parents took me to a local internist who denied that the flu shot had had anything to do with my illness (it was just a coincidence) and promptly gave me penicillin. The penicillin, of course, did nothing beneficial since I did not have a bacterial infection.

When I finally recovered enough to be able to return to work, it still took me several weeks to recover from the bronchial congestion and to regain my strength. After that, I began having one cold after another, frequently losing my voice and going into bronchitis. I would get the flu more than once per season. It was not fun.

During one particularly virulent bout, my doctor first recommended over-the-counter Robitussin. When I cracked a rib coughing, he prescribed codeine. The codeine did knock me out enough to get some sleep and reduce the cough. However, the codeine was so constipating that it gave me hemorrhoids. And on and on. Every time, I took a prescription medication, I would get a display of new symptoms unrelated to the original problem.

Somewhere during this time frame, I had had a summer job with Pfizer Pharmaceuticals. I worked in the you-should-excuse-me "ethical" drugs division as a copy editor. Among other tasks, I was responsible for keeping the Physician's Desk Reference (PDR) articles up-to-date.   The PDR is a compilation of manufacturer-produced medico-legal articles about each drug they make. Each article includes the drug's chemical structure, how it works (if they know or think they do), what it's used for, and the dosages prescribed. It also includes warnings, contraindications, side-effects, and negative results that have occurred with the drug.

In addition, I was responsible for editing monographs written by doctors testing drugs in hospital or clinical settings on human subjects.   I was astounded to discover that very often the testing would be on seven subjects.   One recovered, two showed improvements with some side effects, one had no response, two had serious side effects and had to be removed from the drug, and one died. On the basis of a few studies of that nature, often sponsored by the manufacturer, the drug could get FDA approval.   And once approved for use in one condition, it could be prescribed for any condition.

After several drugs prescribed during pregnancy were dramatically linked to birth defects, many drugs were declared unsafe for women who might be pregnant.   That had to be translated as all women in their child-bearing years who were sexually active.   At that time, there was no way you could be sure you were pregnant until about the sixth week, by which time enormous damage can be done to the embryo (and especially to its developing central nervous system) by drugs.

Because of all this, I started seriously reconsidering my own use of prescription drugs.

I was in the pharmacy one day waiting for a prescription and the pharmacist, hearing my cough and sinus congestion, suggested that I try vitamin C. I was skeptical, but ready for something different than drugs.   I had learned in school that vitamin C cured scurvy. I didn't really know what that was, except that it affected the gums and sailors got it on long voyages. And what did that have to do with curing a cold anyway?

But he was, after all, a pharmacist. He must know. He carried the whole line of Schiff vitamins.   I had never seen that in a pharmacy before. I took the vitamin C, alternating 500 mg of vitamin C with two aspirins every thirty minutes. By the next day, I was better. I continued to take 500 mg of vitamin C every day for many years and stayed healthy. I also noticed that I didn't bruise as easily as before and cuts and other wounds healed very rapidly.

That was the beginning of my interest in nutrition and natural healing.

Another major marker on the road came in 1970, when I became involved with Buckminster Fuller's World Game project.   The World Game players I knew were interested in Adele Davis's nutrition book *Let's Eat Right To Keep Fit*.   I knew about nutrition, of course: vitamin A deficiency causes night blindness, B1 deficiency causes beriberi, and calcium deficiency causes rickets and makes children eat chalk (pica), vitamin

C deficiency causes scurvy. But what could nutrition have to do with being fit? So I read Adele Davis, and at the same time started taking a morning toddy that we called Rocky Road. It was a mix of orange juice, powdered milk, liver powder, yeast powder, sunflower seeds, kelp, lecithin granules, wheat germ and honey. Within two months, Rocky Road cured my lifelong constipation (which I had not even known was a problem).

In 1968, I had had a bad bout of food poisoning which left me with a mild but painful, annoying and inconvenient case of irritable bowel. So I was either constipated or had painful diarrhea. After inflicting some very painful tests on me, my doctor offered a diagnosis but no solution. In 1972, following Davis's suggestion, I started to take calcium supplements. Within two days, the problem was cured and I finally became a true believer in the power of nutrition.

As a child and teen-ager, I was pretty much a normal size in terms of weight. During the year, I would usually vary between a size 10 and a 12. (This was before the current craze for anorexic women and the resizing of garments to 1, 3, and 5.) I would gain five pounds in the winter and lose it in the summer. Back then, pin-up girl Betty Grable was still supposed to be a perfect size 12. But somehow I was made to feel fat.

I started dieting when I was about 14 years old. I don't remember the order, but there was Weight Watchers, and then chocolate-flavored Metrecal (which actually turned into Fudgsicles—how could you tell the difference?). And then my mother took me to her diet doctor, and by the age of 16, I was taking prescription uppers to lose weight and downers to sleep.

Every time I lost weight, I would gradually gain it back plus a little bit more. So by the time I graduated college, I was 25 pounds overweight. By then I was also taking birth control pills.

When I started to work full-time in publishing, I went back to the amphetamine diet doctor and took amphetamines on and off for several years. I looked great but my endocrine system was taking quite a beating, like in the old Timex commercial: "Take's a licking and keeps on ticking"—only more slowly and erratically.

In the late 60's and early 70's, there was the Stillman Diet (or the Scarsdale Diet) and the Drinking Man's Diet—both based on high-protein and virtually nothing else. I tried Stillman once for a week and lost nine pounds, but it was very boring and I felt like I was being punished. I wasn't much of a drinker, so the Drinking Man's Diet didn't interest me. However, the Ice Cream Diet certainly did.

Around 1974, Dr. Robert Atkins published *The Diet Revolution*. The Atkins' Diet (which is back in favor again) changed my life and thinking in many ways. The diet program is based on high-protein/low-carbohydrate, moderate fats, and frequent feeding, eating as much as you want. The dieter uses test strips to measure ketones[1] in the urine. By gradually increasing carbohydrate intake by 5 gms per day each week and measuring urinary ketones with the test strips, the dieter can discover his or her individual tolerance for carbohydrates. This is the only diet plan in which I had ever succeeded. I lost weight. I had plenty of energy. The food was delicious. Sweet cravings disappeared. I could eat in restaurants. I never felt deprived. And I could think and function well. My serum cholesterol and triglyceride levels (both high) dropped to normal.

But something else happened as well. By that time, I was married to my now-ex-husband, and he suffered from mood and energy swings—the adult version of hyperactivity. Think of a Robin Williams character, and please, don't believe the doctor who tells you your child will outgrow hyperactivity. My husband was diagnosed with learning disabilities along with concentration problems—which we were just beginning to understand—and he was trying to complete a Ph.D.

When I went on the Atkins' Diet, my ex decided to try the diet with me to see what I had to put up with. (Where was he for all the torture diets?) He was in heaven. His moods and energy levels were much more even. He felt in control of himself, and his concentration improved. Then we went to a friend's for lunch. Our friend loved food. When we got to her house, we found her 54-inch round country oak dining table buried under a display of exotic foods of all sorts. My husband walked in and helped himself to a very sweet chutney. He almost passed out. He was faint and dizzy and had to lie down for half an hour, while we fed him protein.

This was an alarming reaction, so we went to a top diabetes doctor, who ordered three days of carbohydrate loading followed by a 6-hour glucose tolerance test (GTT). On one of the three days, my husband went to a Viennese bakery for an éclair. It was late afternoon—usually a hypoglycemic's lowest point of the day. He walked out of the bakery straight into the glare of the sun setting in a fiery ball over the Hudson river. He couldn't see straight. He was literally drunk on sugar. He was traveling by bicycle and couldn't keep his balance. He finally found a Checker cab big enough to load the bike into, so he could get home.

His GTT test results were so low and so bizarre that the doctor wanted to put him in the hospital to test for pancreatic tumors. There were none. He was just a severely reactive hypoglycemic on a sugar and high-carbohydrate binge. Six months on a high-protein frequent-feeding diet improved the numbers tremendously. But he had to remain on the program to be able to function well. When he ate artificially sweetened food, he would

---

[1] Ketones are chemicals produced in the body as a product of burning fat. Ketosis occurs when there are insufficient carbodydrates to burn off the ketones. Diabetic ketosis is a disease state. But mild ketosis may be the normal state for many people.

have the same "sugar" reaction while the food was still in his mouth, before he had even swallowed it. So he had to avoid artificial sweeteners as well.

Through our connections with the learning disabilities groups ACLD[2] and The Orton Society, I was also peripherally involved with a non-residential private school for hyperactive and learning-disabled children. A requirement of the school was that each student be on the Feingold Diet. This diet prohibits any white flours or white starches, white sugars, food colorings, preservatives and other chemicals. In the beginning, foods containing natural salicylates, the compound in aspirin, are also prohibited until it can be determined whether the child is allergic to them.

The family was asked to go on the program with the child. The school said that this was to help and support the child. But the school knew that at least one of the parents probably had the same problems as the child. The parent would discover the connection when his or her symptoms disappeared while following the diet.

What happened more often was that the child would soon experience how much better s/he felt. Once the child saw the connection between diet and behavior, s/he usually had no problem adhering to the program. Deals had to be made with the parents, however. Mom could hide her chocolate cake under the bed and eat it after the child was asleep. Or Dad could keep his candy stash in the trunk of the car. The program worked very well except on the day after Halloween when the school was empty of children. The phone would ring off the hook with parents calling to say, "Johnny can't come to school today, because he's climbing the walls."

Other anecdotes included one where an eight-year-old child tested as being allergic to natural gas. The family apartment had a gas stove. The parents were so serious about helping their child that they paid to have the gas stove and gas lines removed and an electric stove installed in their rental apartment. The child improved—and within three days the mother's migraines disappeared. Another child who had seizures as well as hyperactivity and learning problems ceased having the seizures while on the diet. The seizure problem was eventually isolated to calcium propionate—a food additive.

At the same time this was happening, friends of mine opened a halfway house for schizophrenics. Their son had Tourette's syndrome—a multiple tic disorder. And the only effective control they had found was the Feingold Diet and megavitamin therapy. Their large Berkshires home became a half-way house between institutionalization and society. The residents were mostly teen-agers and young adults. They were placed on the Feingold Diet and megavitamin therapy and removed from their prescription (and

---

[2] Association for Children with Learning Disabilities was organized by parents as a self-help group.

non-prescription) psychoactive drugs. As long as they followed the diet, the great majority of them did very well.

In the spirit of the philosophy that says you don't see what you don't believe, western "scientific" medicine would say that these histories are only anecdotal and prove nothing. And until very recently, the official AMA position has been that nutrition has nothing to do with disease.

My point of view is that the anecdotal evidence is overwhelmingly in favor of nutrition being a cornerstone of good health and optimal functioning. And there are no side effects to good nutrition. The scientific studies are plentiful as well, but medicine usually rejects such studies. Now that American medicine has begun to embrace nutrition, medically sponsored researchers are doing their own studies. They translate them into medical language and use the active ingredient of a particular substance. Active ingredients are patentable and therefore cost much more than the vitamins you're used to. They rediscover the power of nutrition and take the credit for this "new" information. But that usually takes 10-15 years. I would rather experiment with good nutrition on myself than lose my life and my joy, waiting for someone to prove it scientifically later.

All of these experiences and many others have brought me over the years to the Sugar Control Program, which was put together by Dr. Victor Frank, the co-founder with Dr. Hal Havlik, of the Total Body Modification (TBM) chiropractic technique, with important input from several sources, including Dr. John C. Thie and the many TBM doctors all over the world involved in TBM's clinical research.

This book itself was actually written for my many patients and students who over the last ten years have begged me for recipes, menus, and survival tips, to help them turn their lives around. I hope it helps you as well.

Dr. Jacqueline Paltis
Greensburg, PA
April 20, 1997

❖ ⌘ ❖

CHAPTER 1—LIFE STYLE AND DISEASE

The Causes of Chronic Disease

❖ ⌘ ❖

Mood Swings	PMS	Rashes
Poor Concentration	Memory Loss	Chronic Fatigue
Headaches	Spaciness	Arthritis
Sugar Cravings	Vaginitis	Irritability
Menstrual Problems	High Cholesterol	High Triglycerides
Obesity	Fibromyalgia	Frequent Colds
Diabetes Mellitus	Yeast Infections	Running Ear
Depression	Low Libido	Joint and Muscle Pains
Allergies	Epilepsy	Low Back Pain
High Blood Pressure	Migraine	Cardiovascular Disease
Hyperactivity	ADD	Learning Disabilities

If you have some or all of the above symptoms or illnesses, and they are making your life miserable, I wrote this book for you. If you are sick and tired of feeling sick and tired, if you are ready to take control of your life and feel well again (or for the first time), I wrote this book for you. If you are well and are looking for ways of staying well, I wrote this book for you.

My goal is to show you evidence—scientific, clinical and anecdotal—that these dis-eases and conditions are nutritionally based; to show you how today's popular high-carbohydrate/low-fat/low-cholesterol diets have actually made all of these problems worse; and to show you how TBM's Sugar Control Program can bring your body and your mind back to normal functioning and guide you to a healthier lifelong eating style. If you are like me, you will want to know what the Sugar Control Program is before you read any further. So, if you can't wait, the program is outlined on page 104 in Chapter 11.

What Is TBM?

Total Body Modification[3] is a chiropractic technique co-founded by Dr. Victor Frank in the 1970's. It is rooted in old-time chiropractic thinking, applied kinesiology, acupuncture and suble electromagnetic energies, and the concepts of functional physiology. Functional physiology is a term I think you will be hearing more often. Physiology is the study of how the body works. Most current medical thinking is based on cadaver physiology. If the living body functioned the same way as a dead one, it would be dead too. Functional physiology is the complex interaction of all aspects of the body from the cellular level up, involving communication, feedback, cell memory, etc.

The human organism has several levels of functioning. But, a major priority system is the sympathetic nervous system, which controls the "fight or flight" reaction. This system is designed for survival. When you are suddenly faced with a lion in the jungle, or with the sight of your son pinned under the wheel of your car, the fight or flight system mobilizes your physical resources, largely through the function of the adrenal cortex, which secretes epinephrine and norepinephrine. It overrides parasympathetic functions of digestion, thinking, muscle repair, cellular healing, etc., and sends your blood supply to your heart and large skeletal muscles, so that you can run, fight, or lift the car with your bare hands.

This same system that protects us so well in emergencies, has not yet adapted, however, to life in the twenty-first century United States. The stresses of today's life style are not the occasional lion emergency, but are instead the constant barrage of overwork, deadlines, car pools, noise, pollution, keeping your mouth shut when your supervisor gets on your case unreasonably, and commuting on LA freeways during rush hour (which can actually sometimes be the equivalent of meeting several lions in the jungle).

In these circumstances, the sympathetic system is "on" all the time, putting a constant strain and drain on the adrenal glands. If the body has an internal problem that it can't fix and the problem is not immediately life-threatening, the brain will wall off the problem and forget about it, in favor of the perpetual emergency.

TBM doctors seek to restore balance and harmony to the human system, essentially to switch the lights back on, balance sympathetic function with parasympathetic function, and reconnect the brain and body control centers with the problem, so the body can remember to heal itself.

Many of us live in fight of flight day in and day out, never really relaxing. When you spend your day like this, there are two ways to get your body to switch over to the balancing parasympathetic side of the autonomic nervous system (to allow for rest, relaxation and repair). One way is to eat a large high-carbohydrate meal. The other way is to do mild, steady exercise for about 30 minutes. There are also some specific breathing techniques that work. Which way do you usually choose?

---

[3] To locate a TBM practitioner in your area, call the TBM office at 801-571-2411, FAX: 801-576-0806 or e-mail: Health@TBMseminars.com

Symptoms

Do you know anyone (maybe even yourself?) who gets sick if s/he takes a vacation? This is actually a healthy response to constant stress. The body's computer decides to use the vacation as down time to activate the Empty Trash command. The body starts to detoxify. But because we have been taught to look at detoxification symptoms as disease—we think we are sick.

Actually, symptoms are evidence that the body is mounting an immune response—they are signs of health and should be encouraged and supported rather than suppressed. Fever, for example, is a defense the body creates to kill harmful germs. The best way to deal with fever is to drink a hot toddy, including a good dose of cayenne pepper, while taking a very hot bath. Wrap up warmly for about an hour afterwards. This will initially increase the fever, so it can do its job faster and more effectively. The body temperature will probably fall back to normal within an hour.

Chronic Degenerative Disease

Chronic degenerative diseases include arthritis, cardiovascular disease, cerebrovascular disease, cancer, AIDS, Alzheimer's, ALS, osteoporosis, lupus and the rheumatoid diseases, and multiple sclerosis, to name but a few. TBM believes that the major causes of all chronic degenerative diseases are:

- ◆ Chronic subclinical dehydration;
- ◆ Poor carbohydrate (sugar) metabolism;
- ◆ Lack of sufficient and quality rest;
- ◆ Interference from electromagnetic fields and radiation;
- ◆ Heavy-metal toxicity.

Dehydration. Water is the regulating mechanism of living systems. Without sufficient hydration, our electromagnetic systems do not function properly. These include the central and peripheral nervous systems and cellular communication, as well as the more subtle energy systems that we in the west are just beginning to understand.

Poor carbohydrate (blood sugar) metabolism is the subject of this book, and we will examine it in detail. When I speak of "sugar," I am referring to refined sugars and carbohydrates and natural and refined starches.

Rest. In true rest, the nervous system shifts to parasympathetic control. This is the regenerative phase that balances fight or flight. In this phase, healing can occur. Although the work week is shorter and we have all the modern conveniences, we Americans put in four to five more hours a day working than did our forebears in the early 1900's. And we never really allow ourselves to rest, either mentally or physically.

As a chiropractor frequently treating herniated disks, I am reminded of the riddle:

Q: What is the difference between a man and a woman climbing the ladder of success?
A: The woman is expected to put the ladder away.

I can tell a man with a herniated disk to take three days of bed rest, and he may. If I prescribe bed rest for a woman with a herniated disk, she may take time off from her outside-the-home job. But she still has a full-time job at home. If she's home, she will keep working. In the case of patients with chronic conditions, I have often written them prescriptions for five days of bed rest. They need permission to rest, because society expects them to keep going and going and going, till they fall over—just like the Energizer Bunny. But when they return to my office after five days of bed rest, they look reborn. The changes are amazing and wonderful.

Electromagnetic Fields and Radiation. We are just big electromagnets, from our nervous systems to our more subtle energies. As such, we can be negatively impacted by electrical fields and radiation. The Earth and the Cosmos have electrical and radiation fields of their own. But man has added electrical circuits, radio waves, television, microwave antennas, high-tension transmission lines, electric blankets, LED clocks, microwave ovens, computer monitors, cellular telephones, and radar. Many of these conveniences have caused degenerative diseases that have been proven; many are suspect. The government is in denial and refuses to acknowledge the scope of the situation. That makes it more difficult to remedy. There are many things that we could do to protect ourselves and keep the benefits of having harnessed electromagnetic energies (to the extent that we have). But not until we admit that there is a problem.

In the meantime, the government and military are involved in top secret projects. In Alaska, there is a program classified as H.A.A.R.P.[4] that seems to be producing symptoms in the human nervous and endocrine systems. The extreme opposition view is that these projects are responsible for the massive and widespread flood damage we have seen in the last few years, for whales beaching themselves in large numbers, for unusual earthquake activity, for airplanes and UFO's falling out of the sky, for 1998's El Nino, and that they will result in the military-industrial complex's ability to use mind control. The government and the military deny all except that it is a safe academic project to study the aurora borealis and the ionosphere as it relates to weather.

---

[4] *Angels Don't Play this Harp*: Advances in Tesla Technology by Dr. Nick Begich and Jeane Manning. EarthPulse Press, POB 20139, Anchorage, AL 99520. Phone 907-249-9111. Fax 907-696-1277. $14.95. Type nohaarp/pandora or just haarp into your Internet search engine to get information.

Heavy Metals. For many years, we have recognized the detrimental effects of lead toxicity on the developing brains of our children. Lead in paints and gasoline was outlawed years ago. Yet children are still being mentally retarded by lead paint. Lead in deteriorating water system infrastructures (the lead in the pipes of your city's water supply system) is probably leaching into your drinking water. Lead solder in tin cans gets into your system and stays there. Alzheimer's has been linked with aluminum toxicity, probably from aluminum cookware. There have been rumors and controversy about toxic problems from silver-mercury dental fillings (amalgams). In Europe, it is malpractice to put them into teeth. In the U.S., it is malpractice to remove them. Recent studies show amalgams disintegrating when exposed to radiation from computer monitors.

And parasites. I would also add parasites as a major cause of chronic degenerative disease, although you don't get parasites unless the other causes are already in operation. Americans tend to think that parasitism is rare in this country. I would estimate, however, that 80 percent of my patients have had one or more types of parasites. Parasites are difficult to diagnose using standard stool samples. Because only one stool sample in a ten-day period may contain parasites and eggs, if you don't get the right sample to the lab, the report may come back: "No parasites."

One of my patients tested positive by TBM methods for roundworms. He asked me how he could have gotten them. I asked him if he had a pet. With great love, he told me about his dog who sleeps with him. A very common route of worm infestation is the flea bite, because the flea's saliva contains parasite eggs, which it injects when it bites.

I suggested he have the dog checked out by the vet. The vet laughed. After all, what could a chiropractor know about whether a dog has parasites? He tested the dog, however, and gave him a clean bill of health. The next week the dog passed a worm ball. Now whether the man got the parasites from the dog or the dog got them from the man, I don't know. I just know parasites are very common, especially among people who are not really well. I put the dog on the same natural anti-parasite program as the man, and both of them got well together.

Testing

To evaluate a patient's health, TBM doctors may use blood and urine tests, stool samples, x-rays, CT and MRI scans, and all of the technology available to modern medicine. But the basic testing tool is the **neuromuscular reflex test**. On the simplest level, this looks like a test for muscle strength. The doctor tests the patient to find a strong muscle or muscle group to use for testing. The shoulder-arm muscle group is commonly used for convenience. The muscle is tested again, but this time the doctor or patient touches a specific body point (for example, the liver point) during the testing. If the strong muscle becomes weak while the liver point is touched, then we assume there is an imbalance in the body's functioning related to the liver. The doctor corrects the imbalance by adjusting the specific pattern of spinal misalignment associated with that point.

Neuromuscular reflex testing has been developing for over 50 years. It is based on medical kinesiology, but has been refined through Sacro-Occipital Technique and Applied Kinesiology (two well-accepted chiropractic disciplines), and acupuncture philosophy.

By using TBM techniques, practitioners around the world have helped patients recover from many different kinds of conditions. In my records there are patients who came in with medical diagnoses of conditions like hepatitis B and C, scleroderma, cirrhosis of the liver, prostatitis, prostate cancer, premenstrual syndrome, menopausal symptoms, infertility, fibroid tumors, goiter, dysplasia, allergies (including those causing anaphylactic shock), chronic fatigue syndrome, fibromyalgia, memory loss, learning disabilities, multiple sclerosis and lupus. I treated these patients with TBM. Patients are usually sent back to their medical doctors for retesting. Many of them were released from my care after their medical doctors (usually reluctantly and disbelievingly) declared them well.

I remember the day a patient diagnosed with cirrhosis of the liver secondary to hepatitis C came in with his latest blood test on a five-foot length of computer paper. The lab had repeated the test five times, because the result was negative. The patient had recovered from a disease that has no cure and the lab was sure their test results couldn't be right.

In another case, where the patient no longer tested for prostate cancer, the urologist who had diagnosed the condition originally was so upset that he sent the patient's "before" records to Cleveland Clinic for a second opinion to prove the patient did have prostate cancer. He didn't, however, send the patient or his "after" tests.

But most people just come in tired, with sinusitis, bowel and skin problems, asthma and low-grade depression, irritability, and loss of interest in sex.. Their medical doctors have offered them no help and no hope. Or they've received drug treatment and it has made them worse in a different way.

In praise of the traditional medical establishment in the U.S., let me say (God forbid!) that if I am ever in a serious accident, take me to the nearest university trauma care center. American medicine has achieved mastery in emergency medical care. Trauma and burn units work miracles. However, I want a team of TBM doctors at my side all the time and, once I'm stabilized, get me out as fast as possible and back into TBM hands.

American medicine and most modern medical systems have missed the whole point about health. At least 50 percent of the medical dollar is spent in the last 10 days of life, using heroic measures to try and keep people alive—whether they want to live at that point or not. Modern medicine focuses on patients from disease to death, ignoring the much longer continuum from optimum health to disease.

Medicine virtually ignores that whole spectrum of health where disease could be prevented. This is reflected in medical testing. Most medical tests are not "positive" (meaning the patient has a problem) until the patient is already quite sick. And the normal ranges—that the lab cites on the report for comparison—are not based on the lab values of healthy people. They are based on the lab values of average people, including a lot of sick people. And as the population gets sicker and sicker (and it is), every few years, the range of "normals" gets wider.

When I look at a blood test, I look at the range of normal values that the lab provides. If the value of my patient's test is more than 10 percent higher or lower than the middle of the normal range, I consider that a sign of too little or too much functioning. It is unhealthy—out of balance—even though the blood test results are considered to be normal (or average). And I always wonder about the values of a system that says if you are sick and your blood test shows it, that's "positive." But if your tests show you to be healthy, that's "negative."

Most laboratory tests were designed to detect outright disease. The neuromuscular reflex is usually much more sensitive. It detects and discovers imbalances in organs, systems, processes and pathology, before the imbalances become diseases with diagnosable names, such as cancer, stroke, diabetes and rheumatoid arthritis.

Sugar Control and TBM

If a patient is in my office, s/he needs to be on the Sugar Control Program. TBM offers specific chiropractic corrections to balance the organs that control blood sugar. These corrections speed the patient back to health and, in most cases, eliminate the possible three- or four-day period of detoxification symptoms that can occur at the beginning of any health program. During that period, the cravings for sugar and refined flour can be a challenge. But if you follow this program in conjunction with TBM treatments, you are most likely to avoid the common detox symptoms of headaches, irritability, the feeling that you have the flu, and/or cravings for sweets and starches. If you do experience these, a treatment by the TBM doctor can eliminate the symptoms quickly and easily without interrupting the cleansing process. If you are not being treated by a TBM doctor, grin and bear it: Eat allowed foods frequently, drink plenty of water, exercise and breathe.

Many patients who have sugar control problems may also have systemic candidiasis, parasites and/or allergies. These problems will also be addressed and corrected by the TBM doctor. It is, of course, possible to use this program without consulting a TBM doctor. But it is easier, faster, safer and more effective with TBM corrections.

The Sugar Control Program is intended to be used under the supervision of a TBM physician so that the program can be tailored for individual needs. The diet presented here is not designed for anyone with kidney problems, Parkinson's disease, for pregnant women or women trying to become pregnant, or athletes. If you are on medication, have diabetes, high blood pressure or any cardiovascular disease or problem, or have had a heart attack in the past year, do not attempt this program without a doctor's supervision. No one should begin a diet or fitness program without consulting a physician first.

For most people, this program represents a big life-style change. This book is designed to help you accomplish that change now. It explains the program to you, how and why it works and how it differs from other programs. It also offers food lists, strategies, recipes, and menu suggestions to help you get your new life style underway.

The Sugar Control Program is an unlimited-calorie, frequent-feeding diet that emphasizes animal protein, beef, and natural, non-starchy carbohydrates (fruits and vegetables), whole grain rice, natural fiber, good quality fats and sufficient drinking water. You will find an outline of the diet on p. 104. There are no calories, or fat-, carbohydrate- or protein-grams to count, no food exchanges, etc.

In many ways, this program is the opposite of the "health" diet that is being popularly and profitably promoted by Susan Powter, Dean Ornish, Cybervision, Richard Simmons, the Galloping Gourmet, Julian Whitaker, the American Cancer Society and the AMA, *ad nauseum*. I have been active in the nutrition field for 25 years. When I first became interested in nutrition to deal with my personal health problems, protein was king. Then, as is usually the case with western medicine, the pendulum swung to the other extreme, and carbohydrate became king. And over the course of the 20-year reign of carbohydrate foods, I have watched friends, family and patients become sicker and sicker as the high-carbohydrate diet has failed abysmally.

❖⌘❖

CHAPTER 2—CHOLESTEROL AND THE CARBOHYDRATE CONNECTION

The Sickening of America

❖⌘❖

The Failure of the Low-Cholesterol Diet

If you have been a "good" American over the past 20 years, your low-cholesterol/low-fat/high-carbohydrate diet probably consisted of egg-white omelets prepared in non-stick skillets with no fat, Special-K or 100% All-Bran cereals with skim milk, white meat chicken with every trace of skin and visible fat removed before cooking, salads with low-fat or lite [*sic*] salad dressings, baked potato with margarine, thin-sliced diet breads, skim milk in your coffee, diet sodas, Equal sweetener, no red meat, no egg yolks, fish prepared without oils, water-packed tuna, pasta salads, etc. Of course, the low-fat programs do allow you to have hard sucking candies, no-fat raspberry-filled coffee cake and low-fat frozen yogurt for dessert.

If you haven't been good, you may have subsisted on The Great American Junk Food Diet of sugar-coated cereals with table sugar added before eating, donuts and coffee, chips, naturally or artificially sweetened caffeinated soda pops, white bread, refined-flour hotcakes, packaged toaster waffles with real imitation table syrup (actually 10 percent maple syrup), frozen prepared dinners, fast-food restaurant meals, and a 6-pack a day of beer aged with formaldehyde and stored in aluminum cans. The junk food diet is a high-calorie, low-nutrition one, made with fats of very poor quality. It is high-fat/high-carbohydrate/low-protein.

Most patients who come to me for treatment of the symptoms listed at the head of Chapter 1, p. 17, have usually been eating some form of either one or both of these diets, including vegetarian diets, packaged-food diets from the diet centers, and the macrobiotic diets. These are programs that have proven over and over that they don't work. Many of these programs are just plain unhealthy for most Americans.

The Sickening of the U.S.

The United States is one of the wealthiest countries in the world and the fattest. During the reign of the low-cholesterol/low-fat/high-carbohydrate diets, obesity has become epidemic in America. Seventy-one percent of Americans are overweight. Comparing 1978 with 1995, obesity in American men has increased 72 percent[5] (79 percent among men 50-59 years old). Among women, it is up 58 percent. As a society, since we don't know how to fight it, we have decided to accept it. Even Barbie is fatter, now.

The incidence of cardiovascular disease has decreased slightly, but cancer has skyrocketed and will outpace heart disease as the number one cause of death in the U.S. by the year 2000. At the present time, one out of four people in the U.S. dies of cancer. And cancer is becoming more and more common in young children.

Diabetes, a disease directly linked to sugar metabolism, has quadrupled in the past 20 years, increasing from 14 million to 16 million cases just between 1990 and 1994. Type II diabetes and insulin resistance have a very high correlation to the development of cardiovascular disease and many other serious degenerative disorders.

Younger and younger people are suffering from cardiac disease and undergoing angioplasties and by-pass surgeries. At the beginning of this century, there was no medical specialty called cardiology in this country, because there was such a low incidence of heart disease.

Scientists and government authorities must see that the low-cholesterol/low-fat/high-carbohydrate diet is failing. But instead of looking for a different or better plan, they say it's our fault, that we are not trying hard enough.

The truth probably is that a high-carbohydrate/low-fat plan does work—when it is based on healthy foods—for about 30-40 percent of the American population. The problem is that no one diet is right for everyone. So the very same diet causes carbohydrate-intolerant people to gain weight while carbohydrate-tolerant people lose weight. We differ biochemically, metabolically and genetically. For people who cannot metabolize large amounts of carbohydrate, a high-carbohydrate/low-calorie diet frequently results in a condition called insulin resistance that triggers the body to store fat.

The popular concept of a low-fat/high-carbohydrate diet as the healthiest eating plan is based on research on cultures whose environment and evolutionary history warrant this diet. The Bantu tribes of Africa, the natives of Papua New Guinea and the Tarahumara Indians of northwest Mexico thrive on such diets. The assumption is that if it's healthy for them, it will work for Americans too. If scientists could find healthy Martians or Venusians, they would probably decide their diet was appropriate for Americans as well. The problem is that these native cultures are composed of homogenous groups that are descended from people that evolved to the diet of their environment. The U.S. may be composed of more different races, cultures, ethnic groups and nationalities than any other country in the world. We can't all thrive on the same diet.

---

[5] According to Charles Hennekens, M.D., Chief of Preventive Medicine. Brigham and Women's Hospital, Boston, MA.

The Health Paradox

The British government recently reported the good news that Britons are dying less from heart disease, strokes, suicides and accidents. Gonorrhea is down even more than they had targeted. But Health Secretary Stephen Dorrell said the bad news is:

> "The number of obese men and women has been rising since the mid-1980's. We know that it increases the risk of heart attacks and strokes and that day-to-day physical activity has declined with technological advances."

The report went on to state that Britons eat far too much fat, with 40 percent of dietary calories being supplied as fat (doctors recommend less than 30 percent). Now, I did learn a little logic in high school and this doesn't fit into any logic I know. If Dorrell's contention were true that eating fat and being obese causes heart disease, and people are doing it anyway, then the heart disease rate should increase. But as people ate more fat and got fatter, heart disease decreased.

If the heart disease rate is decreasing, then people should continue in the behavior that decreases it. Or am I missing something?

Lest facts get in the way of belief, any statistics that do not support the prevailing view of the superiority of the high-carbohydrate/low-fat life style are swept under the rug or labeled contradictions and paradoxes. Here are just a few of the many.

• In 1981, both the University of Denver and Stanford University published 10-year follow-up studies of heart-attack victims who had followed low-cholesterol, low-fat diets for that period. The results of both studies indicated that the dieters had higher than normal rates of cancer, even when compared to other heart disease patients who did not follow the regimen.

• In the 1960's, the American Cancer Society made an 8-year survey of 800,428 people. Those who ate more than 5 eggs per week and considerable red meat and greasy food had slightly fewer heart attacks than those who ate fewer than 5 eggs per week and less of those "dangerous foods."

• Then there is the French paradox. French men have a 50 percent lower incidence of heart disease than American men; French women have a 37 percent lower incidence of heart disease than American women. Yet the French eat far more fat and cholesterol than Americans do and the French smoke a lot of cigarettes (and have the lung cancer rates to prove it!). According to the World Health Organization, however, the French eat 70 percent less sugar than Americans.

Fig 2.1.   Egg Consumption and Heart Disease

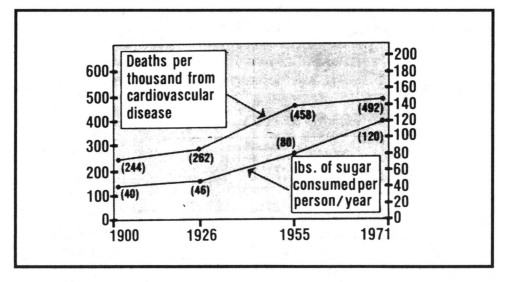

As egg consumption has decreased in the United States, heart disease has increased.[6]

Fig 2.2.   Sugar and Atherosclerosis

The lower line represents pounds of sugar consumption per person/per year. The upper line represents deaths per thousand from cardiovascular disease.[7]

- As egg consumption has decreased in this country, there has been an inverse increase in heart disease. As sugar consumption has increased, there has been a directly proportional increase in atherosclerosis. See the graphs, above.

---

[6] *Oral Chelation Therapy* by Kurt Donsbach. Rosarto Beach, Baja Calif, Mexico: Wholistic Publishers, 1988. 619-428-8585. Page 21.
[7] *Ibid.*

- Now, there's the Spanish paradox.[8] From 1973 to 1990 in Spain, the death rate due to strokes decreased 42 percent—a very significant decrease. What do you suppose happened to the Spanish diet during the same period? As the income of the Spanish people increased during that period, their consumption of meat, poultry, fish, eggs and cheese more than doubled from 6.1 ounces a day to 12.7 ounces a day. At the same time, the Spanish decreased their intake of bread, pasta, rice and potatoes by more than half. And sugar intake, itself, dropped by 35 percent. Is it possible there is a connection?

- Demographic and epidemiological studies from Europe indicate that countries that use olive oil and eat higher amounts of animal protein and beef have lower incidences of heart disease, stroke, diabetes and cancer.

Cholesterol and Heart Disease

Cholesterol is essential to central and peripheral nervous system function, to vitamin D formation, and to formation of sex and adrenal hormones as well as liver bile salts. It is a waxy substance that is present in blood plasma and in all animal tissues. It is a steroid. It is not a fat, but it is found in combination with animal fats. Serum cholesterol is a measure of how much cholesterol your liver makes. Your body requires about 3000 mg of cholesterol per day. A diet high in animal fat provides only about 800 mg. If you do not eat enough cholesterol, your liver has to make it. As with many body processes, there is a feedback mechanism that balances dietary intake against what the body needs to make.

One of the causes of cardiovascular disease is the build-up of calcified cholesterol and fat plaques on the interior walls of blood vessels, much like the hard water build-up of calcium deposits on the inside of water pipes. The build-up causes the lumen of the vessels to become narrower. This narrowing (atherosclerosis) blocks the free passage of the life-giving blood that brings oxygen to all the cells of the body. It can also be involved in heart attack and stroke.

Some studies indicated that high cholesterol levels coexisted with heart disease. So, in spite of what was known about the cholesterol production feedback mechanism, it seemed logical to medical researchers that restricting the dietary intake of cholesterol should prevent high serum cholesterol and thus prevent heart attacks. To prove this theory, the first experiments were done on lab animals. Rabbits and chickens were fed cholesterol and rapidly developed arterial plaques. However, there are major flaws in this method: Unlike humans, these animals are herbivores (they only eat plants) and, unlike humans, in the normal course of events would never eat cholesterol. So there was no way to know whether the results would be the same for humans.

---

[8] *Am Jrl Clin Nut,* vol. 61. Supplement 1995.

The second and possibly more serious flaw in the various cholesterol studies is that about 90 percent of them used oxidized cholesterol as a test material. Oxidized cholesterol tears the inside of artery walls apart. Generally, humans do not eat oxidized cholesterol, except perhaps in powdered whole or skim milk or powdered eggs. There was a study done during the Korean War on cadavers of soldiers. The study demonstrated the presence of arterial plaques even in 20-year-old boys. Perhaps this was due to their diet of powdered eggs and milk (and let's not forget the possible effect of the stresses of war).

So, how do we prevent heart disease? For the last 20 years, the medical answer to this question was to limit cholesterol in the diet. This also meant limiting animal protein, because it usually contains cholesterol. Something had to replace the protein and that something was carbohydrate. The type of carbohydrate, however, did not seem to be that important to the scientists. Blood (serum) levels of cholesterol were used to measure how well or poorly an individual was doing.

This is a plan framed in a system that views the body as a simple machine—like a car engine. And it says that every car engine runs perfectly on the same fuel. In such a system, it seems logical that if you put more cholesterol fuel into the engine, you will find more cholesterol in the engine. For 40 percent of the U.S. population that may be true. But if the body is like any kind of machine, it is more like an oscillator which changes in response to its environment—and changes in what may seem like unpredictable ways.

There are a number of factors that determine the best diet for an individual. One of the most important is genetic evolution. The genetic make-up of about 60 percent of Americans naturally favors a higher protein, higher fat, lower carbohydrate diet for optimum health. In these people, excess carbohydrate (sugar) fuel in their engines turns into higher triglycerides (fats in the blood) and higher blood cholesterol. For these people, low-cholesterol, low-fat, high-carbohydrate diets cause illness not health.

It is not that the information is wrong—it's just too simplistic. There is no one diet that is right for everyone.

Several years ago, the first chink in the low-cholesterol/low-fat/high-carbohydrate armor appeared, when the father of the cholesterol theory of heart disease died. Medical representatives began recanting the cholesterol litany almost immediately. They got as far as saying that in men over age 70 (*JAMA*: 11/2/94), high serum cholesterol is no longer considered a risk factor for heart disease. In fact, it may be a protective factor—we really don't know.

However, these representatives were quickly subdued by lobbyists for the food and drug industries. The food industry is heavily invested in "lite," low-fat, low-cholesterol foods, food substitutes and artificial sweeteners; while the pharmaceutical industry is heavily invested in cholesterol-lowering drugs. I have been told by informed sources that the acceptable level for cholesterol, 220 mg/dL, was artificially lowered several years ago to 200 due to pressure from drug companies. These companies were having problems recouping their research and development costs on their cholesterol-lowering drugs. The market for the drugs was not big enough, so they had to create a need for the drugs.

You may feel very confused, because your TBM practitioner has just told you to eat red meat, butter and eggs—all the foods the medical profession and the media have been trying to get you to quit for the past 20 years. And you are saying, "This can't be right."

But it is right. Time after time, when TBM patients follow the Sugar Control Program, their high blood cholesterol and triglyceride levels fall dramatically in just a few weeks. Overweight patients lose weight eating high-fat foods and eating frequently and in unlimited amounts; while underweight patients gain weight on the very same program. And many vegetarians feel better than they have in years.

Remember, I said health is about functional physiology. The Sugar Control Program gets the body functioning normally again. When people who should naturally eat a low-starch/low-sugar diet (about 60 percent of Americans) eat sugar and starchy carbohydrates for energy, they manufacture fat and cholesterol from them. It is not a mistake in metabolism; it is just the wrong diet for those people.

The Cholesterol Hype

Here's another cardiac paradox: It is common for people with normal/low cholesterol to have heart attacks and for people with high cholesterol to live long and healthy lives. It's time to reverse years of cholesterol propaganda. Serum cholesterol is not an accurate cardiac risk factor, although in some people it may be an indication of poor liver function and poor protein and sugar metabolism.

A charming 87-year-old woman has one of the worst low blood sugar problems I've seen. She eats low-fat cereal, skim milk, a muffin and three cups of coffee for breakfast. By mid-morning, when she runs out of breakfast, she gets very irritable, shaky and less than charming. Her energy, ability to drive, coordination, decision-making, memory and vision are affected. She eats hard candy until lunch to keep her blood sugar up, because, she says, she can't function otherwise. And hard candy has no fat or cholesterol. The same scenario happens in mid-afternoon. She scrupulously cuts all visible fat from her food and removes the chicken skin before cooking. She has been trying to lower her cholesterol on this diet for 20 years. It's still in the same mid-300 range.

This woman exemplifies the cholesterol hype. She has no signs of cardiovascular disease. She has not tried drugs, fortunately, but years of low-fat, low-cholesterol eating have not budged her serum cholesterol. The propaganda is so strong, however, that I cannot convince her—even in the face of her persistent high cholesterol—that this program is not working for her. The Sugar Control Program would improve her energy, memory, moods and arthritis, but she fears it will raise her cholesterol. And besides, she has a sweet tooth (a sure sign she needs to be on Sugar Control) and loves having a medical excuse to eat candy at 11 A.M. She won't even try the Program to see if it will help her.

My favorite cholesterol story is about one of my patients who came in with cholesterol readings in the high 600's (normal is 220) and triglyceride readings in the mid 1400's (normal is 100). She had been on a low-fat/high-carbohydrate program and had tried taking a cholesterol-lowering drug. The drug made her sick. So she came to me as a last resort. I put her on the Sugar Control Program and her cholesterol and triglyceride levels dropped by half in about two weeks. Then we had to dig for the real problem. That turned out to be lead toxicity in her liver. Using TBM techniques, we were able to detoxify the lead in about six weeks. Seven years later, she still follows Sugar Control principles and her cholesterol and triglyceride levels remain in the normal range.

My second favorite cholesterol story is about the wife of a patient. I have never met this woman, but her husband and daughter are patients of mine. I understand Mom is about 4 foot 10 and weighs 98 pounds soaking wet. We put her husband on Sugar Control. She decided to do the program with him, because it was easier than cooking separate meals. When she went for her annual physical two months later, her cholesterol level was 206, way down from her usual reading of 270 on her low-fat, so-called "Mediterranean" diet.

Risk Factors for Heart Disease

Lipoproteins. Cholesterol is not water-soluble, so it must be assisted in its movements in the body. Low-density lipoproteins (LDL's) transport cholesterol from its factory in the liver to the various tissues and body cells. High-density lipoproteins (HDL's) may transport excess or unused cholesterol from the tissues back to the liver, where it is broken down into bile acids and is then excreted.

Lab tests for these lipoproteins[9] are somewhat more indicative of cardiovascular and cerebrovascular risk than is serum cholesterol. Cholesterol attached to LDL's is thought to help build up calcified deposits in the blood vessels (atherosclerosis). So you are at greater risk if you have higher levels of LDL, very-low density lipoproteins (VLDL) and lowered levels of HDL. Higher HDL's are protective and may actually serve to retard or reduce atherosclerotic build-up.

Cigarettes and Smoking. A major risk factor in cardiovascular disease is cigarette smoking, which depresses HDL's (the good guys). Nicotine in cigarettes also adversely affects sugar metabolism by alternately stimulating and then depressing the adrenal glands

---

[9] Lab tests that measure individual types of fat particles in the blood.

(the fight or flight control). The healthiest move would be to quit and become a non-smoker. This would be a great time, because on the Sugar Control Program you can eat frequently and not gain weight. In addition, TBM offers techniques that help detoxify the chemical and heavy-metal residues from smoking that are stored in your body. Other techniques fix the allergy problems that help cause dependence on nicotine and smoking.

The Homocysteine Revolution In 1969, Harvard-trained Dr. Kilmer McCully, M. D., proposed the theory that homocysteine levels were possibly accurate cardiovascular disease risk factors, after observing two children who had died of different forms of CV disease. The only thing McCully could find that the children had in common was high blood homocysteine. McCully's work was effectively suppressed and he lost his job at Harvard. All research money at that time went to cholesterol studies. Finally, almost 30 years later,[10] his valuable information is being accepted and broadcast.

Homocysteine is an intermediate chemical that your liver makes in the process of using methionine and cysteine (protein building blocks). It is a complicated series of steps in which homocysteine appears for a flash and then disappears. Homocysteine is essential to several of the body's chemical processes, but it is also toxic to the lining of blood vessels. It is normally changed so rapidly that little or none gets into the blood. But a surprisingly large number of people do have elevated blood levels of homocysteine. These people may be at increased risk of peripheral vascular, cardiovascular, and cerebrovascular disease. The negative effects of homocysteine may also be aggravated by low HDL levels. Genetic high homocysteine is rare. Two-thirds of those who have high homocysteine blood levels are B-vitamin deficient in B6, B12 and folic acid. Even minimal doses of these vitamins (200 mcg folic acid, 2 mcg B12, and 2 mg B6) are effective in correcting the homocysteine pathway, but all three must be present for proper metabolism of the methionine/cysteine to homocysteine pathway.

Trimethylglycine (also called betaine) has also been shown[11] to normalize high plasma homocysteine even in cases where the B vitamins did not.

The Iron Stores Connection. Until menopause, women have a much lower incidence of heart disease than men. Within two years after the menses cease, women lose their heart protective advantage. How? Researchers have looked at the possible answers. Two main factors make women and men different, and they change at women's menopause. 1.) A woman produces estrogen in her ovaries until menopause. 2.) A woman has a monthly bloodletting as the uterus sheds its lining, until menopause.

---

[10] McCully, Kilmer. *The Homocysteine Revolution* (see Bibliography); and "Atherosclerosis, Serum Cholesterol and the Homocysteine Theory: A Study of 194 Consecutive Autopsies" in *The American Journal of the Medical Sciences.* 299:4 (4/90). Pp. 217-221.
[11] Monatero Brens, C., et al. "Homocysteinuria: effectiveness of the treatment with pyridoxine, folic acid, and betaine" in *An Esp Pediatr* 39:1 (7/93). Pp. 37-41

Estrogen production was eliminated as the answer when researchers noticed that younger women who had hysterectomies (surgical menopause) also lost the heart protection even when their ovaries were left intact. The ovaries produce estrogen. In other words, whether she was producing estrogen or not, a surgically post-menopausal woman lost her heart protective factor. So estrogen was probably not the answer.

That leaves the monthly blood loss. When blood is lost, iron is lost. Men have 300 percent more stored iron than premenopausal women. After menopause, when women stop shedding the uterine lining monthly, their iron stores increase to a level comparable to that of men. At the same time, their heart disease rates increase proportionally.

Support for the idea that iron stores are the difference that makes the difference also comes from the disease hemochromatosis. This is a disease in which excess iron builds up in the body's tissues. People who suffer from hemochromatosis usually develop heart disease. So the implication is that iron stores may be involved in heart disease.

Studies have been done so far by Uka Salinin and they are compelling. Further research is needed into the connection between iron stores and heart disease. Until the results are in, I recommend that men and post-menopausal women donate blood several times a year. These two groups should not take iron supplements, unless there is blood loss from ulcers or injury. There is plenty of iron in the Sugar Control Program. Your body saves it, stores it and recycles a lot of it. The iron at issue is not the iron circulating in the blood, but the stored iron. Your iron stores can be safely depleted without any anemia or energy loss occurring. Anemia in older people frequently is a result of B12 and folate deficiency (see the homocysteine section, p. 33) and copper toxicity, not iron deficiency.

What To Do?

For most people, getting off the high-carbohydrate roller coaster is a must for good health. The Sugar Control Program, emphasizing whole foods and high quality fats and oils, usually improves the lipid picture for people who need this type of diet. The Sugar Control Program usually brings serum cholesterol, triglycerides, lipoproteins and blood-sugar readings to normal quickly, because the body begins to function in a healthful way. Overweight people generally lose weight healthily on the Program and their blood pressures normalize. (In addition, TBM offers several specific blood pressure corrections, if needed.) And most people are amazed at how energetic and alive they feel, how stable their moods and emotions are, how well they sleep, how good their skin and eyes look, and how flavorful healthful food tastes once the sugar is out of their systems.

❖ ⌘ ❖

CHAPTER 3— PROTEIN BUILDING BLOCKS

Macronutrients

❖ ⌘ ❖

Recent conversations with friends, family, and acquaintances have convinced me that before I throw any more words around like protein and carbohydrate, we need to get some nutrition definitions clear. Many people are very uneducated about the food they eat and about nutrition in general.

A friend of mine has suffered with arthritis and related skin conditions for years. I recommended over and over that he eliminate milk from his diet for at least two months to see if that would help. (Milk is implicated in many conditions such as arthritis, asthma, acne, sinusitis and constipation.) We live 500 or so miles apart and visit about once a year. He met me at the airport one year and told me delightedly that he had finally taken my advice and stopped using milk. Over the next day, I watched him have pancakes (made with milk), a milkshake (made with milk), a cheeseburger (cheese is made from milk), a frozen yogurt (made from milk), and a piece of cake (made with milk). Finally I said, "I thought you said you had stopped using milk?" And he replied, proudly, "I did, I'm not drinking any milk!"

Then there was the time my mother called me about this new weight-loss method she had seen on the Oprah talk show. My mother has been an unsuccessful follower of the low-fat, high-carbohydrate diet and if I mention the Atkins' diet (p.13) as an alternative, she gets angry. Apparently on this particular show, a woman doctor was interviewed by Oprah. I still have not discovered who the doctor was. She had weighed close to 300 pounds and tried many diets. My mother said that the doctor said she finally figured out what her problem food was and eliminated it from her diet. With fear and trembling, I asked what the doctor's problem food was. I was expecting to hear about another high-carbohydrate/low-fat diet. But, lo! and behold, my mother told me the problem food was carbohydrate. I replied, "That sounds like Atkins' diet."

And my mother said, "But I don't eat a lot of carbohydrates!"

So I asked, "What about that bagel you had for breakfast?"

And my mother said, "Bagels are carbohydrate?"

And then last spring, I was in a kosher-style delicatessen. I asked the counterman if they had whole-wheat Passover matzos (traditional flatbread). He told me that whole wheat couldn't be used on Passover. I replied that I always purchased whole-wheat matzo on Passover. Again he said no. Beginning to doubt my own sanity, I finally asked him what he thought regular matzo was made from.

"Flour—it's made from flour."

"And where does flour come from?" I asked

He looked at me uncertainly and said, "Wheat?"

These conversations with otherwise intelligent and knowledgeable people have shown me that many of us know very little about the food we put into our bodies. We must eat to live. In order to maintain our bodies, we have to replenish them. Just as we put gas and oil in our cars, or water and fertilizer in our plants' soils, we must nourish ourselves. If we put low-grade gas in our cars, they knock and ping, but they still go. Well, on the wrong diet, we knock and ping as well, but we keep going for the time being.

We must supply macro- and micronutrients to our bodies, most of which they are incapable of making themselves: carbohydrates to burn for energy; protein to rebuild and repair tissue; fats to build tissue and hormones; vitamins, minerals and enzymes to help the chemical reactions work; and water. Plants are able to make their own food from chlorophyll, the green pigment which gives plants their color. However, even plants still need sunlight, water, and minerals from outside to accomplish photosynthesis.

This chapter and the next five form a group that discusses these nutritional fuels and co-factors in some detail. I have separated the chapters to make the reading easier.

The macronutrients are called protein, fat and carbohydrate. It is important to understand what these macronutrients are, because most health and weight-loss diets manipulate the ratios between the intake of the three macronutrients to produce results. Proteins and carbohydrates supply 4 calories per gram and fat provides 9 calories per gram.

What Is Protein?

Protein is the building block of the body—it is essential to the structure and function of living things. It is necessary to every cell in the body. Of the solid part of the human body, an overwhelming 90 percent is collagen—a protein structure that holds everything else together. Proteins are made up of carbon, nitrogen, oxygen, hydrogen, and sometimes contain sulfur, phosphorus, iron or other minerals. They are large, complicated molecules formed of chains of amino acids bound together by peptide bonds, and folded over and twisted on themselves. Muscle tissue is made of protein. Hormones and hemoglobin are proteins. Enzymes, which help us digest our food and drive chemical reactions in our bodies, are protein. Neurotransmitters, which carry electrical messages from one nerve to another, are protein.

Proteins are necessary in almost all cellular functions: muscle contraction; antibody production; and blood vessel expansion and contraction to maintain normal blood pressure. Protein malnutrition retards growth and development of intelligence in children, and causes fatigue. A protein-deficiency disease common in some developing nations of Asia, Africa, and South America is kwashiorkor, which afflicts children of ages 1 to 4 who are being weaned from protein breast milk onto starchy carbohydrate foods.

Human beings can make protein from amino acids. There are 29 amino acids, 22 of which are used by humans. Of the 22 we use, we are incapable of making 8-10 of them. These 8-10 are called essential amino acids and must be supplied in the diet.

Complete Protein

To complicate things even more, a complete protein food must contain all the 8-10 amino acids in a certain proportion to each other to enable the human body to use them as whole protein. If a protein source does this, it is called complete and efficient. If not, it is incomplete and/or inefficient. Eggs, for example, are a highly efficient source of complete protein, because 98 percent of the egg is usable in the correct ratio for humans. Beef has complete protein, but is only about 50 percent efficient. That means that the 50 percent of the amino acids that are excess to the correct proportion will be broken down to individual amino acids and stored in a free amino-acid pool to be used for various jobs.

For the most part, complete proteins are found in animal sources of protein: eggs, beef, poultry, game, fish, milk, cheese, yogurt. The only animal source of protein that is incomplete is egg white. Both muscle and organ tissue are protein.

Vegetable sources of protein are usually found in the seed portion: nuts, seeds, legumes (chickpeas, soybeans), lentils (split peas), grass seeds (wheat and rye). The dormant seed contains stored energy for the growing plant. When the plant sprouts, it uses up some of this starch to make protein. So sprouts contain more protein than seeds. All vegetable sources of protein are incomplete for humans. That means that a given plant that contains usable protein does not contain all 8-10 of the essential amino acids. Even though a protein food is incomplete, it can be combined with a complementary food that contains the missing amino acids.

Protein Combining

Plant proteins should be combined: Rice and beans, for example, are a complementary combination supplying complete protein. In order for the body to use the plant proteins as complete, the complementary proteins need to be eaten within an hour of each other. The highest quality plant proteins are found in tofu, tempeh, sprouts and spirulina.

Traditional diets combine vegetarian protein in complementary groups and can lead us to good protein combinations. Corn and beans; rice and beans; rice and milk; wheat, sesame and soy; are complete protein combinations—in the right proportions. In general, combine a legume (dried beans, buckwheat, peanuts, alfalfa and lentils) with a grain (wheat, rye, corn, millet, rice).

Vegetarians, especially those who do not include milk or eggs in their diets, frequently suffer from protein malnutrition, because they do not combine their vegetable proteins; and vitamin B-12 deficiency, because they do not eat Brazil nuts (the only vegetarian source of B-12). Much of the "vegetarianism" that I see in the U.S. today seems like just a high-minded excuse to eat junk food.

In plants, available protein is found in seeds, that is lentils, legumes, grains, seeds and nuts. The seed is a part of the plant from which a new plant can be grown. While it is true that every plant cell contains protein in the cell membrane, cell wall and nucleus, it is also true that this kind of protein is not available to human nutrition. So while lettuce and spinach technically contain protein, this protein is not counted in human nutrition, because humans can not normally digest it. In order for you to use the kind of protein found in a grass stalk, the grass has to be digested by a termite, or through the 4 stomachs of an animal that chews its cud and then turns grass into beef. So you would need to have four stomachs and chew your cud—or have termites in your stomach to do the job yourself.

Amino Acids

You may already have heard some of these names of amino acids, because they are being used therapeutically as medicines.

You don't need to remember this list, but the names of the amino acids are:

- l-alanine
- l-arginine
- l-asparagine
- l-aspartic acid
- l-carnitine
- l-citrulline
- l-cysteine
- l-cystine
- gamma-aminobutyric acid (GABA)
- l-glutamic acid
- l-glutamine
- l-glutathione
- l-glycine
- l-histidine
- l-isoleucine
- l-leucine
- l-lysine
- l-methionine
- l-ornithine
- l-phenylalanine
- DL-phenylalanine
- l-proline
- l-serine
- l-taurine
- l-threonine
- l-tryptophan
- l-tyrosine
- l-valine

Tryptophan, for example, makes people sleepy and it used to be the best natural over-the-counter choice for insomnia. However, several years ago, the FDA pulled it off the U.S. market, because a contaminated batch from Japan resulted in several deaths. On the other hand, prescription drugs are the third leading cause of death in the U.S. Approximately 20,000 people a year die just from side effects of ibuprofen. The FDA is not about to remove it from the market. Nor, after repeated incidents of product-tampering with Tylenol did the FDA keep Tylenol off the market—once tamper-proof packaging was created. The Japanese lab that was involved in the tryptophan contamination has an otherwise impeccable reputation.

But you have to follow the money to understand the FDA's reasoning. Tryptophan is the body's fuel for manufacturing serotonin, a hormone that aids in sleep and is anti-depressant. Prozac was the first psychoactive prescription drug that helped the body make serotonin in significant amounts. Prozac is patented and as such is much more expensive and more profitable than nutritional tryptophan. Tryptophan was removed from the market the year before Prozac was introduced, probably to eliminate the competition with Prozac. I have heard speculation in the health-food industry that the Japanese lab was sabotaged, so the FDA could get at the tryptophan. I have no evidence. By the way, significant amounts of tryptophan occur naturally in turkey and milk. Tryptophan is now available by prescription, or OTC as 5-hydroxy-l-tryptophan.

In general, this area of amino-acid therapeutics is one where the FDA has exerted a lot of pressure to turn amino-acid food supplements into prescription drugs. The FDA said, when it was trying to put through new labeling laws a couple of years ago, that the over-the-counter availability of nutritional supplements was a "disincentive" for people to use the far costlier prescription drugs.

The following is a list of how some of the amino acids are used to affect health and disease in both prevention and cure. When there is good nutrition and digestion, the body extracts the amino acids from food, but these amino acids are also used as nutritional supplements to replace nutritional deficiencies.

L-carnitine is a non-essential amino acid made in the liver and kidneys from lysine and methionine. B6, C, B3 and iron are also needed to make it. Carnitine promotes energy production by enhancing fat-burning in the mitochondria (the energy powerhouse of each cell). It is useful for lowering triglyceride levels and raising HDL cholesterol levels, and in treating cardiomyopathy, angina, cardiac arrhythmias, and cirrhosis of the liver. For fat-burning, 500-2000 mg daily in divided doses between meals have been recommended. Use only the l-carnitine form. Capsules are probably the best form.

L-cysteine is the body's precursor (along with glycine and glutamic acid) to make l-glutathione—the most powerful antioxidant/free-radical scavenger (see p 61). Sulfur-bearing, l-cysteine is useful in treating hair loss and skin conditions like psoriasis. It helps protect the lungs of smokers and is beneficial in asthma, bronchial disease and bacterial infections. It helps rid the body of the heavy-metal toxicity of copper, cobalt and molybdenum.

L-glutamic acid is a precursor of glutamine and glutathione. **L-glutamine,** a precursor of glutathione, is used in alcoholism, sugar cravings, impotence, fatigue, epilepsy, senility, depression, schizophrenia, mental retardation and ulcers. Glutamine is vital for the structure and function of the small intestine and is used in leaky gut syndromes. It enhances gut immune function by decreasing bacterial activity and increasing secretory IgA (an immune system defense). Glutamine is now considered conditionally essential, because the body cannot make enough during times of starvation, injury, surgery and infection. When patients are fed intravenously after surgery, the gut lining atrophies in a few days from lack of use. Bacteria can then translocate through the gut and affect other systems. The resulting multiple system failure can cause death. It is very important to supplement glutamine when feeding patients by tube and by mouth.

L-glycine, another precursor of glutathione, has been shown to reduce plasma homocysteine levels, lower VLDL's, increase muscle mass and decrease fat content. It helps prevent epilepsy and has been effective in treating bipolar depression. The nervous system, immune system and prostate gland depend on it as well.

L-lysine is helpful in treating Parkinson's disease. It is excellent as a preventative and curative for cold sores and shingles, both caused by the herpesvirus. It also aids in tissue repair, impaired calcium absorption, and lead detoxification.

L-methionine is a rich source of sulfur. It is used to treat depression, schizophrenia, Parkinson's disease, skin and hair disorders, gall bladder dysfunction, rheumatic fever, toxemia of pregnancy, and copper and other heavy-metal toxicity.

L-taurine is an anti-spasmodic agent, produced in the gall bladder. It is required by the heart and the brain to prevent heart attacks and seizures. Studies of the brain chemistry of epileptics have shown depressed levels of taurine. It aids in fat digestion and digestion of the fat-soluble nutrients (vitamins A, D, E, F and K). Just something to think about when your surgeon says you really don't need that gall bladder anymore.

L-tyrosine is the body's precursor along with iodine to make thyroxin (thyroid hormone). It is used to treat anxiety, depression, alcoholism and drug withdrawal. It is also beneficial for endocrine imbalances involving adrenal, pituitary and thyroid function.

How Much Protein Is Enough?

This is not an easy question to answer. The U.S. government's recommended dietary allowance (RDA) is 0.8 grams of protein per **kilogram** (2.2 pounds) of body weight per day for an average adult. That comes out to about 25 grams or 200 calories a day for an average weight woman, or about 15 percent of her diet. In general, U.S. government dietary recommendations err on the low side for everything except carbohydrate. They recommend about 12-15 percent of the daily diet as protein, a little more than enough to prevent outright disease states.

The basis of the current USDA recommendations for daily protein, carbohydrate and fat percentages come from studying the diets of the Bantu people of Africa, the Tarahumara Indians of Mexico, and the natives of Papua New Guinea. These are three very healthy groups who still eat their native diets. They have been thriving on these diets for thousands of years. That does not mean that you will also.

Most of the clinical experience I've had with patients tends to support the idea that people are healthiest when they eat the purest diet they can find of foods determined by genetic factors: their blood type, endocrine type, and possibly ethnic background. So if you are pure or even predominantly Bantu, the current U.S. dietary recommendations will probably work very well for you. If not, you need to look elsewhere for guidance.

Henry Bieler, in his book *Food Is Your Best Medicine,* says the proper protein percentages in diets are related also to the geographic latitude in which the gene pool developed. Starting at the North Pole, the Eskimos ate a very dense diet that was almost entirely composed of protein and fat. They were one of the healthiest groups of people on our planet, until they began eating western foods. As you move farther south toward the equator, there is more of a mix between protein and other foods. At the equator, much more of the diet is composed of fruit and water-containing foods with a lot of the protein coming from fresh raw coconut meat, which contains the special kind of methionine that is vital to the Sugar Control Program.

Recent studies[12] with athletes used as a baseline the U.S. government protein recommendations. They found that athletes-in-training lose body mass when their protein intake is only at the recommended level. Body mass increased when protein intake was increased to 1.6 g/kg[13] of body weight per day. But impressive strength gains of 5-6 percent were observed in world-class lifters, over several months of training, when they increased their protein intake to 3.5 g/kg of body weight per day. Weight lifters need more protein than other athletes, because they are building muscle. Recommended protein levels for athletes are about 50-60 g/day:

Class 1—Strength, Speed, Endurance (weight-lifting, shot-put, javelin, men's gymnastics). Protein 2 g/kg body weight/day.

Class 2—Speed, Strength, Endurance (sprinting, jumping, boxing, wrestling, karate, judo. Protein 1.6 g/kg body weight/day.

Class 3—Endurance (cycling, tennis, cross-country, running, skiing). Protein 1.4 g/kg body weight/day.

Athletes should not eat more than 30 g protein at a meal to protect their kidneys. They should eat at least six meals a day with 40 percent of the diet coming from vegetables, fruit and complex carbohydrates. Carbohydrates should be taken before, during and after training or competition as the muscles can only store about 650 mg of carbohydrate.

In their book *Protein Power,*[14] Drs. Michael and Mary Dan Eades recommend a minimum amount of protein between 0.5-0.9 grams of protein per day per **pound** of lean body mass (LBM). The variation depends on activity level.

Example: If a 170-pound man has 80 percent LBM; that means he has 136 pounds of LBM. If he is moderately active, exercising about three times a week, he needs at least 0.6 g of protein/pound of LBM/day. Multiply LBM (136) by 0.6 g and you get 81.6 g of protein per day or 326.4 calories of protein. Say he was eating 2000 calories a day—that would be 16 percent of his diet as protein.

However, the Eadeses also recommend eating more protein than the minimum amounts. There are reference books available to help you figure out how many ounces of food that amounts to.[15]

Clinically, I have usually found that my patients who remain healthiest and most vibrant follow nutritional guidelines that I set up for them by evaluating factors like height,

---

[12] "Do Athletes Need More Dietary Protein and Amino Acids?" by P.W.R. Lemon. *International Journal of Sports Nutrition.* 5:S39-S61, 1995.
[13] A kg (kilogram) equals 2.2 pounds.
[14] Pp. 156-8.
[15] USDA *Composition of Foods,* and Netzer's *Encyclopedia of Food Values* are two good sources.

circumference to determine dominant and recessive endocrine types. We combine this information with blood type to determine the individual's best diet program. In this system (see p. 139 for *The 8 Endocrine Biotypes*), the minimum recommendation for protein is usually between 50 and 66 percent of the daily intake. That may seem like a lot by today's standards, but remember those standards probably do not relate to what is necessary to your optimum health. I believe that the profound deterioration in the health of the U.S. population as a whole over the past 20 years has been largely, if not entirely, caused by the change in the government's and medical community's dietary recommendations of a low-fat/high-carbohydrate diet for everyone.

Most of the nutritional information that is popularly disseminated by the medical establishment and its mouthpieces, the print and broadcast media, is not based on sound experimentation or even sound principles of functional physiology. So the recommendations, especially when they are unnatural or extreme, and tamper with natural foods, are usually wrong and usually create more illness rather than wellness.

It reminds me of the USDA's warnings in the late 70's about not using wood cutting-boards, because they are insanitary. They were concerned that wood would spread salmonella and *E. coli* infections. Plastic is obviously much better. Nobody had ever studied the issue. The USDA just made a pronouncement based on what seemed like common sense. Well about 10 years later, someone[16] did do the experiment. The results were that wood was much safer than plastic. Wood seemed to contain an intrinsic anti-germicidal property, while plastic actually promoted the growth of germs.

We had already noticed plastic's ability to promote germ growth in the epidemic of toxic shock syndrome that plagued women in the early 80's. It turned out that the women who got sick were using plastic-fiber tampons, while the women who used natural-fiber tampons did not have a problem.

Anyway the USDA's response to the wood-is-better experiment was that they were sticking to their recommendations until more studies were done. And it's true, more studies were needed, but there were no studies supporting the original USDA recommendations. They were sticking to the no-study recommendations anyway. And I still hear on TV that plastic cutting boards are better.

So the recommendations for how much protein is enough continue to range between 12 and 66 percent. Barry Sears in *The Zone* recommends 30 percent for everyone. But there is no one diet that is right for everyone. The government is sticking to its guns, in spite of the evidence. You may need to work with a doctor or nutritionist who is not afraid of protein in order to find the right amount and type of protein for you.

---

[16] Dean O. Cliver and Nese O. Ak, microbiologists at the University of Wisconsin, Madison, reported in *Science News*, 2/6/93.

❖ ⌘ ❖

CHAPTER 4— CARBOHYDRATES FOR QUICK ENERGY

Macronutrients

❖ ⌘ ❖

When I talk about sugar in this book, I am talking about carbohydrates. Carbohydrates provide calories for quick energy, and the natural foods that contain them are frequently rich in vitamins, minerals and enzymes. Carbohydrates are starches and sugars that are primarily found in plant sources of food. Carbohydrates can be simple or complex. A simple carbohydrate, a simple sugar, is made up of a five- or six-sided ring of carbon atoms. Each carbon atom in the ring has two available attachment sites for atoms and molecules containing oxygen, hydrogen or carbon. Sugars usually contain one or two rings. A complex carbohydrate (or polysaccharide) is made up of more than two rings.

Your body breaks carbohydrates down to the simplest sugars, in fact, to blood sugar—which is glucose. There are no essential carbohydrates. That means you don't have to eat them, because your body can make carbohydrates from other food sources, like protein.

Sugars, being relatively simple forms of carbohydrate, are digested and assimilated rapidly and can provide quick, short-term energy. Natural simple sugars are found in fruits and fruit juices, in sugar cane and in sugar beets.

Starches, being polysaccharides, are more complex and are found in dried peas, beans, grains, potatoes, etc. They are bigger molecules with many more rings than sugars, but they break down to simple sugars. In fact, as soon as you begin chewing starch, the saliva in your mouth begins converting it to sugar—that's why that Saltine cracker turns to a sweet taste before you swallow it.

Where's the "Sugar"?

When I talk to many patients about "sugar," they tell me they don't eat any. That means they don't put any white granulated table sugar in their morning cereal, coffee or tea, or on their grapefruit. (And if they don't, they are likely to be using artificial sweeteners, but more about them later.)

When we talk about sugar in relation to the Sugar Control Program, we are using the word loosely to mean any food that breaks down in the digestion to simple sugar, raises the blood sugar level, and stimulates the production of insulin—especially any concentrated sweetener (sugar, fructose, honey), refined white, enriched or even whole grain flour

If my patient is eating a commercial breakfast cereal (with the exception of unfrosted shredded wheat), at least 50 percent of the product is sugar. Read the label. Bear in mind that any word ending "-ose" is a sugar. Perhaps the third ingredient is sugar. But listed separately may also be dextrose, maltose, fructose, and corn syrup solids. Add 'em up—there's often more sugar than cereal.

But what about the cereal? The cereal is made of refined grains. The healthiest, most nutritious parts of the seed—the germ (protein and oil) and the bran (fiber)—have been removed. The remaining starch portion has been "fortified" with eight or so synthetic vitamins. So except for some chemicals, the cereal product is all refined carbohydrate—all "sugar." In other words, it raises the blood sugar level and, therefore, forces the body to secrete the hormone insulin.

Add milk (especially skim) to the cereal and you add milk sugar (lactose). When you remove the fat from a quart of whole milk to make skim milk, something has to take up the space in the quart. That something is a little more protein, but also a little more carbohydrate. And it goes on from there: Bread, pasta, cereals, pastry, ice cream, desserts, candy, crackers, croutons, pancakes, waffles, bagels, breading on foods, flour and starches to thicken soups, sauces and gravies and sugar to sweeten them, ketchup, commercial salad dressing made with sugar—the sugar's in there.

Carbohydrates are beneficial when eaten in the form of whole fresh fruits and vegetables with all of the fiber intact. Fruits and vegetables contain vitamins, minerals, enzymes, and antioxidants. They are also alkaline, and dark green leafy vegetables and zucchini especially help to neutralize the acidity of animal protein.

The fiber in the whole plant is vital to your health. Most people know, at the very least, that sugar causes cavities in teeth. And yet people who eat whole unrefined sugar cane do not suffer from those effects, because they are eating a whole food with the fiber intact. That brings us to a primary issue with carbohydrates: refining or milling of grains.

Refined vs. Complex Carbohydrates

In the natural state, there are simple carbohydrates (fruit) and complex carbohydrates (polysaccharides, such as whole grains). Most foods made of grain—bread, cereal, converted rice, and other grain products—in supermarkets and bakeries in the U.S. are made from refined flour. Refined flour offers many advantages to manufacturers and retailers. The germ (which contains most of the nutrients) and the bran (which contains the roughage) are removed, so the grain does not become rancid and can be maintained on store and pantry shelves for up to two years after milling. This refined flour forms a softer, sweeter product, and it is not subject to insect infestation.

But personally I wonder: If insects won't eat it, why should I?

From the 1900's through the 1930's, the milling interests in this country waged a huge propaganda war on the American public, medical profession, and government to get them to accept refined white flour. When white flour first came out, people who depended on bread as a staple developed pellagra, beriberi and other deficiency diseases and the medical profession objected. Eventually these problems were handled by adding a few cheap synthetic B-vitamins to the flour. Just enough to prevent deficiency diseases, not enough or of good enough quality to provide good nutrition for health. They call this "enriched."

In 1930, the milling industry finally bribed enough people in the government to get nutritionists at the Department of Agriculture to issue a statement that said:

> Bread, either white or whole wheat, is always an economical source of energy . . . in any diet. The form may be left to the choice of the individual when the remainder of the diet is so constituted as to contribute the necessary minerals, vitamins, and any necessary roughage.[17]

What they were saying was: This bread is devoid of nutrition, we know that, but it's okay to eat it if the rest of your diet makes up for the lack. The problem is, many people eat up to a third of their daily calories in the form of bread and refined flours. Think of people who have a packaged cereal for breakfast, a white-bread sandwich for lunch and pasta for dinner. How are they going to make up for a third of their missing nutrients?

One of the most important implications for human health is that refined grains are pure starch and force the body to produce a lot of insulin in order to reduce the level of glucose in the blood. We will see the importance of this in the chapter on eicosanoids (see p. 97) and in the chapter on carbohydrate metabolism (see p. 87).

People and animals remain healthier on whole unrefined foods than on refined foods stripped of their nutrients. When the change from unrefined to refined foods occurs rapidly, diseases like pellagra and beriberi are epidemic. When the change occurs slowly, the human body's survival mechanisms allow the body to adapt. So outright disease does not appear, but there is also a lack of abundant health and degenerative disease develops over time. Because these diseases take so long to appear, people frequently don't suspect the link. In Denmark during World War I, the government forbade milling of grains because of scarce energy resources. Even though it was wartime, Denmark's death rate fell by 34 percent.

---

[17] *The Poisons in Your Food*. William Longgood. New York: Simon & Shuster, 1960.

Royal Lee, who founded the Standard Process nutrition company, made vitamin supplements by compressing whole foods. His company's vitamin C preparation contains only about 1-1/2 mgs of vitamin C with all its synergistic components, like bioflavonoids, found in the vegetable source material. His C was physiologically more effective than 1000 mgs of ascorbic acid, the "active" or refined ingredient in the vitamin C complex.

Recommendations About Carbohydrates. In general, eat fresh fruits and vegetables for the bulk of your carbohydrate intake. On the Sugar Control Program, you are also permitted unlimited amounts of roasted rice and two slices of sprouted grain bread per day. Good sources of carbohydrate after the training diet are legumes, lentils, whole seeds, raw nuts. If you must eat bread and pasta, make sure it's in small quantities and that it is whole grain not "enriched."

Fiber

Fiber and bulk are parts of plant-source foods that are largely indigestible to humans. We just do not have the appropriate enzymes in our digestive systems to break them down. Even though we can't digest them, they have proven to be very important to human digestion and to health. Fiber is very deficient in the American diet, because the refining process removes fiber from most food, especially grains and seeds. This is one of the reasons I believe that refined grain products, like bread, cereal, pasta and flour, should not be called enriched. They should be called "impoverished."

The following list includes most kinds of fiber and bulk, where to find it in food, and how it promotes health. The food sources mentioned emphasize the foods on the Sugar Control Program and usually omit those foods not included in Sugar Control. Fiber and bulk, though indigestible, are of vital importance to the function of digestion and thus to the health of the whole being. They are divided into insoluble and soluble types of fiber. In general the insoluble fibers work on the digestive system and the soluble ones have detoxifying effects, help lower cholesterol levels, and reduce insulin levels.

Cellulose helps peristalsis (the gut motion that pushes digesting food along), scours the gut of unwanted debris to keep it clean, and helps to provide bulk to fecal material. It helps prevent varicose veins and hemorrhoids (varicose veins of the rectum), colitis, irritable bowel, diarrhea and constipation. By removing cancer-causing chemicals from the gut wall, cellulose helps prevent colon cancer. Colon cancer is one of the most prevalent cancers in the U.S., because the general diet is so deficient in fiber. Cellulose is an indigestible fiber found in the outer layer of vegetables and fruits and wheat bran. It is found in apples, pears, carrots, broccoli, green peas and beans, whole grains, and Brazil nuts. Its is also found in lima beans and beets.

Hemicellulose is an indigestible complex carbohydrate that absorbs water into the large intestine and so increases the bulk of the fecal material, which helps it move more easily through the gut. This relieves both simple constipation and also the bowel pockets of rotting debris that cause diverticulosis. It helps prevent cancer. It is found in the outer layers of wheat (wheat bran), apples, cabbage, bananas, green beans, peppers, greens and pears.

Lignin lowers cholesterol levels and prevents gall stones, because it binds with bile acids. It aids diabetics by slowing the rise of blood glucose after a carbohydrate meal. Sources include carrots, green beans, peas, whole grains, Brazil nuts, peaches, tomatoes, strawberries, as well as potatoes.

Pectin is a soluble fiber found in apples, carrots, bananas, cabbage, citrus fruit and okra. It is also in beets and dried peas. It is used in making jellies and preserves. Pectin slows absorption of food after meals, which is useful for diabetics and those with other sugar-handling problems. It helps remove heavy metals and toxins from the body and is useful during radiation therapy. It also has cholesterol-lowering effects.

Gums and Mucilages help regulate blood glucose by slowing the rise in blood sugar after carbohydrate meals. They also aid mildly in lowering cholesterol and help remove toxic waste from the body. For the purposes of the Sugar Control Program, the mucilage in psyllium seed husks would be acceptable. Psyllium is a good intestinal cleanser and stool softener. Commercial psyllium products, are, I think, overprocessed. Natural forms of psyllium seed husks are available at health food stores.

Oat Bran (not on the Sugar Control Program) is the most well-known of the soluble fibers and has received much propaganda, largely because oatmeal is a major product of the agri-business Quaker Oats. This is the perpetual joke of "nutritious" food in America. Oat bran has been shown in studies to have a mild cholesterol-lowering effect. Now the simplest and most healthful way to get oat bran would be to eat hot, cooked steel-cut oats—a pretty natural form. But the most popular ways to get oat bran are:

1. the oat-bran muffin (which contains enough sugar, adulterated fat and refined flour to more than counteract any beneficial effects of the bran);
2. microwaved instant oatmeal, which is so processed that it may keep you alive, but won't nourish you, and;
3. Cheerios—whole grain oats are listed as the most plentiful ingredient followed by three types of sugar and refined starches. You can also get Cheerios in a sugar-frosted version, making the same health claims.

Now I am a firm supporter of capitalism. Unfortunately, the value systems of most capitalists in the food industries in the U.S. only include their bottom line. And their bottom line these days rarely has to do with high quality. When you are listening to the commercial version of health news and advice, always remember, "Show me the money!" Many research projects are funded by vested interests. The news is brought to you in print and over the air-waves by commercial sponsors. And the AMA—whose official position until just recently has been that nutrition has nothing to do with health at all—is in control of what most of the media have to report about health.

When a medically approved source gives the media information about health, no second opinion is needed. But when a "complementary" or "alternative" health professional gives the information, the media have to have a balancing opposing medical opinion, as though it were a political debate. And, in general, the medical authority who is interviewed has no training or expertise in the subject at hand.

A leading AMA "quackbuster" often testifies against alternative medicine. When he was cross-examined in one case last year (*Alt. Med. Rev.*, v2:2, p. 81, 3/97), he admitted under oath that he was an expert in consumer strategy. (I don't know what that is—but it is not nutrition, on which he was supposed to be the expert.) This MD had written about coenzyme Q10, stating that there was no evidence that supplements of it actually raised blood levels of it and further that it might be toxic to some people. But he admitted that prior to publishing the article, he had never read any scientific studies about CoQ10 (and there are many), and he could cite no study demonstrating toxicity. He stated he was not an expert on CoQ10. He further stated, when questioned about the effectiveness of ginkgo biloba for tinnitus, that he had never reviewed the literature on any herb that he could think of, although he had been presented as an expert witness on these issues.

I remember a series done by the TV program *Good Morning America* about 20 years ago. It was about taking vitamin and mineral supplements. They presented a decent report, interspersed with an interview with the chief of internal medicine at an important New York hospital. His opinion was that you probably couldn't hurt yourself taking vitamins, it would just give you expensive urine. In other words, don't waste your money on vitamin supplements. This "authority" figure had dark circles under his eyes—the kind that indicate either parasites or a congested liver, due to too much coffee or too little protein, and a pasty complexion. He could have used some expensive urine.

Recommendations About Fiber. Emphasize vegetables and fruits that are high in fiber. These fruits are satisfying, healthful and low in carbohydrates. The best foods in this category are broccoli, kale, chard, leafy green and cruciferous vegetables. And berries!!

If you eat plenty of fruits and vegetables on this Program, especially those listed above, you will have an abundance of fiber in your diet. Half a cup of raspberries contain more fiber than five oat-bran muffins. You may find when changing from whatever kind of diet you were eating to Sugar Control that you have some constipation. You may want to supplement some psyllium for a few days. If you have irritable bowel syndrome, however, just wait. Psyllium may be too irritating for you to use at first. Glutamine is very healing to the gut lining. Any constipation should normalize within a few days, especially if you are getting TBM treatments with your Sugar Control Program.

CHAPTER 5—FAT: THE MISUNDERSTOOD NUTRIENT

Macronutrients

❖ ⌘ ❖

In cutting edge nutritional research, fat is one of the areas most studied at this time and most misunderstood until recently. The United States has to get over its fat phobia for both weight loss and/or true health.

Fats are essential to good health. They are involved in the make-up of hormones. The outer membrane of each cell is a lipid (fat) compound. Many diseases, ranging from skin conditions to death, can occur when there is not enough dietary fat of the right kinds. Deficiencies in essential fatty acids (EFA's) can result in skin lesions, delayed growth and maturation, learning disabilities and behavior problems, visual, arthrititic and reproductive problems (from PMS to menopausal hot flashes to infertility), and in liver and kidney disorders. These conditions have been successfully treated with nutritional essential fatty acids. The right kinds of fats also protect us against cancer and heart disease.

In the peripheral nervous system, the myelin sheath, which helps transport the message down the nerve so rapidly, is fat. The brain, itself, is 60 percent fat. Many neurological diseases are involved with nutritional defects involving the fatty structures, and high-fat diets have been very successful in treating some of them, like multiple sclerosis and intractable seizure disorders. The 1997 TV program *Do No Harm*, depicted a high-fat diet for treating epilepsy that has been successful for decades. And the movie *Lorenzo's Oil* depicted a rare disorder, adrenoleukodystrophy, and its control through a nutritional oil. Both of these films were based on real cases.

Common signs of essential fatty acid deficiency include dry skin, goose-flesh texture on the skin of the upper arms, hair loss, brittle nails, excessive ear wax, persistent ear infections in children, and increased susceptibility to colds and infections.

Fat and Fat Terminology

Fats and oils are neutral compounds that are semi-solid, solid or liquid at room temperature. They are not water soluble, but do dissolve in ether, glycerin or other fats. Fats are derived from both animal and plant sources. Butter, lard, bacon drippings, suet, rendered chicken fat, shortening, and vegetable and nut oils, are all fats. Fat is found in many foods including animal flesh, nuts, coconuts, seeds, grains, avocados, milk and cheese. And remember, cholesterol is not a fat.

Fat breaks down in the digestion to glycerin and units (monomers) called fatty acids. Fatty acids can be made in the human body from sugar. That's one of the reasons the high-carbohydrate diet doesn't work for a lot of people: In people who are not genetically adapted to that diet, fat is produced in their bodies from the excess carbohydrates they eat (see carbohydrate metabolism, p. 87). It doesn't take much carbohydrate. In addition, the less fat they eat, the more fat they produce. This fat is stored, and it cannot be reconverted to sugar.

Essential Fatty Acids (EFA). Linoleic acid cannot be manufactured by most mammals— so it is essential, but it is plentiful in the diet. Linolenic and arachidonic acids are also termed essential, because they can pinch-hit for linoleic. But they can actually be made from linoleic acid. Linoleic acid can be found in safflower oil, flax seed oil, and sesame oil.

Fig 5.1. Omega-3 and Omega-6—Symptoms of Deficiency

Omega-3	Omega-6
allergies cardiovascular problems high or low cholesterol circulatory problems eczema eyesight problems immune deficiencies learning difficulties nerve problems osteoarthritis rheumatoid arthritis viral illness weight management	acne allergies cardiovascular problems dehydration dry skin fatigue food sensitivity immune deficiencies liver problems mood swings osteoarthritis premenstrual syndrome weight management

Omega-3 and -6 classifications are based on the chemical structure of the basic fatty acid chain. Omega-6 is linoleic acid and omega-3 is alpha linolenic acid. The omega-6's are abundant in the U.S. diet and include gamma linolenic acid (GLA) and arachidonic acid (AA). Omega-6's are converted in the bodies of healthy people to omega-3's. But some people cannot make this conversion successfully and they are better off taking omega-3 oils directly. The omega-3 oils have been almost eliminated from the American diet.

These include North Sea fish, flax seed, canola and walnut oils. Lower quality omega-3's include soybean and wheat germ oil. You should have a ratio of at least 1:1 omega-3 to omega-6 oils. The actual ratio in the American diet is more like 1:25.

EPA (eicosapentaenoic acid) and **DHA** (docosahexaenoic acid) are found in fish oils and can also be made in the body from linolenic acid. It is the DHA end product that is necessary for human health. The omega-3 fish oils are a better source, because they do not need much conversion. There is a DHA-only product made from blue-green algae. EPA and DHA prevent coronary heart disease and stroke. DHA is a main component of the synaptic membranes in the nerves and a lack of it has been linked to depression. Researchers[18] believe that depression linked to alcoholism, MS and childbirth may all be due to a lack of DHA and can be corrected by increasing the dietary intake.

Saturated vs. Polyunsaturated Fats. There's been a lot of rhetoric in the last 20 to 30 years about saturated and unsaturated fats. The propaganda has all been in favor of the unsaturated fats. The saturated fats have been practically blacklisted.

What's the difference? Fats are composed of long chains of carbon atoms. Each carbon atom has four arms, where other atoms or molecules, like hydrogen, can attach. If two carbons in the basic chain have a double link to each other, there are fewer places for hydrogen atoms to attach and the fat is said to be monounsaturated (olive oil). If there are two or more carbon double bonds, the fat is polyunsaturated. If there are no carbon double bonds, all of the receptor sites are occupied with hydrogen, and the fat is said to be saturated. Saturated fats are animal fats, like butter, lard, and suet, and are solid at room temperature. Unsaturated fats come from fish (fish liver oils) and plants (canola or rape seed, avocado, peanut, corn, safflower) and are liquid at room temperature.

In the early 1950's, when doctors first started doing kidney transplants, there were problems with organ rejection. A patient's immune system would recognize the transplanted organ as a foreign invader and try to reject it. Medicine knew for a long time that a diet high in polyunsaturated oils causes immune system suppression. So they prescribed high doses of polyunsaturated oils to help transplant patients combat organ rejection by suppressing normal immune system function. This was before anti-rejection drugs were developed.

When the transplant patients began to develop higher-than-average incidences of cancer, doctors were perplexed. In those days, medicine did not believe that cancer was related to immune system suppression, so they made no connection. When anti-rejection drugs came along, the information was forgotten and, as usual, rediscovered 20 years later by a new generation of medical researchers. In the meantime, unsaturated fats were loudly and

---

[18] American Journal of Clinical Nutrition, Vol. 62, July 1995, pp. 1-9.

erroneously proclaimed by medical nutritionists to be wonderful and saturated fats useless and, worse, injurious.

Around 1980, two 10-year follow-up studies were published, one by Stanford University and one by the University of Denver. Both studies looked at the health of men who had survived heart attacks and had made life-style changes, including exercise and the low-cholesterol/unsaturated-fat diet that has been prescribed from about 1970 on. The conclusion of both studies was that there was a higher-than-normal incidence of cancer in these patients compared to heart attack survivors who did not follow the diet.

Hydrogenated Fats. When the polyunsaturated craze hit the U.S. in the 60's, butter was thrown out with the baby and the bath water. Of course, people still wanted a spread that looked and tasted like butter. But polyunsaturated oils are liquid at room temperature. What to do? Well, the chemists decided to engineer the synthetic addition of some hydrogen atoms to receptor sites on the carbon chain by forcing hydrogen atoms in under high heat and pressure.

This process destabilizes some of the carbon chain bonds to create a partially hydrogenated trans fatty acid. Trans fatty acids promote those cellular reactions in your body that result in inflammation, PMS, excessive platelet aggregation, vasoconstriction, bronchoconstriction, etc. Add some synthetic food coloring and a bunch of other chemicals and *voilà*—margarine: The health food of the 60's that causes both cancer and heart disease, as well as many other health problems.

Trans fatty acids are found in margarine and in many other processed foods like crackers, soups, cookies, TV dinners, breads, etc. I recommend that you stop using margarine and any processed foods made with margarine immediately! Inquire in restaurants what they use to sauté omelets and other foods. Most restaurants who pay lip-service to health concerns are still using margarine, and margarine-like spreads. Educate them. Demand real butter. Better still, real organic butter.

Butter, which is naturally saturated but not hydrogenated, contains vitamin A and is an excellent food used in moderation. It also has a protective x-factor (found in eggs as well) —something about it that we do not understand yet, which promotes health. With a very little effort, you can clarify butter to make ghee. There are a number of reasons to use ghee: Ghee retains butter's taste; It is no longer a milk product; It can be stored for months at room temperature; It doesn't burn in cooking To prepare it, melt the butter in a saucepan over low heat and skim off the milk solids as they rise to the top. Store the ghee in a covered container on shelf. Refrigeration is okay as well.

I think fats were dismissed from the American diet because of all the fats only butter and marine liver oils have any vitamins or other nutrients and they have twice the calories of protein or carbohydrate. Researchers thought they were useless and inefficient.

Fat and Weight

In the 40's, the New York City Health Department administered a free weight-loss program. Jean Nidetch took it and created Weight Watchers. Originally, Weight Watchers, removed all fat from the NYC diet (other than what one might find in skim milk or lean beef). In the first years, many dieters ended up with gall bladder problems, because of this lack of dietary fat. Fat is required to stimulate complete emptying of bile from the gall bladder. So a scant tablespoon of oil per day was added back into the diet.

Interestingly, fat deficiency contributes to obesity in several ways. When there is linoleic acid deficiency, the body retains as much water as possible. Low-fat dieters frequently exhibit swollen ankles, hands, etc. When there is insufficient fat in the diet, the body converts sugars even more rapidly into fat. As a consequence, the blood sugar drops dramatically which creates a powerful craving for more sugar and carbohydrates. The dieter eventually or immediately gives in—or just suffers and makes everyone around him or her suffer. A hundred calories of fat is very satisfying to the appetite. To make up for not having that tablespoon of fat, an obese person is likely to crave and eat 500 calories of carbohydrate.

What To Do

Eat fat. Eat more fat than is currently being recommended. You usually don't really have to worry about how much fat, because amazingly it is really self-regulating. But be sure to eat high-quality fat. Your diet should probably include 25 to 35 percent fat from all sources—with a ratio of at least 1:1 omega-3 to omega-6 fatty acids. Recent studies show that reducing fat below 25 percent has no effect on cholesterol levels anyway—even if cholesterol were actually the issue.

But, please note that some research shows control of symptoms in diseases like multiple sclerosis from eating less than 20 percent fat/day dietarily. The restriction does not, however, produce cure. And the diet is supplemented with omega 3 and 6 oils.

You should include a minimum of a tablespoon of olive oil, flax seed oil or other high quality oil in your diet daily to help your gall bladder[19] operate more healthfully and efficiently. My optimum choice for butter would be sweet (unsalted) butter from raw organic cream, but it just is not available. Second choice—organic grade AA pasteurized butter. Butter is one food of which women, especially, should eat organic sources.

For cooking, you need stable fats. Use olive oil (preferably extra virgin), butter or ghee. Sautéed and stir-fried foods are healthful, but avoid deep-fat frying. Do not use unsaturated oils for cooking, because heating them causes trans fatty acids to form.

---

[19] And if you are suffering gall bladder pain or bloating after meals, check with your TBM doctor. These problems can usually be fixed fairly easily and naturally through TBM

Oils

Oils add great benefit to your health and to the taste of your foods and the satisfaction you get from eating those foods. But they need to be used properly to promote health— otherwise they can create degenerative diseases.

A primary issue with oil is rancidity. If left exposed at room temperature, oil will become rancid. When this happens, it smells like paint thinner. It is unpleasant and you will know it. Rancid oils destroy vitamins in your body, especially vitamin E, and therefore interfere with oxygenation of the cells. Whole grain flour left for a month on a shelf will become rancid. It's amazing the amount of mildly rancid oil that creeps into the diet, especially from commercial foods like peanut butter and movie popcorn. Even at home, we often serve mildly rancid foods, like mayonnaise and nuts, without realizing it.

Since oils do get rancid, store them in a cool dark place and refrigerate after opening. Oil should last 6 months that way. Some oils will become solid when chilled. Just run some hot water over the bottle till enough melts for use or take it out of the refrigerator to soften for 15 minutes before you use it. Since cold-pressed oils can easily become rancid, it is advisable to take vitamin E, an oil-soluble antioxidant, to prevent oil rancidity in your body. You can also empty a vitamin E perle into a bottle of oil to protect it.

The other big issue is how oils are processed. Traditional methods use an old-fashioned cold press, the kind used for pressing apples for cider or grapes for wine. There is also a cold expeller-pressed method. If your oil is produced this way, it should say so on the label. Agri-business uses high heat to extract oils from seeds and nuts. This produces a higher yield for less money, and much longer shelf-life. However, heat processing denatures oil and makes it unhealthful.

For some people, olive oil seems to be an acquired taste. Olive oil is monounsaturated and figures prominently in the diets of European countries that have lower heart disease and stroke rates. Extra virgin olive oil is from the first pressing of the olives. It is the most healthful. Virgin olive oil is the second pressing. A light olive oil has less of the olive taste. Where olive oil would interfere with flavor, as in oriental stir fry, use sesame seed oil (which is stable enough to heat). For cooking, try mixing ghee (p. 53) with olive or sesame oil for a great taste. For salad dressing, use olive oil, or unsaturated oils such as safflower, sesame seed, walnut, and rice bran, which are best eaten uncooked. Most unsaturated oils, except olive and sesame, are too unstable to stand up to high heat.

The best quality oils are cold-pressed: European olive oils have been made this way traditionally, but beware! With the huge American demand for this product, some European manufacturers have started cutting corners to make more product more cheaply. They have been using high-heat methods to extract oil. And they have been passing off the heated products as extra virgin olive oil and selling it at extra virgin olive oil prices.

Do not use mineral oils internally. They are made of petroleum. Your body can't absorb them, and they rob you of nutrients. Would you think of eating Vick's Vapo-Rub or Vaseline petroleum jelly? They are just hardened mineral oils. In fact, I usually use vegetable oils even externally for cosmetic, massage, and medicinal purposes.

Oil Supplements

Borage Oil is one of the richest sources of gamma linolenic acid (GLA), a key regulator of immune system T-lymphocyte activity. GLA is made in your body, but there are many things that can block its synthesis, ranging from magnesium deficiency to high intake of poor quality fats.

Black Currant Oil contains linoleic acid and alpha- and gamma linolenic acid. Use for treating inflammation, hypertension due to vasoconstriction, uterine constriction as in PMS, thyroid dysfunction, muscle cramps, skin conditions and homocysteinuria, a risk factor for cardiovascular disease. Alpha-linolenic should be limited in the diet (p. 98).

Evening Primrose Oil (EPO) contains a high level of GLA. It helps protect against cardiovascular disease, PMS, menopausal symptoms, MS, arthritic inflammation, high serum cholesterol, liver disease and high blood pressure. Because of its hormonal effects, avoid or limit use of EPO in breast cancer. (Black currant is a good substitute.)

North Sea Fish Oils, are far and away the best oil supplements, because they are very high in omega-3 fatty acids, containing DHA EPA. Carlson Labs has a good Norwegian salmon oil. Dale Alexander produces a good quality cod liver oil. Eating salmon, cod, herring and mackerel also provide the oils. You need at least three servings per week. Be aware, however, that most salmon on the market today is farmed and probably does not contain as high a quality of oil.

Dale Alexander's instructions for using cod liver oil work well. Use unemulsified oil (make sure the label says free of heavy metals and PBB's): mix one tablespoon of oil in a small covered jar with an ounce or two of orange juice or whole milk. Shake vigorously and drink on an empty stomach (at least three hours after eating.) Don't eat for an hour. The best time to do this is first thing in the morning, especially if you exercise before breakfast. Last thing before bed works as well, if you don't eat after dinner. This is excellent for arthritis. Most recent research, however, has been done with oil perles taken with meals and the results have been good.

Fish liver oil, as you will see, helps promote the production of Series 1 eicosanoids (p 97) in the cells. It relieves arthritis, works better than pharmaceutical blood thinners (often rat poison), lowers serum cholesterol, makes your hair and skin look wonderful, is helpful against psoriasis, contains vitamin A and D, improves vision, helps prevent colds, and much more.

Octacosanol, concentrated wheat germ oil, has been shown to improve endurance in athletes. It reduces cholesterol.

Flax Seed Oil is a source of omega-3 and omega-6 unsaturated fatty acids. It is helpful to those who have blood fats that are too high or low, immune system problems, eczema, and diets high in refined foods. It also helps with calcium metabolism. Take about one tsp. per 100 pounds of body weight. Mix the oil (1:4) with a sulfured protein such as cottage cheese or plain yogurt. Or use it on salad when the meal includes a sulfur protein, such as cheese or egg yolks. Flax seed oil is highly promoted by the health food industry for its vegetable lignans, which have been demonstrated to be powerful weapons against cancer and viruses. But it contains high amounts of omega-6 which have to be converted to omega-3. As far as I can tell, if flax seed oil is not taken with sulfured protein, it is also capable of overproducing series 2 eicosanoids (p. 97) and having consequent negative effects. I personally prefer North Sea fish oils to flax oil, but with marine oils, you have to deal more with environmental pollution.

There is an algae-based supplement that is pure DHA. Solgar makes one. This may be the simplest solution.

Dietary Recommendations: Fats and Oils

- Eat 25-35% of your diet as high quality fat.
- Eat a 1:1 ratio of omega-3 to omega-6 oils.
- Eat a 2:1 ratio of unsaturated to saturated fat.
- Use extra virgin olive oil, butter or ghee for cooking.
- Do not deep-fat fry foods. Sautéing is acceptable.
- Use raw cold-pressed unsaturated oils for salads. Walnut, safflower, sesame, and rice bran are beneficial. Do not heat them.
- Avoid or limit canola, soybean, corn and flax seed oils.
- Avoid margarine and hydrogenated trans fatty acids.
- Use a variety of oils and oil supplements, varying them day to day.
- Take vitamin E daily to prevent rancidity of oils—400-1600 IU/day.
- Get EPA DHA omega-3 from North Sea fish and fish liver oils.
- If you are sensitive to arachidonic acid, limit it in the diet, see p. 100.
- Eat a low-carbohydrate diet to suppress insulin and promote glucagon.

❖ ⌘ ❖

CHAPTER 6— ANTIOXIDANTS AND VITAMINS

Micronutrients

❖ ⌘ ❖

Note

[My very wise and very talented husband[20] suggested that this chapter and the next, while containing vital information, slowed down the main flow of ideas in this book. He suggested that I put this information in an appendix, and he is right. But for some reason, I can't seem to do it. So, I suggest that you skim these chapters now, and then use them for reference information later on.]

Vitamins, minerals and antioxidants are called micronutrients. Micronutrients do not provide calories for energy. Instead they are cofactors in the millions of chemical reactions that have to take place in the body all the time. Normal body temperature (97-99 degrees) is too cool to support a chemical factory without help. So cofactors, enzymes and co-enzymes are needed to speed up the reactions. Although they make the reactions go, they are not changed in the reactions. Magnesium and B-vitamins, for example, act as cofactors at various stages of the complicated Krebs cycle, which makes energy in and for each cell of your body.

ANTIOXIDANTS

Free radicals (no, not Madonna) are the bad guys. They are molecules roaming through our bodies looking for oxygen they can grab onto to balance their electrical charge. Most free radicals are formed within our bodies. They cause degeneration and aging. There are three known free radicals: superoxide, hydroxyl and peroxide. They may be formed as a result of:

- normal metabolic processes;
- exposure to radiation (electromagnetic, cosmic, ultraviolet from the sun, x-ray, microwave, etc. or;
- exposure to toxic chemicals.

---

[20] Sam Wieder is the author of the audio-tape program "Wake Up and Win: How To Stress-Proof Your Body and Ignite Your Energy." 1996. $19.95 + $3.00 shipping. Order from Sam at POB 963, Greensburg PA 15601. Phone 724-832-7459 FAX 724-836-8606.

Free radicals are believed by many to be responsible for aging and degeneration of all types. The short list includes skin aging or wrinkling, cataracts, cardiovascular disease, age-related pulmonary function impairment, rheumatoid arthritis, chronic bronchitis, asthma, kidney disease, strokes and ME (the virus that causes chronic fatigue).

A rusty nail has been oxidized by oxygen in the air to create the rust. Free radicals in the body cause a similar kind of oxidation or rust. One free radical can damage a million cells and it has a special affinity for DNA and RNA molecules—which contain the master blueprints for cell reproduction.

The body also makes free-radical scavengers. These chemicals act like little microscopic PacMen engulfing and destroying the enemy radicals. The PacMen scavengers are: superoxide dismutase (SOD), methionine reductase, catalase, and glutathione peroxidase.

Nutritional antioxidants are also free-radical scavengers. There are several different groups of antioxidant free-radical scavengers. Vitamins A, E and C are important antioxidants (see vitamins, p. 62), as is the mineral selenium (see p. 78).

Antioxidants and the precursors to antioxidants in our diets come largely from raw fruits and vegetables. Because many people do not eat these foods and because our world now bombards us with so many more free-radicals and free-radical generators, it has become important to supplement antioxidants. In fact, I believe, if I could only supplement one thing, I would choose a good combination antioxidant formula.

Bioflavonoids

Bioflavonoids are complex chemicals in fruits and vegetables that make them red, yellow, orange and blue. They are usually found with vitamin C. They are very plentiful in the white rind of citrus fruit. When you eat citrus, peel it crudely, leaving a lot of the white on and eat the white between the sections. Tiny amounts of rind may be used in recipes for flavor. A half a grapefruit contains almost a whole day's supply of the RDA of vitamin C. The membrane is full of pectin, which lowers cholesterol and LDL (pectin, p. 48). Grapefruit and other citrus contain limonene and other flavonoids. Limonene is a bioflavonoid which may reduce breast tumors. Red grapefruit also contains lycopene (p. 61), a carotenoid, which may fight prostate, cervical, bladder and pancreatic cancers. Bioflavonoids have positive biological activities and multiply the effects of vitamin C.

Fig 6.1:   Bioflavonoids Benefit Health

Anti-inflammatory	Promoters of good eicosanoids by
Antioxidant	inhibition of arachidonic acid (pp. 100)
Ulcer preventative	Inhibitors of harmful eicosanoids (p. 97)
Vitamin C enhancing	Anti-viral
Free radical scavenging	Strengthens capillary membranes
Anti-histaminic	Removes heavy metals from body

Major classes of bioflavonoids include:

- Flavans—catechins, epicatechins
- Flavanones—hesperidin, hespertin, naringin, naringenin
- Flavones—chrysin, apigenin, luteolin
- Flavonols—quercetin, rutin, rhamnetin, kaempferol, myricetin
- Chalcones—hesperidin methyl chalcone, phloretin
- Anthocyanidins, Proanthocyandins (pycnogenols)

Carotenes. There have been about 600 carotenoid bioflavonoids isolated in foods. Of these only 14 are known to be absorbed into the bloodstream. Beta-carotene is a precursor of vitamin A, which is essential to vision and to the integrity of all the mucous membranes and skin. A precursor is a substance your body uses to make something else: in this case, vitamin A. Beta-carotene is the most well-known of the carotenoids and the most studied, but it is far from the most effective. Here are the names of some of the other carotenoids that have been discovered. You'll probably be hearing a lot more about them soon as we discover how they are used in the human body to promote health and longevity.

- Alpha-carotene   }
- Beta-carotene}
- Gamma carotene   }
- Beta-cryptoxanthin
- Alpha-cryptoxanthin
- Neurosporene
- Pro-gamma-carotene
- Zeta-carotene
- Phytofluene
- Phytoene
- Lycopene
- Lutein
- Zeaxanthin

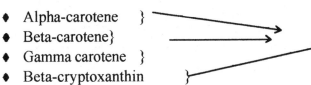 Precursors to **Vitamin A**

The carotenoids are found in dark-green leafy vegetables and give the color to yellow and red vegetables and to flowers like marigolds. Chlorophyll gives plants their green color and helps them manufacture carbohydrates. In the autumn, chlorophyll subsides and the hidden colors of the carotenoids are unmasked. Then we see orange, yellow and red carotenoid colors that were there all along. The carotenoid vegetables and nutritional supplements offer protection against many kinds of cancer, cataracts and heart disease. Carotenoids appear to be both anti-germicidal and also to increase the activity of natural killer cells. There is a significant link between longevity and plasma carotenoid levels.

Lycopene. The healthy prostate gland contains high levels of the carotenoid lycopene. Recent studies have shown that cooked tomatoes and tomato sauce (but not tomato juice)

Lycopene. The healthy prostate gland contains high levels of the carotenoid lycopene. Recent studies have shown that cooked tomatoes and tomato sauce (but not tomato juice) concentrate lycopene and have a significant correlation with the prevention of prostate cancer. The action seems to be enhanced by cooking the tomatoes in olive oil and to be related to lycopene's role as an antioxidant.

Lipoic acid, at first thought to be a B-vitamin type of cofactor, has been shown to have both powerful antioxidant and pro-oxidant capabilities. It was discovered over 50 years ago. It is only within the past few years that its antioxidant properties have been discovered. It protects lipoproteins, preventing LDL's from being oxidized into the "bad" cholesterol that forms atherosclerotic plaques. Lipoic acid is a nerve protector. In Europe, it is used to treat conditions such as diabetes, diabetic peripheral neuropathy, amanita mushroom poisoning, liver disorders (including alcoholic cirrhosis), and strokes. It is a liver protectant, enhancing liver function, clearing metabolic poisons and healing liver pathology. It is a critical co-enzyme in cellular respiration and amino acid metabolism. It lowers blood glucose levels, modulates immune function and inhibits HIV virus. Lipoic acid also renews spent vitamin E and stimulates the body to produce glutathione (see below). It is the only antioxidant known to be active in the brain and it may prevent strokes as well as rehabilitate nerves damaged by stroke.

Co-Enzyme Q10 is a vitamin-like substance resembling vitamin E. It is a very powerful antioxidant, which is normally present in human tissue, but decreases with age. It is involved in immune system function and is very effective in the treatment of heart disease, tumors, and leukemia. It reduces the side effects of chemotherapy. It can be beneficial in allergies, asthma, schizophrenia, Alzheimer's disease, obesity, candidiasis, and MS. It protects the stomach lining. Applied topically to the gums, it helps reattach the dental ligaments. Early studies used 10-30 mg doses, but more recent studies are using 200-300 mg doses very successfully. CoQ10 is found in mackerel, salmon and sardines. Small amounts are made in the body, and supplementation may only have therapeutic benefits if the patient actually has a deficiency.

Glutathione (GSH), a tripeptide, is probably the most important antioxidant, because it can detoxify both water- and fat-soluble peroxides. We make it in our cells from its precursor amino acids: cysteine, glycine and glutamine. GSH is found everywhere in the cell. It is very versatile and can change all types of free radicals (peroxides, superoxide free radicals, hydroxyl radicals, and singlet oxygens) to inert and nontoxic compounds, which are then eliminated through the urine. It has a wide range of activities, but is most active in the lungs and liver. GSH production diminishes with aging. Combining 5-9 fruits and vegetables a day with GSH supplements can slow aging as well as heart disease, high blood pressure, diabetes and cataracts. A GSH supplement with precursors, such as NAC plus selenium and vitamin C is better. But in more advanced problems, it is beneficial to use some reduced glutathione as well.

VITAMINS

Vitamins are carbon-based compounds that the body requires to perform its metabolic functions. With few exceptions, however, the body is incapable of making these chemicals. They must be obtained from food. Vitamins are classed as water soluble or fat soluble. The water-soluble vitamins (B-complex and C) are not stored in the body and are excreted in the urine (water). The fat-soluble vitamins (A, D, E, K) can be stored in the body in fatty tissue. It is possible, therefore, to build up toxic levels, especially when using synthetic sources of the vitamins. When using natural sources, it is very difficult to reach toxic levels. However, too much of a vitamin or mineral can produce symptoms similar to deficiencies of that vitamin or mineral, or may produce fatigue, diarrhea and vomiting.

Fat-Soluble Vitamins

◆**Vitamin A** helps to prevent aging, cancer and other degenerative diseases. It is integral to membrane integrity. Membranes are the skin inside your body—the mucous membranes in your nose, for example, and the lining of your entire digestive system. Vitamin A is also involved in the chemical reactions of vision. It is, therefore, involved in nightblindness and photophobia. Because of its involvement with mucous membranes, vitamin A is essential to immune function. It is also directly related to healthy skin and thus to acne.

Vitamin A comes in several forms. The active form is retinol. Carotenoids (of which beta-carotene is the best known, but not the best) are both antioxidants and also pro-vitamins. A provitamin is a substance out of which your body makes an active vitamin. Fish liver oil contains highly concentrated vitamin A. Liver and butter are good sources. Green and orange-yellow vegetables and fruits also contain carotenoid provitamin A.

People with underactive thyroid function (a highly underdiagnosed condition) should take vitamin A and not beta-carotene, because they have trouble making the vitamin from the carotenoid precursors or provitamins.

◆**Vitamin D,** acting with parathyroid hormone and calcitonin, is involved in calcium metabolism, helping to move calcium from intestines to blood and from blood to bone. Vitamin D deficiency interferes with absorption of phosphorus and calcium and results in a bone-deforming disease called rickets in children and osteomalacia in adults. Psoriasis frequently responds to D3 supplementation.

Vitamin D is converted in the liver and kidneys from precursors and from exposure to ultraviolet light. Anyone with liver, gall bladder or kidney problems may have difficulty with this conversion, resulting in osteoporosis. The active forms of vitamin D are ergocalciferol (vitamin D2) and cholecalciferol (vitamin D3). Vitamin D3 was misclassified as a vitamin—it is really a hormone.

Sources of vitamin D are fish liver oils, fatty salt-water fish, eggs, butter, alfalfa. Cholesterol-lowering drugs, steroids, mineral oil, and antacids interfere with D absorption. Some diuretics upset the calcium/vitamin D ratio. Take vitamin D with calcium.

◆**Vitamin E** is an important antioxidant. Antioxidants prevent aging, cancer, and CV disease. Vitamin E is useful in circulatory problems, including blood clots and varicose veins, in fibrocystic breast disease, PMS, menopausal symptoms, and sexual potency. It aids in wound and burn healing and, when applied topically can prevent new scars and heal old ones. It is more effective at treating and preventing blood clots than prescription blood thinners (some of which have the same ingredient as rat poison) and has no side effects. Vitamin E enhances oxygenation of the cells. The brain cells, which are particularly dependent on oxygen, derive great benefit from vitamin E supplements. It is very useful in depression and fatigue and to stabilize emotional disorders. Take instead of aspirin to help prevent stroke and heart attack.

Vitamin E demonstrates some of the fallacies of "scientific" testing. The Shute brothers in Canada did much research on vitamin E in the treatment of heart disease and angina, and found it to be very effective. Scientists in the U.S., however, were unable to replicate their findings. The reason was simple. The Shute brothers used a concentrated whole-food form of vitamin E for their studies. In the U.S., scientists used a fraction of vitamin E—the active ingredient, not the whole complex. Using the fraction, U.S. researchers could not replicate the Shute brothers' results and so they declared the Shute brothers' work to be invalid.

Here's another example of magic bullet thinking: It used to be recommended that vitamin E not be used for patients with high blood pressure, because vitamin E elevated blood pressure. In the short term, vitamin E does elevate blood pressure. This is a typical event in a natural healing cycle. There is an aggravation of symptoms (a good sign that the body is mounting a defense) before the improvement occurs. In fact, E can be helpful for treating some hypertensives. Recommended dosages of vitamin E vary from 200 IU to about 1600 IU. For each tablespoon of oil in your daily diet, add 100 IU[21] of vitamin E to protect yourself from the oil becoming rancid in your body.

When starting on vitamin E, begin with 100 IU/day and gradually increase your daily dosage to 400 to 1600 IU. Tocotrienols are an anti-tumor factor found in the gamma tocopherol fraction of vitamin E. They are plentiful in palm and rice bran oils. It's better not to take vitamin E with mineral supplements, because E is a mineral chelator. The exception to this is selenium, because E reduces selenium's possible toxic effects.

Food sources of vitamin E include whole raw nuts, seeds and grains and unrefined vegetable oils made from them, but E is completely lost when the oils are refined or

---

[21] We don't know what the exact ratio should be yet.

hydrogenated. It is found in the wheat germ which is removed in milling and it is not one of the eight synthetic vitamins put back into "enriched" flour. Before the popularity of white "enriched" flour, our daily intake of vitamin E was about 150 IU a day. Now, if the vitamin is not supplemented, someone on the average U.S. diet gets about 7 IU a day.

◆**Vitamin F**, or the essential fatty acids (EFA's), are discussed above under Fats (p. 50). Extra EFA's are needed by people who do a lot of mental work. EFA's are found in raw nuts, seeds and grains, and in cold-pressed vegetable and fish oils.

◆**Vitamin K** is made to a limited extent by bacterial flora in the human gut. It is required for making blood-clotting factors, and may have a role in bone formation and osteoporosis. It is also involved in the conversion of glucose into glycogen for liver storage. Food sources include alfalfa, broccoli, dark-green leafy vegetables, Brussels sprouts, cabbage, egg yolks, liver, and safflower oil.

Water-Soluble Vitamins

◆**The B-Complex** vitamins are important in maintaining healthy nerves, skin, eyes, hair, liver, mouth, and the muscle tone of the gastro-intestinal (GI) tract. They are involved in cellular energy production and are useful in treating depression, schizophrenia, anxiety and alcoholism. Older methods of studying B-vitamins indicated that the whole complex should be taken together, in a specific ratio. This, however, no longer appears to be the case, although if you need a therapeutic dose of B1 for fibrocystic breast disease, for example, you should take a B1-complex containing a high dose (250 mg) of B1 combined with a lower, but balanced dose, of the rest of the complex of other B vitamins.

◆**Vitamin B1 (thiamine)** is involved in circulation and in the manufacture of hydrochloric acid in the body. The neurological disease beriberi is caused by thiamine deficiency. It occurs in those eating a low-protein, highly refined-carbohydrate diet. In China, rice is the staple food. In the 1930's, they began to mill rice in China to make the polished rice product you get in Chinese restaurants today. Only the wealthy could afford the processed rice. When they started eating it, they suffered an epidemic of beriberi as a result of the sudden nutritional deficiency in the refined rice.

Thiamine has recently been implicated in a long and growing list of symptoms that may be a result of the high-carbohydrate diet. Benign breast lumps may be effectively treated with B1. It affects energy, growth and learning, and is needed for normal muscle tone of the digestive system and heart.

Sources include whole-grain rice, egg yolks, fish, organ meats, pork, poultry, asparagus, broccoli, Brussels sprouts, Brazil nuts, plums. Antibiotics, sulfa drugs, and birth control pills destroy thiamine.

◆**Vitamin B2 (riboflavin)** helps form red blood cells and antibodies. It is active in cell respiration, growth, and in metabolism of the macronutrients. It is important in eye function and can relieve eyestrain and help prevent cataracts. It assists in oxygen use in tissues and is necessary for good skin, hair and nails. Cracks and sores around the corners of the mouth may indicate B2 deficiency. Deficiency may cause fetal damage.

Food sources include cheese, eggs, fish, meat, poultry, spinach, yogurt, asparagus, avocado, broccoli, Brussels sprouts, Brazil nuts.

◆**Vitamin B3** (niacin, niacinamide, nicotinic acid) is needed for proper circulation and healthy skin. It aids in metabolism and helps produce hydrochloric acid. Niacin megadoses have been used effectively to treat depression, schizophrenia, Tourette's syndrome, alcoholism and hypercholesteremia. However, high intake of niacin can give false-positive liver blood tests and may cause liver damage. Niacin causes a flush for about half an hour with redness and itching. Doses should be increased slowly starting with 50 mg at a time. **Pregnant women and people suffering gout, peptic ulcers, glaucoma, liver disease and diabetes should use high amounts with extreme caution**. Niacin is energizing and stimulating; niacinamide is sedative. In general, limit daily doses to under 600 mg. Food sources include beef, broccoli, carrots, cheese, eggs, fish, milk, pork, and tomatoes.

◆**Pantothenic Acid B5**, the anti-stress vitamin, helps in the production of adrenal hormones and antibodies and is involved in energy production. It is needed by all cells in the body, and helps in normal functioning of the GI tract. It is useful in treating depression, anxiety and hypoglycemia. Sources include beef, eggs, salt-water fish, human milk, pork, and many fresh vegetables.

◆**Vitamin B6 (pyridoxine)** is one of the most important single nutrients, affecting physical and mental health. It is involved in cancer immunity, liver function and menstrual cycles. It helps prevent atherosclerosis, and is useful in treating allergies, PMS, arthritis, asthma and carpal tunnel syndrome. During childbearing years, women require 300 mg. per day.[22] B6 is also available in a precursor form as pyridoxyl-5'-phosphate. Serum homocysteine levels are a more accurate risk factor for cardiovascular disease than serum cholesterol. Homocysteine (p. 33) is an intermediate liver product that is toxic to the lining of blood vessels. The destructive action of homocysteine can be counteracted in most cases by supplementing B6 (along with B12, folic acid). A 1998 (*JAMA*, May) study showed a risk reduction for heart attacks in women to be 50 percent with intake of as little as 400 mcg of folic acid and 3 mg of B6. **In Parkinson's disease, limit intake to 2 mg/day.**

---

[22] For the time being, therapeutic doses of B6, above 250 mg/day, should not be used during pregnancy. One study indicated that it might be involved in birth defects. But it should be started again postpartum.

Food sources: carrots, chicken, eggs, fish, meat, peas, spinach, avocado, banana, brown rice, cabbage and cantaloupe. Anti-depressants, estrogen replacement and birth control pills increase the need for B6. Deficiency can be a trigger for encapsulated tumors.

♦**Vitamin B12 (cyanocobalamin)** aids in cell formation and longevity. It is needed to digest and absorb foods, make protein, use carbohydrate and fat, and to produce energy. It prevents nerve damage, maintains fertility and promotes normal growth and development. B12 is produced in the GI tract from intestinal flora. People with digestive problems, including older people, may be unable to synthesize sufficient amounts. These people suffer from pernicious anemia. B12 is one of the B-complex vitamins involved in homocysteine metabolism. Since Brazil nuts are the only vegetable food with B12, vegetarians should eat raw Brazil nuts or supplement B12.

Food sources include blue cheese, clams, eggs, herring, kidney, liver, mackerel, milk, and seafood. Blood thinners, potassium supplements, and anti-gout meds may block absorption of B12.

♦**Biotin** aids in cell growth, metabolism and fatty-acid production. It is necessary for the utilization of the B-complex. It is necessary for skin sweat glands, nerve tissue, bone marrow, and healthy hair (and may help prevent hair loss in some men). Seborrhea, especially in infants, may indicate biotin deficiency.

Biotin is synthesized in the GI tract from foods and is found in cooked egg yolk, salt-water fish, meat, milk, and poultry. A substance in raw egg white (ovidin) depletes the body of biotin, and rancid fats and saccharin interfere with its absorption.

♦**Choline** is necessary for nerve transmission, gall bladder and liver function and lecithin formation in the liver and intestines. Lecithin is an emulsifier that homogenizes fat and cholesterol into tiny particles that can be used by the tissues, so choline minimizes excess fat in the liver. Choline aids in hormone production and helps metabolize fat and cholesterol. It is essential to brain function and memory. Choline is useful in treating Parkinson's disease and tardive dyskinesia. It should be taken by anyone who does a lot of mental work. It is also useful for those with high-stress life styles and in menopause. As a supplement, it is available in lecithin, but phosphatidylcholine supplements have far higher amounts of choline. In foods, it is found in egg yolks, meat, and milk.

♦**Folic Acid** is also brain food. It helps make energy, new red blood cells and healthy new cells. Folate-deficient women are 20 times more likely to develop cervical cancer. It is useful for treating cervical dysplasia, depression and anxiety. Folic acid deficiency may result in a red, sore tongue, and in high homocysteine levels (p. 33).

During embryological development, folic-acid deficiency causes neural tube defects like spina bifida. Although it was strongly indicated that folic-acid deficiency was implicated in spina bifida, the FDA decided to sit on the information during 10 years of testing. In those 10 years, thousands of cases of spina bifida could have been prevented with a small harmless dose of folic acid. Any woman of child-bearing years should be taking it.

A lot of folic acid in the diet can mask B12 anemia in blood counts. B12 anemia can lead to brain damage. If you suspect, vitamin B12 deficiency, based on symptoms, get an inexpensive serum vitamin B12 test to be sure. Folic acid consumption does not interfere with the serum B12 test. However, women all over the world have been taking 1000 mcg of folic acid a day for 20 years with no harm. Folic acid is so important in the prevention of cervical cancer and atherosclerotic heart disease, I recommend 800-1000 mcg/day.

Food sources include whole grain rice, cheese, chicken, green leafy vegetables, lamb, liver, milk, oranges, organ meats, pork, salmon, and tuna. Folic acid and B12 are antagonistic to each other in that they compete for the same receptor sites in the blood. It may be beneficial to take them separately as supplements. In that case, take B12 in the morning to early afternoon and folic acid later in the day into the night. Oral contraceptives increase the need for folic acid. **Folic acid is contraindicated in hormone-related cancers and convulsive disorders.**

◆**Inositol** is important in lecithin formation, and therefore in fat and cholesterol metabolism (see choline, on page 66). It stimulates hair growth and prevents atherosclerosis. It is found in fruits and vegetables, meat and milk. Heavy caffeine use depletes inositol.

◆**PABA (Para-Aminobenzoic Acid)** is part of folic acid and aids in the utilization of pantothenic acid. PABA is an antioxidant which, when taken internally, protects against sunburn and cancer, assists in the metabolism of protein and in the formation of red blood cells. It is rumored to restore gray hair to its natural color (200 mg after each meal), when the gray is caused by stress or nutritional deficiency. It has been used to treat vitiligo and other skin pigmentation disorders. Because PABA interferes with the action of sulfa drugs, the FDA made it a prescription item in dosages over 30 mg. This effectively curtailed most of the PABA research.

PABA is found in kidney and liver. For sunburn protection, 1 gm/day is recommended for a week prior to sun exposure.

◆**Vitamin C** is an antioxidant. It is required for tissue growth and repair, adrenal function and healthy gums. It is needed to form collagen, the most abundant tissue in our bodies. Scurvy, which is marked by spongy gums and loosening teeth due to breakage of collagen cross linkages, occurs with vitamin C deficiency. Vitamin C has so many uses that it is difficult to list them all. It protects us against pollution, infection, toxicity, and blood clotting. It promotes wound healing, immunity and prevents bruising. Vitamin C is used to cure the common cold, and in treatment for AIDS and cancer. Vitamin C comes in many forms. Ascorbic acid is the "active" ingredient, but when you take natural forms of C in synergistic combination with all the products with which it exists in nature, its effect is multiplied a thousandfold. For years, Standard Process has made a 1-mg natural vitamin C that has the effect of 1 gm of ascorbic acid. Until recently, this was the form I used with hypoglycemic patients, because ascorbic acid can make people more insulin-resistant. Combining bioflavonoids with C can produce the same multiplying effects.

Humans have lost the capacity to make vitamin C, although healthy sheep, for example, manufacture about 15 gms/day. I usually recommend between 1 gm and 15 gms/day depending on the situation. Excess vitamin C is lost in the urine, and when your body's tissues are saturated, you get diarrhea. That's a simple way to know your limit. If you get diarrhea, cut back by 500 mg-1 gm/day.

Vitamin C is found in green vegetables, berries, citrus fruit, asparagus, avocado, beet greens, broccoli, Brussels sprouts, cantaloupe, collard greens, kale, mangos, mustard greens, onions, papaya, parsley, green peas, sweet peppers, persimmons, pineapple, radish, rose hips, spinach, strawberries, Swiss chard, tomato, turnip greens, watercress.

Because vitamin C is easily destroyed, (and may not be in foods by the time they reach your table), I recommend supplements. Aspirin, alcohol, analgesics, anti-depressants, blood thinners, birth control pills, and steroids destroy vitamin C in the body, so if you are using these, take extra vitamin C. Cigarette smokers should add 25 mg/cigarette/day to a base intake of 1-2 gms. So a pack-a-day smoker should take a minimum of 2500 mg of vitamin C a day. Vitamin C interferes with the action of sulfa drugs and Diabinase, an oral diabetic medication. In pregnancy, limit your intake or a rebound effect may cause scurvy in the infant. When decreasing vitamin C dosing, after an illness, for example, reduce the dose in increments over a period of time to prevent a rebound effect. When facing surgery, limit vitamin C for several days to prevent hemorrhage.

Linus Pauling, two-time Nobel Prize winner, made a third career of studying and experimenting with high doses of vitamin C. If he is any example of the effect of high doses of vitamin C, then everyone should be taking it. He lived in polluted southern California until the age of 93 and worked vigorously until the end of his life.

◆**Vitamin P (bioflavonoids, p. 59)** are not true "vitamins." However, they enhance the absorption of vitamin C, usually coexist with vitamin C in nature, and should be taken together with vitamin C. There are many bioflavonoid compounds, including hesperidin, quercetin, rutin and pycnogenols. They relieve pain and bruising in athletic injuries and reduce symptoms associated with bleeding and low serum calcium. They act with vitamin C to protect capillary walls. They are anti-bacterial, promote circulation and bile production, lower cholesterol levels, and prevent cataracts. They have been used to treat oral herpes. Quercetin (which should be taken with bromelain) is used in asthma treatment and for allergies. Bioflavonoids are antioxidants.

Food sources of bioflavonoids include the white part of the rind of citrus peel, peppers, buckwheat, black currants, grape seeds, apricots, rose hips, and acerola berries.

❖⌘❖

CHAPTER 7— MINERALS

Micronutrients

❖⌘❖

Like vitamins, minerals are not manufactured by the body and so must be supplied in the diet. They are necessary as cofactors and catalysts in chemical reactions. They are needed to make up the proper composition of the body fluids: blood plasma, lymph, and cerebrospinal fluid. They help form blood and bone and maintain nerve function.

People and animals are basically made chemically of organic compounds, consisting of atoms and molecules of carbon, hydrogen, oxygen, nitrogen and phosphorus. These chemicals bond together in a special way. None of the normal chemicals that make up these organic compounds are like the kind of minerals that make up rocks. In fact, those chemicals are called inorganic. But we do need these rock minerals to perform special jobs in our bodies. They act as cofactors in chemical reactions in the same way vitamins do (p. 58). The fact that organic compounds and minerals do not mix is important in understanding the best ways to get minerals from the diet or in food supplements. Eating a rusty nail will get iron into your body, but it is unlikely that much of that iron will get to become part of your body—it will simply be eliminated out the other end.

Minerals that we can use are broken down into tiny crystals in the earth by natural forces of erosion. Then microbes in the soil break them down further. The minerals are taken up by plants. The plants with the minerals in them are then eaten by animals. Man gets minerals either by eating plants directly, or by eating animals that ate the plants, or by using sea salt.

The minerals in the plants and animals that we eat are, for the most part, chelated compounds. Chelate comes from a Greek word meaning *claw*. An organic molecule, usually a complicated protein, shaped like a claw grabs hold of a mineral and holds on to it. Hemoglobin is an organic chelate binding iron. Its function is to carry oxygen to all the cells of the body. Amino-acid chelated minerals are the most digestible and easily assimilated forms of minerals for human consumption.

When the European immigrants began farming in the U.S., they had virgin soil full of minerals. The Thanksgiving story tells how the Native Americans of Massachusetts taught the Pilgrims to plant corn. Along with the seed corn, they buried a fish. The fish provided natural fertilizer to both the plant and the soil. So the Pilgrims started out with natural farming methods. Other natural farming methods include crop rotation, green manuring, mulching and composting to replenish the soil with minerals and other organic material. Flood plains of river valleys used to be some of our most valuable farm land, because the flood waters would naturally fertilize the soil. But we have built levees and dams to control floods. Then we built homes and cities on the flood plains, so now we have to prevent the floods to protect the homes.

Natural fertilization and soil-conditioning methods have been replaced with cheaper petrochemical-based fertilizers which add potassium, nitrogen and phosphorus to the soil and nothing else. Where natural farming methods are ignored, the played-out soil turns to dust and just blows away as in the Dust Bowl during the Great Depression in the 1930's. When the minerals are not in the soil, they are not in the plants. Our commercial food supply is now very deficient in magnesium and in most of the trace minerals.

This soil depletion is only one of the reasons it is more healthful to eat organically grown sources of food. Organic farming uses natural methods to fertilize and condition the soil and the plants. Fresh organically grown foods will generally contain more nutrients than commercially grown foods. After farm land has been abused for years, it takes at least seven years of replenishing and restoring the soil before it can grow healthy crops. The government is currently trying to make it illegal to label foods organic.

◆**Boron** aids in calcium uptake. Supplementing 2-3 mg/day in post-menopausal women and older men helps prevent bone loss. It also relieves symptoms of menopause such as hot flashes. It should be found in leafy vegetables, fruit and nuts. Limit intake to 3 mg or less per day.

◆**Calcium** is vital to the structure of strong teeth and bones and the genetic materials of RNA and DNA. It helps maintain regular heartbeat, muscle contraction and nerve transmission. It is essential to blood-clot formation, helps prevent colon cancer and is necessary to prevent bone loss (osteoporosis). It activates enzymes, including lipase.

To build bone, humans need about 1 gm of calcium/day with about an equal amount of phosphorus and half as much magnesium. Vitamin D must be present as well, along with B-vitamins, vitamin C and zinc. Additional magnesium is needed by the body for other pathways. It is one of the most important minerals of body function.

Because calcium is so important to so many processes, the body has several mechanisms to make sure the blood level of calcium remains stable. When the blood level of calcium falls, the parathyroid gland liberates calcium from joints and bones and sends it to the blood. When there is excess calcium in the blood, the thyroid gland can deposit it back into body structures.

Recent experiments and observations confirm that calcium supplementation (combined with the other synergists) slows down the rate of bone loss, but it doesn't replace bone already lost. Highest amounts of bone loss occur during sleep, so nutritionists are recommending that calcium supplements be taken in the evening. However, weight-bearing exercise increases the rate of new bone growth dramatically. A good program for older people might combine 3-5 miles per day of walking with mild weight-training 3 days a week. Recent studies with people over age 70 have shown rapid increase in bone density with weight training.

The best forms of calcium to take are hydroxyapatite from freeze-dried bone; citrate; aspartate; and amino-acid chelate. Calcium lactate will relieve nighttime leg cramps, but will not prevent bone loss. If you take the same form of calcium year in and year out, your body may stop absorbing it. So it is recommended that you rotate among several forms of calcium (aspartate, citrate, amino-acid chelate, and hydroxyapatite), changing from one to another every 3-4 months.

Taking calcium supplements toward the beginning of a meal is preferable, because the stomach needs to be in a state of higher acid production to break the calcium down for digestion. Although an antacid may be an inexpensive source of calcium (and therefore better than other antacids that contain aluminum), it is very difficult to assimilate this calcium. Most of the time, you get what you pay for.

The catch is that the antacid is designed to reduce stomach acidity, thereby creating an environment in which calcium cannot easily be broken down. In addition, the calcium source is calcium carbonate (limestone), which is very hard to digest anyway. For these reasons, antacids are a very poor form of calcium supplementation. It is probable that indigestible forms of calcium from milk and antacids, for example, may actually promote osteoporosis as well as contribute to arthritic spurs and kidney and gall stone formation.

Antacids are the most precribed drugs in the U.S. but they are just a symptom-chasing way to deal with gastro-intestinal problems. When I interview patients with widespread vague joint pains and instability, I always inquire about antacid use. Antacids interfere with calcium absorption, and so the body begins to rob the joints of calcium to maintain optimum blood levels. With TBM treatments to turn digestion back on and supplementation with hydrochloric acid and/or pancreatic enzymes, most digestive problems can be cleared up in a healthful way.

If you eat the bones, canned salmon and sardines are good sources of calcium. Other good sources are dark-green leafy vegetables, almonds, asparagus, brewer's yeast, broccoli, cabbage, collards, dandelion greens, dulse, filberts, raw goat's milk, raw-milk cheeses, kale, kelp, mustard greens, oats, parsley, prunes, sesame seeds, turnip greens, whey and raw-milk yogurt.

There are some other guidelines that will help you use your calcium supplements healthfully. Spread calcium supplements out in several smaller doses for better absorption. Iron and calcium interfere with each other and should not be taken together. Calcium and zinc are antagonistic to each other and should also be taken at separate times. Most multiple vitamin/mineral supplements will give you all these antagonistic minerals together.

Some foods that are high in calcium also contain oxalic acid, which blocks calcium absorption in some people. They include soybeans, kale, spinach, rhubarb, beet greens, almonds, cashews, chard and cocoa.

Here's a test to see if your calcium supplement is absorbable. Drop a pill into a glass of water. If it hasn't dissolved within 24 hours, you probably cannot digest it.

Diets high in sugar and refined carbohydrates block calcium absorption and your body actually has to use some of its calcium to process the sugar. This may explain why people on diets high in sugar and refined carbohydrates develop so many types of diseases that are related to calcium metabolism (see Weston Price, p 135).

There are several good combination supplements that contain all the synergists the body needs to absorb calcium and several designed primarily for post-menopausal women. Such a supplement should contain all the minerals we have mentioned in relation to calcium absorption: calcium, at least half as much magnesium, phosphorus, and vitamin D. It should also contain: boron, silica (or horsetail or shavetail grass), and ovary and, possibly, adrenal tissue. Post-menopausal women are at the highest risk for developing osteoporosis, but it also affects men—it just takes longer.

Synthetic estrogen is prescribed for post-menopausal women to protect against osteoporosis. However, recent studies show that after the women stop taking the estrogen, usually in their early sixties, their bone loss accelerates so rapidly that they catch up with their non-estrogen-using sisters within a year (*N Eng J of Med.* 10/14/93). So in their seventies and eighties, when hip fractures and vertebral fractures are most likely to occur and to be life-threatening, they have lost as much bone as if they had never used estrogen. These women are at just as high a risk for osteoporosis. And they have exposed themselves to the additional risks of synthetic hormones—cancer, heart disease, breakthrough uterine bleeding, etc.

There are many good nutritional supplements, herbs, homeopathic remedies, and foods that allow a woman to pass through an uneventful menopause without exposing her to unnecessary risk. Menopause is not an estrogen-deficiency disease, but a normal passage in a woman's life. But we see here in action another negative effect of the high-sugar and-carbohydrate diet. It wears out the adrenal glands. When a woman reaches menopause and the ovaries stop manufacturing estrogen, the adrenal glands should kick in with an estrogen-like hormone. But her adrenal glands are so wiped out from dealing with sugar and stress that they are too tired to manufacture estradiol.

Here's another calcium myth shattered. Pasteurized milk products are not good sources of calcium, because the heating process has caused the calcium to combine with casein (you know, the stuff from which they make Elmer's glue) into calcium caseinate. This is not easily absorbed. It's been estimated that only about 5 percent of the calcium in pasteurized milk can be absorbed by humans.

If you have a tendency to form stones, talk to your TBM practitioner about simple, inexpensive and effective treatments for dissolving kidney and gall stones, and for balancing your body chemistry and your endocrine glands to prevent formation of new stones. And take the right calcium supplements.

◆**Chromium or Glucose Tolerance Factor (GTF)** is involved in the metabolism of blood sugar and keeps it stable, while helping to produce energy. It also helps make cholesterol, fat and protein. Low chromium levels are implicated in coronary artery disease. Researchers estimate that two-thirds of the American population has sugar metabolism problems (hypoglycemia, insulin resistance, syndrome X, or diabetes. See the chapter on Carbohydrate Metabolism, p. 87). In the U.S., our food supply is woefully deficient in chromium, probably contributing to our high cardiovascular disease and diabetes rates.

Chromium picolinate has been widely advertised for weight loss, but there is no great advantage in the picolinate form except to acid endocrine[23] types, like thyroid and thymus, who absorb picolinates better than they do the other forms of minerals like citrates, aspartates, or vegetable cultures.

Chromium should be found in brown rice, cheese, meat, whole grains, legumes, chicken, dairy products, calf's liver, mushrooms and potatoes. However, because our soil is deficient in chromium, you may not find it in food grown in depleted soils. Because of its importance in sugar metabolism and cardiovascular disease, I consider chromium an important mineral to supplement, up to 1200 mcg/day.

◆**Copper** aids in bone, collagen, nerve, hemoglobin and red blood cell formation. With zinc and vitamin C, it forms the elastin of connective tissues. It is involved in healing, energy production, skin coloring and the sense of taste.

Osteoporosis is a sign of copper deficiency. Another sign is the inability to drink more than a sip of water at a time.

Copper can leach into foods from cookware (including copper-bottom pots) and into water through copper plumbing. It is found in many foods: almonds, avocado, barley,

---

[23] Richard and Laura Power. *The 8 Endocrine Biotypes.*

beet greens, garlic, lentils, liver, mushrooms, nuts, oats, oranges, organ meats, pecans, radishes, salmon, seafood, soybeans, and green leafy vegetables.

Copper can be depleted by excess zinc and vitamin C. Men who take zinc for prostate health should supplement copper (2 mg/day) or they may develop weak joints or arthritic symptoms.

◆**Germanium**, a recently discovered trace mineral, helps bring oxygen to body tissues. Studies have found that 100-300 mg/day caused improvement in a wide range of chronic degenerative diseases like rheumatoid arthritis, food allergies, high cholesterol, candidiasis, chronic viral infections, cancer and AIDS. It is also a pain-killer. Production is limited, so this can be an expensive supplement.

Food sources include aloe vera, comfrey, garlic, ginseng, shiitake mushrooms, onions and suma.

◆**Iodine** is the trace mineral necessary for the thyroid gland to manufacture hormone, so it is involved in the myriad of thyroid functions: energy, weight control, hair and nail growth, depression, concentration, and memory. Iodine deficiency in children can cause mental retardation. It has recently been linked to breast cancer in adults. Iodine deficiency causes goiter, an enlargement of the gland (seen in the external throat), when the thyroid can't produce enough hormone. There is some evidence that infants whose mothers were deficient in iodine (and selenium) may be more prone to sudden infant death syndrome (SIDS). There is also evidence that many people diagnosed with Alzheimer's disease are actually suffering from hypothyroidism that could be treated easily.

Sources of iodine include salt-water seafoods (fish, shellfish and seaweeds), asparagus, dulse, garlic, lima beans, mushrooms, sea salt, sesame seeds, soybeans, spinach, summer squash, Swiss chard, and turnip greens.

Some foods block the uptake of iodine by the thyroid. They are called goiterogenic (causing goiter) and include Brussels sprouts, cabbage, cauliflower, kale, peaches, pears, spinach, and turnips. Consider eliminating them if you have goiter or another underactive thyroid condition.

To determine if you have a thyroid problem, a good marker test is basal body temperature (BBT).[24] Shake down a thermometer. Put it at your bedside. When you awake in the morning, before you get out of bed, take your temperature. The prescribed method is an underarm temperature for 10 minutes. (These directions are from before digital thermometers were invented.) A fever thermometer will work, but a basal body temperature or ovulation-predictor thermometer will be easier to read.

---

[24] Broda Barnes, M.D. and Lawrence Galton. *Hypothyroidism: The Unsuspected Illness.*

Do this for three days in a row at the same time each morning. For menstruating women, it is best done from the first or second day of the menstrual cycle on. A normal thyroid should give you a temperature of 97.8-98.2 degrees Fahrenheit. If the numbers are consistently below 97.8, you may have an underactive thyroid. If the numbers are consistently above 98.2, you may have an overactive thyroid. The BBT will give you an indication long before thyroid blood tests will, because it is very sensitive and because it measures function. Blood tests are inaccurate, both because you have to be very sick before they test positive and because they measure factors in the blood not function in the cells. And the thyroid blood tests don't measure the complicated interactions between the thyroid, adrenal and pituitary glands, and the liver.

One of the most common problems I have found as a TBM doctor is the presence of lead toxicity in the thyroid gland, preventing normal function. This usually occurs in combination with a serious emotional event. Using TBM techniques and nutritional supplementation to chelate the lead, we have been able to stimulate the thyroid to function normally again.

Recent research from England and the U.S. indicates that iodized salt[25] may be causing an epidemic of thyroid problems—just what it was designed to prevent. People in the midwest U.S., who had little access to iodine-containing salt-water fish and sea vegetables, often developed goiter. To help prevent this, it was decided that salt should be iodized for everyone—not just those whose diets were deficient. Too much iodine in an otherwise adequate diet is causing both hypo- and hyperthyroid problems. (And now iodized salt also contains 15 percent sugar to keep it free flowing.)

Extra iodine is also found in expectorants, antiseptics, drugs and contrast dyes for radiography.

♦**Iron** carries oxygen in the red blood cells, which then carry the oxygen to the body cells. Aside from oxygenation of blood, iron has many important roles. It is essential for many enzymes involved in growth and resistance to disease.

Deficiency symptoms include fatigue due to poor oxygenation (anemia), brittle hair, spoon-shaped nails, ridged nails, hair loss, pallor and dizziness.

Iron absorption can be enhanced by taking iron with vitamin C. An acidic stomach is also necessary, so take iron between meals or at the beginning of meals. Other nutrients that enhance iron absorption are copper, manganese, molybdenum, vitamin A and B complex. Vitamin E and zinc are antagonistic to iron absorption, as is calcium. Most therapeutic forms of iron, such as iron oxide, ferrous fumarate, and iron gluconate are poorly absorbed. Most of this unabsorbable iron is excreted in the stool. Consequently the stool

---

[25] "What Doctors Don't Tell You." Vol 7:7, 11/96.

turns black and hard, and constipation may occur. These iron pills may contain stool softeners to prevent the constipation, but that doesn't improve your body's absorption of the iron. The bottom line is that if you don't absorb it, your body can't use it. My recommendations for iron supplements are Ferrofood (Standard Process) and amino-acid chelate. Because of recent studies about iron's possible relation to heart disease (p. 33), I do not recommend that adult men or post-menopausal women supplement iron unless they have iron deficiency anemia. In pregnancy, there is a period of pseudo anemia, because the blood volume is expanding. If your serum ferritin (stored iron) is okay, don't take iron supplements. You can deplete your circulating hemoglobin and still not have anemia.

Excess iron can build up in tissues as occurs in hemochromatosis, cirrhosis of the liver, diabetes and heart problems. Therefore it is preferable to take multi-mineral supplements without iron or copper. Then you can control your iron intake by using separate iron and/or copper supplements. Some conditions, such as rheumatoid arthritis, candidiasis, bleeding ulcers, chronic herpes, heavy perimenopausal periods, and cancer, may result in iron-deficiency anemia of both circulating and stored iron.

Taking an aspirin a day to prevent stroke causes minute amounts of capillary bleeding and can lead to anemia. The capillary bloodletting may actually be what makes the treatment effective. Think about giving blood a few times a year instead, and taking fish-liver oils, selenium and or vitamin E to prevent platelet aggregation.

Iron is readily obtained from the diet in eggs, fish, liver, meat, poultry, green leafy vegetables, whole grains. Lesser sources include avocado, dulse, kelp, lentils, legumes, parsley, peaches, pears, prunes, pumpkins, rice, sesame seeds and soybeans.

Iron is stored by the body in the liver, spleen and bone marrow. One of the liver's functions is to recapture and recycle iron. But iron is lost to the body through strenuous exercise and heavy perspiration, bleeding ulcers, heavy menstrual cycles, and chronic illness.

♦**Magnesium** assists in calcium and potassium absorption. It is vital to cellular energy production in the Krebs cycle, and to nerve and muscle impulses. It protects arterial walls and aids in mineral metabolism. It is one of the most important functional minerals in the body. In spite of all the propaganda about calcium supplements and osteoporosis, it is likely that magnesium deficiency is more of a problem than calcium.

Magnesium is used in chronic fatigue states, insomnia, irritability and depression. It aids in preventing dizziness, muscle weakness and twitching, heart disease and high blood pressure. Because magnesium is similar to calcium in electrochemical activity, it can replace calcium at receptor sites in chelated (see p. 69) compounds in the body. So magnesium can be used (orally or by injection) to break up the calcium deposits that bind arterial plaques to the inside of the artery walls.

Alcoholics and children of alcoholics are frequently deficient in magnesium, vitamin B6, folic acid and zinc. Many of their mental, emotional and physical symptoms can be greatly relieved with adequate supplementation of these nutrients.

Magnesium should be easily obtainable from the following: dairy products, fish, meat, seafood, apples, apricots, avocado, banana, whole grain rice, garlic, kelp, lima beans, nuts, peaches, salmon, sesame seeds, green leafy vegetables, and whole wheat. However, since magnesium is depleted in the soil, many foods do not contain the levels that they should.

The body's need for magnesium increases with alcohol and diuretic use. Diuretics are drugs that flush water out of the tissues. This body water often contains dissolved minerals. Magnesium need increases because your body's ability to use it decreases with the use of fluoridated water, high amounts of zinc, oxalic acid, cod liver oil, and vitamin D. Because magnesium is deficient in the soil and is such a vital mineral, it should be supplemented. If you are taking a gram of calcium, take at least 500 mg magnesium. Take an additional 500-1000 mg of magnesium separately. Magnesium (as in milk of magnesia) may cause loose stools or diarrhea.

♦**Manganese** is needed in trace amounts for protein and fat metabolism, healthy nerves, immune system function and blood-sugar regulation. It is required for energy production, bone growth, and reproduction. It is necessary to iron-deficient anemics and for the use of B1 and vitamin E. It's needed to oxidize fats, produce enzymes and metabolize purine. The intervertebral disc material in the spine is made up largely of manganese, which should be used therapeutically in intervertebral disc degeneration and slipped and herniated discs.

Avocados, nuts, seeds, seaweed and whole grains are primary sources of manganese. Secondary sources include blueberries, egg yolk, legumes and lentils, pineapples, spinach and green leafy vegetables.

♦**Molybdenum** is essential in trace amounts for nucleoprotein metabolism and in the excretion of the end products in the urine. It is helpful in treating sensitivity to MSG and sulfites (food additives) and strong aromas, like perfumes and solvents. It is found in the liver and bones.

Deficiency states are associated with disorders of the mouth and gums, with cancer, and with impotence in older men. Deficiency states occur with diets high in refined, processed foods and high sulfur intake. Too high an intake of molybdenum (over 15 mg/day) may produce gout and may interfere with copper metabolism.

Food sources are beans, cereals, legumes, peas and dark-green leafy vegetables.

♦ **Phosphorus** is necessary for bone and tooth formation, cell growth, heart muscle contraction and kidney function. It aids in energy production. Balanced amounts are needed with magnesium and calcium to promote absorption of all three minerals.

Phosphorus is high in junk food diets, especially with consumption of carbonated beverages and soda pops, which contain phosphoric acid. Excess phosphorus will increase bone loss and osteoporosis.

Phosphorus is abundant in asparagus, bran, corn, dairy products, eggs, fish, garlic, legumes, nuts, sesame and sunflower seeds, meats, poultry, salmon and whole grains.

♦**Potassium** is important for a healthy nervous system and regular heart rate. Every cell in the body has a sodium-potassium pump which regulates fluid balance. This pump is specialized in nerve cells to create electricity for nerve impulses. Potassium is an important catalyst in chemical reactions, helps regulate transfer of nutrients to the cells, and is needed for hormone secretion. Night-time leg cramps are effectively treated with a mineral supplement containing potassium, calcium and magnesium.

Potassium and sodium levels must be in a proper ratio in the body. The sodium-potassium pump in each cell creates an electrical charge along the cell membrane. This keeps water in balance inside and outside the cell. The pump is specialized in nerve cells to create the electrical impulse that carries nerve messages between the brain and the rest of the body.

Because this sodium-potassium relationship is so important, the kidneys are designed to waste potassium and save sodium. The use of diuretics and laxatives causes potassium deficiencies, because they eliminate potassium from the body. When the liquid protein diets were the rage in the 70's, several people died of heartbeat irregularities due to potassium loss. Kidney disorders can raise potassium blood levels. Potassium levels must be regulated carefully in kidney disease. Deficiency has been implicated in fatigue states.

Potassium can be found in dairy foods, fish, fruit, legumes, meat, poultry, vegetables and whole grains. Good potassium sources are apricots, avocado, bananas, kiwi, whole-grain rice, dried fruit, garlic, nuts, potatoes, winter squash, wheat bran and yams.

♦**Selenium** is an important antioxidant, especially when combined with vitamin E, with which it also works to produce antibodies and protect the heart. Selenium is required for pancreatic function and for tissue elasticity. Deficiencies have been linked to heart disease and cancer. Use selenium instead of aspirin to prevent heart attack and stroke.

Selenium should be found in Brazil nuts, broccoli, brown rice, chicken, dairy, garlic, liver, meat, onions, salmon, seafood, tuna, vegetables, wheat germ, and whole grains.

◆**Silicon (Silica)** is essential for bone and collagen formation, and for healthy hair, skin and nails. Silica prevents arteriosclerosis and counteracts the effects of aluminum in Alzheimer's disease and osteoporosis.

Boron, calcium, magnesium, manganese and potassium aid in uptake of silica. Food sources include alfalfa sprouts, brown rice, horsetail grass herb, mother's milk, bell peppers, soybeans, leafy green vegetables and whole grains.

◆**Sodium** maintains proper fluid balance and pH in the body. It is needed for stomach, nerve and muscle function. Sodium deficiency is rare, because the kidneys save sodium. However, deficiency symptoms include confusion, low blood sugar, weakness, lethargy and heart palpitations—all symptoms of acute dehydration.

Although doctors have been warning for years about sodium being a culprit in heart disease and hypertension, recent experiments refute those findings. Tests in this country using iodized salt showed no significant increases in blood pressure among normal people and only a slight increase in those who already had hypertension. A recent study in the Netherlands used Celtic sea salt to treat hypertensives and their blood pressure decreased with the use of the sea salt.

Salt cravings are a sign of generalized dehydration. Chronic subacute dehydration is one of the prime causes of degenerative disease. Almost all foods contain some sodium.

◆**Sulfur** disinfects the blood, resists bacterial infection, protects the protoplasm of cells, and is necessary to collagen formation. It is an acid-forming mineral and aids in oxygen-hydrogen reactions, stimulates bile secretion in the liver for fat digestion, and protects against toxic substances. It is a powerful defender against radiation and pollution, slows aging and extends life.

Sulfur has a very distinctive odor when cooked. It is contained in broccoli sprouts and broccoli, Brussels sprouts, legumes, cabbage, eggs, fish, garlic, horsetail grass, kale, meat, onions, soybeans, turnip, and wheat germ. It is also found in the sulfur-bearing amino acids: l-cysteine, l-lysine, l-cystine, and l-methionine.

◆**Vanadium** is important in cellular metabolism and in the structure of bones and teeth. It is involved with growth and reproduction and inhibits cholesterol synthesis. Deficiency may be linked to cardiovascular disease, kidney disease, infertility and infant mortality. Vanadium has been implicated in blood sugar disorders.

Vanadium is not easily absorbed. It is antagonistic to chromium, which is also important in blood sugar metabolism. The two supplements should be taken at different times of the day. Tobacco interferes with absorption of vanadium. Food sources are fish, vegetable oils, and olives; also snap beans, dill, meat, radishes, and whole grains.

◆**Zinc** is important in reproduction and to the health of the prostate and other reproductive glands. It is required for protein and collagen formation, and promotes immunity and wound healing. Zinc is inhospitable to viruses. Deficiencies lead to itching and to impairment of the special senses of taste and smell. Zinc is needed to maintain vitamin E in the bloodstream.

A balanced dose is about 45 mg. More than 100 mg/day can depress the immune system; while doses under 100 mg/day can enhance it. Diarrhea, kidney disease, cirrhosis, diabetes, and phytates in grains and legumes can lower body levels of zinc. The proper zinc-copper balance should be maintained. Hard water, or copper leaching into drinking water and food, can upset zinc levels.

Food sources of zinc are egg yolk, fish, lamb chops, legumes, lima beans, liver, meat, mushrooms, oysters, pecans, poultry, pumpkin seeds, sardines, seafood, seeds, soy lecithin, soybeans, and sunflower seeds.

RECOMMENDED DIETARY ALLOWANCES (RDA)

There are a complicated set of daily dietary recommedations created by the FDA and by the non-profit independent Institute of Medicine for levels of macro- and micronutrients. They are worthless for promoting health, because they were generally calculated as the minimum amount of the nutrient needed—multiplied by two—to prevent deficiency disease. The RDA and USRDA simply tell you how much you need to prevent getting really sick. They offer no guidelines about how much you need to be really healthy. Even at these low values, the government estimates at least 40 percent of the U.S. population is suffering from deficiencies of one or more of these important nutrients.

I have not made many specific recommendations for daily intake amounts for supplements. A person with a cold or flu needs four times as much vitamin A and three times as much zinc as normal. Requirements change with age; diet; mental, physical and biological stress; genetics; efficiency of digestion; smoking; and environmental exposures. Your TBM practitioner can help you determine what, how much and what formulation supplement you need at this time, and for how long you need to take it. When beginning the Sugar Control Program, it is best to supplement as little as possible, especially if you have secondary infections and parasites. Supplementation will only feed the microorganisms and larger parasites and make them stronger. The emphasis should be on cleaning up the system and repairing the digestion.

The Institute of Medicine is in the process of establishing the RDI (Reference Daily Intake), of nutritional requirements to promote health. The new level for calcium for women is 1200 mg per day. They are currently working on folic acid and B vitamins. The new recommendations will be published over the next few years and will be adopted by the U.S. government.

❖ ⌘ ❖

CHAPTER 8—WATER

The Regulating Principle of Life

❖ ⌘ ❖

Without air, we cannot survive for more than a few minutes.
Without water, we cannot survive for more than a few days.
Without food, we can survive for months.

Although the human body is about 75 percent water, western thinkers look at the 25 percent solid matter of the body and assume (because it is solid) that it contains the regulating functions. But it is the larger portion of the body, the solvent—the water— that is the regulating matter.

The mistaken notion that the solid portion is the regulator underlies most medical thinking and leads to the use of drugs and surgery to treat illness. It is something akin to negative space in a painting. Non-artists usually look at a portrait of a woman as being the regulating influence of the painting. But the parts of the painting that are not the woman can be even more important to the painter and exert more control over the image.

Have you ever seen the brain-teaser silhouette picture of two people facing each other in profile? If you concentrate on the periphery, you see the profiles. If you stare at the center, the space between their faces becomes a goblet and you forget the profiles. Here's another of those. I think it originated with The Semantic Institute.

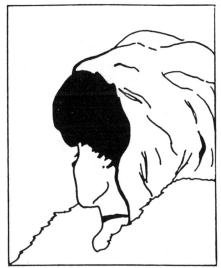

Figure 8.1. Do you see an old woman or a young one?

It is water that allows the electromagnetic energies of the body to function optimally. This form of energy provides the most important communication system of living organisms. There are three large flowing water systems in the body:

- ♦ the plasma, in which the blood circulates;
- ♦ the lymph, which cleans up the body;
- ♦ and cerebrospinal fluid, which feeds the brain.

The only difference among these waters of life is what is dissolved in them. At some point, these waters flow into the blood for cleaning and exchange. Water is eliminated in the urine, feces and perspiration. It must be replaced. Do you know what a standing pool of water looks like when there's no fresh inlet and outlet? That's right: pond scum, green algae. Imagine a process like that going on in your body.

In the human body, when there is not enough fresh water coming in, the body begins rationing water. The brain takes priority. The brain, which is only about 2 percent of the total body weight, uses as much as 20 percent of its water. People who die of exposure to cold die much more rapidly when their heads are uncovered, because they lose so much water, and heat, from their heads.

The only thing that will hydrate the body is water. Other fluids that you drink are simply solid food in fluid form. If you put lemon juice in the water, you are drinking lemonade, not water. Juice, seltzer, club soda, Perrier, coffee, tea, milk and beer are not water. Most of the things we dissolve in water are actually diuretic. That means they use up the water they are dissolved in and then drain some of your body's stored water as well. If you drink a cup of coffee, it robs you of your own water to digest the coffee. If you add cream, that's more water for every cup of coffee. Add sugar, and you lose even more water.

The living principal seems to be if **you** add anything to water, it's not part of your water ration. If you add a few drops of lemon juice to make the water taste better, you have lemonade—not water. If you add Celtic sea salt to replace lost minerals, it's not water. But if it comes out of the tap filled with chlorine and fluoride—it is still water—you didn't add anything.

On average, Americans now consume more than 50 gallons of soda pop a year, but only 40 gallons of water a year.[26] That's one large glass per day of water, rather than the ten glasses I recommend for a 125-pound person.

Thirst and dry mouth are the acute symptoms of dehydration. But rather than reach for a glass of water, we have been educated to drink soda pop, coffee, tea, juice, alcohol, etc. These substances do not replace the water.

---

[26] "Alternatives." Dr. David G. Williams. Mountain Home Publishing. VI:22, p. 170.

We completely ignore the body's signals of chronic dehydration, because they are the symptoms we have learned to suppress with over-the-counter and prescription drugs. Morning sickness of pregnancy, hypertension, and gall bladder pain are a few symptoms of chronic dehydration. So are food cravings. So when you are hungry, drink a glass of water, first. Often the cravings will disappear. Dehydration leads to gall and kidney stones, asthma, hypertension, dyspepsia, ulcers and diabetes, to name but a few conditions. These are the symptoms of chronic dehydration. Dry mouth is the last symptom of chronic dehydration.

Your TBM practitioner will probably correct your body's ability to metabolize and utilize your water, and s/he will also harmonize you to the water you drink. You'll be urinating more frequently at first. But that's good, because your body will also be detoxifying a lot of waste products in the early phases of the Program and you want to get rid of them. The water will help in the elimination process.

Water Pollution

Unfortunately our drinking water supply is severely contaminated, as is all the water on the planet. It is probably safer to drink tap water today than it was in the nineteenth century. The contaminants are just slower to kill us than cholera and typhoid were, and therefore, harder to isolate.

It was reported in 1996 that the immune systems of marine mammals (seals, porpoises, etc.) are depleted by about 20 percent due to exposure to PBB's in the water contaminating the fish they eat. They eat the same fish we do. What do you suppose the PBB's are doing to us?

Public water supplies are badly polluted. If it is not the water itself with all kinds of microscopic sewage, industrial and medical waste poured into it, then it is the additives like chlorine and fluoride that we put in the water to protect ourselves. There is so much chlorine in tap water that if you take hot showers with the door closed, you could be poisoned. The U.S. government recommends taking cooler showers and says that within a few years, every American household will need water filtration. If you have a good private well, congratulations, but have it tested.

Aging public water system infrastructures contain lead and other heavy metals, and intractable parasites, like *Giardia lamblia*.

An incomplete list of what tap water in the U.S. can contain includes: bacteria, such *as E. coli* and *salmonella*; viruses; parasites, such as *Giardia* and *Leptospirosis*; dissolved organic chemicals, such as pesticides and herbicides; dissolved inorganic chemicals; heavy metals such as lead; microscopic bits of toilet paper; chlorine and fluoride.

Natural sources of water are easily contaminated. Be very careful collecting water from a public spring unless it is tested frequently. When camping and hiking, purify all drinking water. Animal dung, or a dead animal in the water, upstream can contaminate any water downstream—no matter how pristine the wilderness may look. And the microorganisms *Leptospirosis* and *Clostridium* are pandemic in water.

Water Purification

There are a number of different types of water purification devices and systems. The government says we will all need home purification units within a couple of years. The charcoal and charcoal-silver filter systems that attach to your faucet give you some protection and shower filters that screw onto your shower pipe are very helpful. People usually tell me how good my hair looks. I recently realized it was because of my shower filter. When I bathe at a hotel with my regular shampoo and soap from home, my hair and skin do not look or feel as good as when I use filtered water. However, these filters at best remove chlorine and large things like bacteria. They don't touch lead, dissolved gases, PBB's, viruses, etc. For that you need either a very good distiller or a reverse osmosis unit.

My personal preference is a **reverse osmosis** (RO) unit with good carbon and carbon-silver pre-filters and a carbon post-filter. Make sure the company has a good reputation, because the quality of the RO membrane can vary widely. The filtered water is pushed through a very fine membrane that only the water can get through. The water may then be stored in a tank and sent to a final post-filter for "sweetening" when you open the tap. You also want to be sure that the system backflushes to keep it clean. The main drawback to the system is that it does waste water. The filters and membrane have to be replaced on a regular basis according to the manufacturer's directions.

You can get one-glass-at-a-time RO units for camping, to counter-top, to under-the-sink, to whole-house units. A number of soft-drink and beer companies have installed RO-type units in their production lines, because the taste of their products is so affected by the variation in tap waters in their different manufacturing locations. The city of Cancun, Mexico, has installed an RO unit for the city water, so (in Cancun, anyway) you can drink the water. These systems—sometimes called nanofiltration—have larger holes in their membrane than home systems.

The other good system would be a good **distillation** unit. Distillation works by boiling the water to steam. As the steam rises, heavier-than-water pollutants and contaminants precipitate out. The purified steam rises and is then cooled. It reliquefies in cooling, minus the contaminants. There are many grades of distiller. Only a very good one can remove everything. What I don't like about distillation is that the water is cooked beyond 190 degrees (see The Kouchakoff study, p. 137). I don't know of any unit under $1000 that eliminates all the impurities. And, I have no scientific proof of this, but it seems to me that because the remaining impurities have been heated, they now have a higher energy rate and may be even more harmful. Some of these contaminants can be removed with a carbon post filter.

Either kind of unit can sell for anywhere from $350 to $1500 for a countertop to an under-the-sink model. In both cases, RO and distillation, dissolved minerals are removed along with the contaminants. This may give the water a negative charge and cause it to leach minerals from your body. Celtic sea salt and multiple-mineral and trace-mineral supplements can easily replace the lost minerals.

Activated carbon filters can only remove organic pollutants like insecticides, herbicides, and PCB's, some industrial chemicals, and chlorine. In theory and practice, carbon filters provide a breeding ground for bacteria. As far as I know, no studies have borne this out. But the studies may all have been done on previously chlorinated water. Only use this kind of filter if you have chlorinated water. The filter should be changed every year.

Silver-impregnated carbon filters are supposed to be the answer to the bacterial overgrowth problem, but the water does not remain in contact with the silver long enough to be effective. The filter should be changed every year.

Ceramic filters can remove dirt, large parasites like *Cryptosporidium* and *Giardia lamblia,* but are ineffective against organic pollutants or bacteria. They should be combined with carbon filters.

Ozone gas is bubbled through water, killing bacteria, viruses, algae and parasites. It's used effectively in swimming pools and spas. It does not eliminate enough things or well enough to be used for drinking water.

Ultraviolet (UV) light kills *E. coli* and *salmonella,* as well as viruses. It doesn't kill everything, however. Nor will it eliminate heavy metals or organic contaminants. It should be used in combination systems.

Water softeners do not purify water.

Bottled Water

Bottled water is unpredictable. Instead of harassing people who want to be healthy and in charge of their lives, the Food and Drug Administration (FDA) should be regulating the water industry. Instead the FDA has merely adopted the very minimal guidelines of the Environmental Protection Agency (EPA). And then it may test a given bottling company about once in five years. Anything can happen in five years. The consumer has no guarantee that the bottle of water that s/he pays more for than gasoline is any better than what comes out the tap. In fact, it could be what comes out of a tap. On a trip in Mexico, a friend of mine saw young boys filling labeled water bottles from a garden hose and sealing the bottles. The bottles looked just like good unopened bottled water.

This kind of abuse also happens in the U.S. There are some reputable springs, but you must rely on popular magazines and health-food industry publications to keep track of what's going on at the source.

Another problem in the water industry is that there are no regulations governing sanitation. They do not have to use sterile containers. Bottles are usually shipped without their caps. Anything can get into them before the water is put in. Bottles don't have to be disinfected before use. There are no hygiene regulations regarding workers, and bottles are often capped by hand. Since no disinfectant, like chlorine, is used in the water, any microorganism that gets into the bottle can grow. For this reason, bottled water should not be used after 60 days, unless it is filtered before drinking.

In the U.S., bottled water is a three billion dollar per year industry, with little or no regulation. By definition that means there is a lot of incentive for unethical activity.

What To Do

Since you are going to be drinking a lot more water, a good filtration or distillation system is worth the investment in your health. Find a reliable water purification company that deals with more than one kind of system (see Mail Order, p. 222), so they can advise you about what you really need for your situation. Don't buy more than you need and be sure you combine systems to get what you really need.

Although it may involve a hefty outlay of money, a good filtration system is healthier and, in the long run, less expensive than drinking bottled water.

❖ ⌘ ❖

CHAPTER 9—CARBOHYDRATE METABOLISM

The Ups and Downs

❖ ⌘ ❖

Let's talk about blood sugar. Blood sugar is the only fuel your brain can use. In order to be usable by your brain, your blood sugar must be maintained at a certain level—between 60-110 mg of glucose per dL of blood. Blood sugar is the simple molecule glucose.[27] Glucose is not usually found in food (except grapes). Blood glucose can be a breakdown product of carbohydrate, protein and/or fat. Sugars and starches (carbohydrates) are most easily and rapidly broken down in your digestion to blood sugar.

Your body has a system of controls to regulate its blood sugar levels. The orthodox view is that blood sugar is under the control of the pancreas and adrenal glands. When glucose enters your blood after a meal, the blood sugar level rises from a resting or fasting level of, say, 80 mg/dL to 120 mg/dL. This 120 level is too high. So your pancreas secretes a hormone called insulin, which helps carry the excess sugar into the liver, fat cells, and muscles for storage as glycogen, a starch. When the blood sugar levels fall between meals, the adrenals send out chemicals to raise the blood sugar levels by reconverting the stored glycogen into glucose and slowly returning it to the blood stream. A normal glucose curve looks like this:

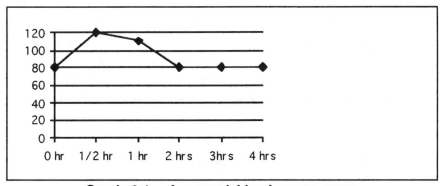

Graph 9.1. A normal blood sugar curve.
The vertical axis is mg glucose per dL blood.

---

[27] The white crystals in your sugar bowl are sucrose, a disaccharide. It is made of two molecules of glucose bound to each other chemically. It must be broken down to be used. It can be used as glucose in the body, but for many readers of this book, it is more likely to be converted to fat.

In the normal graph 9.1, the blood sugar rises after you eat, returns to the normal level within two hours, and stays there.

Disorders of Carbohydrate Metabolism

There are several disorders related to carbohydrate metabolism in which one or more of the blood sugar controls becomes faulty and dysfunctional, resulting in blood sugar levels that are too high or too low. I'm going to discuss the most common types here.

Diabetes

In diabetes, the blood sugar is too high (hyperglycemia). With the advent of drugs, we tend to think of diabetes as a rather benign disease, but this is far from the case. High blood sugar affects the kidneys, the peripheral nerves and the retina of the eye. Over time, after the diabetic damage has been done, the organs affected degenerate according to the pattern of disease for that organ. In the kidney, we see hypertension accelerating the disease. The need for dialysis is common. Blindness both as a result of the disease and insulin use is frequent. Peripheral nerve damage leads to tingling and loss of sensation in the feet, especially. The feet are prone to sores and ulcers, which may be ignored, because the diabetic can't feel them. Sores or ingrown toenails left untended often lead to gangrene and amputation, even in this day and age. Angina, blocked arteries, and heart attack are more common in diabetics than in non-diabetics and occur at an earlier age.

Juvenile Diabetes (JD) is the most well-known type and involves destruction of the pancreatic cells that secrete insulin. The result is too much glucose in the blood (hyperglycemia), so much so that it spills over into the urine. There has been speculation within the past few years that this condition may be the result of Coxsackie or other viral infection destroying the insulin-producing beta-cells of the pancreas. This may possibly be combined with a genetic predisposition to diabetes. Antibiotic suppression of the viral infection may cause mutation of the microorganisms. In one study, a very high number of juvenile diabetics reported a severe viral infection within a year prior to the onset of their diabetes. In another study, juvenile diabetics showed antibody activity. Juvenile diabetes usually appears under age 30. Symptoms are frequent urination, thirst and weight loss.

Adult-Onset Diabetes is non-insulin dependent. It may have the same viral base as JD, but with a longer gestation. It usually occurs in people over age 30 and may be associated with obesity. The insulin-secreting cells of the pancreas seem to be unaltered, but may be smaller than usual. The patient still manufactures insulin, although not enough. The body may also resist using the insulin. Medically these patients are usually controlled with non-insulin drugs, though they may require insulin from time to time.

Diabetics usually do well on the Sugar Control Program, because the foods on the Program do not stimulate much insulin production. Insulin-dependent diabetics, with a combination of the program and the TBM adjustments, are frequently able to reduce the amount of insulin they require. This can add years to their lives. And there are more profound TBM treatments that may produce even better outcomes for diabetics.

In adult-onset diabetes, the combination of dietary change and TBM treatments frequently allows patients to demonstrate normal blood and urine tests and to come off their medication altogether.

Medical doctors, for the most part, have learned to rely on drugs for treatment of diabetes, and rarely advise much in the way of diet. Most of the diabetic patients I have treated were not even educated to the medically accepted food exchange diabetic diets (which contain much too much refined carbohydrate anyway) or to the long-term effects of the disease.

If you have been diagnosed with diabetes, and are taking prescription drugs, do not attempt the Sugar Control Program without the assistance of both your TBM doctor and your medical doctor. You must own a glucometer, know how to use it and use it daily to control your insulin or other diabetic drug dosages.

If you have kidney or Parkinson's disease or are an athlete, the Program will have to be modified for you so that you do not eat too much protein.

Other less common causes of blood sugar increase include thiamin deficiency, myocardial infarct (heart attack), brain damage, severe trauma, convulsions, Cushing's disease, acromegaly, severe liver disease and pancreatitis.

Reactive Hypoglycemia

The less well-known disorders of carbohydrate metabolism are reactive hypoglycemia and dysinsulinism—recently labeled syndrome X. In **reactive hypoglycemia**, the patient's fasting blood sugar is usually in the low normal range. There are rapid fluctuations in blood sugar, which leave the brain bouncing off the walls of the inside of the skull. These changes affect mood, concentration, intelligence, decision-making, even eyesight (see p. 17 symptoms). People who have their prescription lenses fitted during a low blood sugar trough may be fitted with lenses that are two or three diopters wrong.

Standard medical testing, including a three-hour glucose tolerance test (GTT), is typically negative and the fasting glucose level is within normal limits (not healthy, just average), so medical doctors are inclined not to believe in this disorder and to recommend psychotherapy or Prozac to palliate what they see as "psychosomatic"symptoms. But if the doctor took the trouble to talk to patients the day after the test, s/he would discover that the patients were forced to pull off the road on the way home from the test to take a nap. They couldn't drive, couldn't see straight, had a headache, couldn't concentrate and/or were disoriented, if not lost altogether, and couldn't make reasonable decisions. The better test is a six-hour GTT. However, even when this test is performed medically, readings are taken too infrequently to be accurate and the patient's subjective symptoms are usually not recorded nor respected. So the test is inaccurate.

Hypoglycemia was first recognized medically in 1924 by Dr. Seale Harris. Dr. Harris was honored by the AMA for this work, which the AMA then promptly forgot or ignored. Dr. Harris noticed that the blood sugar of certain patients would rise rapidly—but not into the diabetic range—after eating a meals of simple carbohydrates, or after ingesting alcohol, caffeine, nicotine, etc. Then the blood sugar levels would fall dramatically. This is reactive hypoglycemia. Patients have similar reactions to those of diabetics, without having diabetes. The problem is not that the blood sugar rises too high, but that the reactions occur too rapidly for the brain to be able to adjust easily.

I don't usually recommend the six-hour GTT, because it is so hard on the patient (see p. 14 for a description of one GTT test). The diagnosis can be made on the basis of a simple multiphasic blood test, urinalysis, symptomatology and response to the diet. I only use the six-hour GTT if the condition has to be proven for a legal and/or insurance entity, or if the cause seems to be non-diet related. The most common scenario is that, at fasting levels, the blood sugar is normal or low-normal.

In a six-hour GTT, the subject eats a carbohydrate-loading meal,[28] then fasts for about six hours. The subject then drinks a sugar-water solution. The blood sugar rises rapidly to, say, 150 mg/dL and then plummets rapidly often to below the original fasting level. And it may continue to drop from there. Blood sugar should be measured and plotted every 15 minutes throughout the test. With the development of the glucometer, the test itself is easier to perform.

The blood sugar level may start at 70 mg/dL, rise to 150 after the sugar-water solution is drunk, fall rapidly back to 90 and continue to drop until, in the sixth hour, the blood sugar may be 50. The subject should not be allowed to do things during the test that would affect blood sugar, like eating, deep breathing, napping, aerobic exercising, or smoking. It is very important that the test subject record his personal, subjective reactions at each blood draw during the test. Sometimes this information is more important than the lab values. Low blood LDH (lactic dehydrogenase) <140 and low blood pressure are usually associated with reactive hypoglycemia.

---

[28] This is the great American breakfast: 2 eggs, 2 slices of some form of white bread (bagel, roll, English muffin) with butter and jam, home fries, bacon, orange juice, coffee or tea with sugar.

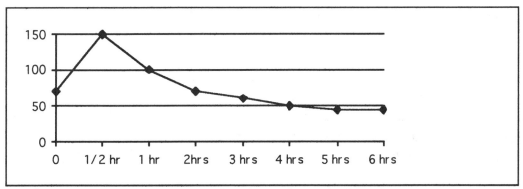

**Graph 9.2. A common reactive hypoglycemia blood sugar curve.
The vertical axis is mg glucose/dL blood.**

In a few cases, other kinds of hypoglycemia may be associated with inborn errors of metabolism, defects in enzyme systems, pancreatic or extra-pancreatic tumors, starvation, and disorders of various glands and organs (hypothalamus, pituitary and adrenals, nerves, kidneys, and liver). These are known medical disorders that will be found by medical testing. But by far, the most common cause of symptoms is a diet high in refined carbohydrates and caffeine, which disturbs the blood-sugar regulating systems of the body.

A flat curve on the GTT graph may be associated with hyperactivity and learning disabilities. It may also indicate a heavy-metal body burden. A hair mineral analysis would confirm or rule out heavy-metal toxicity. Other curve shapes may indicate conditions such as adrenal insufficiency (Addison's disease).

When the blood sugar level drops precipitously, the survival mechanism of the body takes over to demand quick energy. The body's survival object is to feel well enough to make it through the next half hour or so. Like Scarlet O'Hara, the body will think about it (health) later. The sympathetic nervous system, which is in charge of "fight or flight," declares an emergency. It demands a Snickers' bar, or a cigarette and a cup of coffee, or a donut and coffee. A caffeinated soda pop, diet or regular, will also do in a pinch.

The priority is to make it through the emergency. It doesn't matter to the sympathetic nervous system that the strategies it uses for survival will harm you in the long term. The priority is: "If I don't do this now, there won't be a long-term anyway."

A candy bar provides quick energy in the form of sugar, while the cigarettes and coffee provide nicotine and caffeine, which are short-term adrenal stimulants. In either case, the burst of energy from these substances is short-lived and in a half an hour, there is a demand for more of the same—or a nap. People with an undiagnosed sugar control problem usually use one of two behaviors. The more common of the two is to kick the adrenal glands frequently during the day with candy, chips, cookies, Diet Coke, Mountain

Dew, coffee and/or cigarettes. Recently, stimulating herbs have been added to this list, chiefly maté, ma-huang and kava-kava.

The other behavior is to eat only at dinnertime. This is common with weight-conscious people. They know that once they start eating, they can't stop, and they are only hungry for the sweet and carbohydrate foods that make them fat. Consequently, they postpone breaking their fast as long as possible. Some eat lunch. Many drink coffee and diet soda all day and only eat dinner. Then they snack compulsively until bedtime.

Syndrome X has been around for a long time, but it didn't have a name (not that syndrome X is much of a name). It has also been called dysinsulinism and insulin resistance. It is probably a progression—as the patient ages and the organs become more dysfunctional—from reactive hypoglycemia toward adult-onset diabetes.

In syndrome X, the pancreas produces insulin in response to rising blood sugar levels, but the body ignores the insulin. Blood sugar remains too high, so the pancreas secretes more insulin (measurable in the blood), and the blood sugar drops suddenly. The symptoms are similar to those of reactive hypoglycemia. There are sweet and starch cravings, and it is associated with obesity. The lab picture is of somewhat elevated, though still normal blood glucose, high triglycerides, high cholesterol, and higher blood pressure. The lipid profile will also show elevated LDL's and lowered HDL's. Normal triglycerides should be 70-110 mg/dL and should be half the serum cholesterol level. In syndrome X, triglyceride levels are often double the cholesterol levels.

TBM and Blood Sugar Disorders

The medical community believes that sugar-control disorders are primarily pancreatic or adrenal problems. So their standard treatments are based on drugs that target those organs, and sometimes diet based on counting food-exchange values.

In TBM,[29] however, we believe that the liver is the dysfunctional organ in most of these conditions. In 1973, Johns Hopkins Medical School published a report of 5000 diagnosed diabetics, who were studied at autopsy. All of them demonstrated liver involvement. In 98 percent of the cases, they found liver involvement only. These are the non-insulin-dependent diabetics, the reactive hypoglycemics and the syndrome X patients. In only 2 percent of the cases did they find pancreatic and/or adrenal involvement, and these people had liver involvement as well.

This was a large and important medical study and we expected to see it in medical textbooks by 1993—it takes about 20 years for new information to reach the textbook

---

[29] Victor Frank. "Diagnosis and Control of Sugar Metabolism Function." ICAK Research Paper, 1973.

level. It appears to us in TBM that the Hopkins study has been suppressed so that doctors can continue to prescribe, with good conscience, pancreatic drugs, including the recently developed, patented, and very profitable, synthetic insulin.

In TBM, clinical findings in over 1000 cases of blood-sugar malfunctions, reported by 1973, support the findings of the Johns Hopkins study that the liver is the controlling organ in these syndromes. We believe there are two functional disturbances.

The first problem is faulty communication between the liver and the pancreas, and between the liver and the adrenal glands. The liver cannot maintain the feedback loop (a kind of running dialogue) that lets the pancreas and adrenals know the blood glucose status. Methionine (an amino acid) is the chemical messenger in this communication, but the liver does not have enough of the right kind of methionine, the kind found in red meat and coconut, to do the job.

The second problem is that the liver's switches for blood-glucose control are set too high at one end and too low at the other. For optimum functioning of human systems, blood glucose concentrations should be between 70 mg/dL at the low end and 110 mg/dL at the high end. Because the high-end switch is set too high, the blood-sugar level rises dangerously high, before the liver finally reacts to inform the pancreas. In response to the emergency, the pancreas secretes too much insulin. The blood sugar levels fall drastically. And you feel as though the bottom fell out.

Because the low-end switch is set too low, the liver doesn't communicate with the adrenals until too late. The adrenals react in a panic to raise the blood sugar levels. They raise them too high. And you are on a roller-coaster ride, up and down, of energy and mood swings.

In addition, methionine is the limiting amino acid (kind of a smallest common denominator) for the liver to process both sugar and protein. In either a junk-food diet or a high-carbohydrate/low-fat diet, there is very little of the right kind of methionine present to do these jobs adequately.

The Sugar Control Program is a low-stress diet that requires the pancreas to secrete only small amounts of insulin to control blood sugar and that supplies adequate amounts of the right kind of methionine. It allows the organs and functions of blood-sugar control to rest and rejuvenate. And, combined with specific TBM treatments, it allows optimal balance to be restored between insulin and adrenal hormones.

In TBM, we recognize three types of functional blood-sugar miscommunication patterns: hypoglycemia or low blood sugar (25 percent); hyperglycemia or high blood sugar (25 percent), and oppositic blood sugar (50 percent). The oppositic pattern is the roller-coaster pattern described above. Reactive hypoglycemia and syndrome X fall into this pattern. But we see this same pattern of blood-sugar peaks and valleys in people who have diabetes mellitus, although the pattern occurs at the diabetic blood-sugar concentrations. And, the numbers may fluctuate even more wildly. I have seen diabetics go through 100 or more point changes within 15 minutes.

Sugar and Allergy/Sensitivity

In TBM, we have broadened the limited medical definition of allergies to include any substance that causes disharmony in the functional physiology of the body. In this regard, we consider sugar to be the primary allergy. The body can easily be restored to normal functioning through the Sugar Control Program and the specific sugar-control TBM corrections.

Dysfunctional carbohydrate metabolism is involved with other food and environmental allergies or sensitivities in two major ways. The first way is that the junk-food and high-carbohydrate diets, which can lead to sugar-control dysfunctions, also support the overgrowth of systemic candidiasis.

Candida albicans is a normal inhabitant of the human gut. It is a yeast. It co-exists with the intestinal bacteria *Lactobacillus* and *E. coli*. Many common factors of our daily lives will enable the candida to multiply very rapidly and take over in the gut. These factors include the use of antibiotics, cortisone and other steroids, and the birth control pill. When one of these factors comes into play, dietary sugar and high-carbohydrate foods stimulate the overgrowth of the yeast, because that is what the yeast love to eat.

The yeast begin to multiply so rapidly that they begin to mutate into a more complex organism called a mold. The mold is capable of punching its way out of the intestine, causing leaky gut, and getting into the rest of the body. The damage done to the intestine allows proteins to leak from the gut (and germs to translocate) into the body's tissues. The body recognizes these misplaced proteins as foreign invaders and mounts a defense to get rid of them. So now, every time your body meets that protein, it reacts defensively The symptoms of that defense appear as sensitivities to normal foods.

Another provocation for allergies or sensitivities occurs because the digestion of both carbohydrates and proteins is faulty due to the lack of proper methionine in the liver. Again, the body recognizes these partially digested proteins as foreign substances and mounts a defense to fight them off. When both carbohydrate and protein digestion is faulty, we often see environmental sensitivity to things made from petrochemicals: perfumes, newspaper ink, exhaust fumes from your car, natural gas from your stove, cleaning and cosmetic solvents, outgassing formaldehyde from objects in your home. The list is almost endless. The defense symptoms that you would experience in these cases are not standard IgG- and IgE-mediated symptoms. You do not get hives, rashes, red, itchy eyes, or go into anaphylactic shock. Instead, you experience headache, fogginess, fatigue, inability to concentrate, claustrophobia, joint pain and swelling, visual disturbance, seizures—a whole range of symptoms that do not appear to be related to allergies.

The first step in controlling and curing these sensitivities is the Sugar Control Program. Once blood sugar is under control, we can also treat the other allergies with specific TBM techniques. However, we cannot use these allergy-correction techniques to fix sugar, because when we do, we find the body loses control of blood-sugar balance.

A Sugar Control Patient's Case History

The story of one patient I treated for sugar-handling problems shows the many aspects that can be involved. While at college, Wendy had gone on the Fit for Life diet. Fit for Life is a very low-protein vegetarian diet. She felt wonderful for about a year and then started to feel terrible. When she finally got to me, she had been suffering for about six years with fatigue, inability to concentrate, muscle weakness, depression and weight gain. After Wendy got sick, she tried to continue to follow the precepts of Fit for Life, but had pretty much degenerated into a junk-food diet pattern. Over the years, I have had many patients like Wendy, who came to me for help, after an extended period on a low-protein vegetarian diet.

Wendy had a secondary systemic candidiasis infection, which I treated while she followed the Sugar Control Program. I had to trigger out (using TBM) her past use of birth control pills, which is probably what set the stage for the candidiasis infection. She also demonstrated parasites called nematodes. These are parasites that are found in root vegetables[30] like carrots and potatoes. They eat sugar. They are not killed at normal cooking temperatures.

I treated Wendy for nematodes using a TBM correction method and a homeopathic remedy. This is usually very effective, and she began to feel a lot better, but not really great. And the nematodes kept reappearing. After several months, she finally realized that she was eating health food potato chips for snacks, and that that was where the nematodes were coming from.

She stopped eating the potato chips. We got rid of the nematodes. But she still could not tolerate any level of carbohydrate without getting weak, fatigued and depressed.

About a year after this patient first came to me, I read a book called the *Cure for All Cancers* by Dr. Hulda Regehr Clarke. Dr. Clarke believes that cancer and most other

---

[30] Don't buy root vegetables if they have knobs with root hairs growing out of them. These are nematode nests. You can't cut them away, because the whole vegetable is infested. And you can't cook them away, because the temperatures required are much higher than those at which you cook.

diseases are caused by parasites, especially the liver fluke lodging in the liver and there meeting up with a store of propyl alcohol. Using some of these ideas, I checked this patient, using TBM testing methods, and found a parasite in the pancreas. We treated her, again using TBM treatments, followed by a month-long regimen of herbal vermifuges (substances that kill worms). By the fourth day, she began to regain her former vitality and zest for living, and her neuromuscular reflex tests for sugar control finally remained strong.

One last adjustment still had to be tweaked. I found that the head and body of her pancreas were fighting each other. We call this sibling rivalry in TBM. I harmonized the two parts and the patient has been well ever since.

She remains primarily on a modified Sugar Control Program, but can go off the plan occasionally and enjoy a carbohydrate meal or a dessert without falling apart. She retains her strength, her pleasure in living. And she now has both a dog and a significant other—pleasures which she was too depressed to enjoy before Sugar Control.

This was an unusual case and complicated one. Most people achieve excellent results much more rapidly and easily than this patient did.

❖⌘❖

CHAPTER 10—EICOSANOIDS

The Key to Health

❖⌘❖

I have seen the beneficial effects of higher protein, low-carbohydrate diets for over 20 years: weight loss, lowered levels of cholesterol and triglycerides, better blood-fat lab pictures, increased energy, emotional stability, and success in business and relationships. But other than empirical and clinical results and an intuition that this was the right course for so many people, I had no "scientific" explanation of how this could be so. Especially when everywhere you look, the good news of low-fat, high-carbohydrate dieting is shoved in your face. I guess if they make the good news big enough, you won't be able to see all the studies that show the program is not working. But then I started hearing about eicosanoids and I believe they may be the key to why the Sugar Control Program is so healthful for so many people.

Eicosanoids

Translated into English, "eicosanoid" means something with 20 atoms. Eicosanoids are chemically similar to hormones, but rather than being made in a specific endocrine gland like the thyroid gland and dumped into the blood, they are actually manufactured by every cell in your body. They act inside the cell in amounts so tiny that they have been undetectable until recently, and they disappear instantaneously.

Even though you (and your doctor) may never have heard the term "eicosanoid" before, you probably have heard of prostaglandins. They are one type of eicosanoid and were discovered about 60 years ago in the prostate gland.

Eicosanoids are a very powerful set of chemicals and a little bit goes a long way. There is a balanced set of eicosanoids. We tend to think of them as "good" or "bad," but the bad ones (Series 2) do things we need, like make blood clots when we are wounded or mount an inflammatory response when we are injured. The problem is that if we overproduce bad eicosanoids and underproduce the good ones (Series 1), the bad ones seem to turn on us and attack, producing joint inflammation, headaches, menstrual cramps, abdominal pain of ulcers, rashes, arterial plaquing, asthma, and auto-immune diseases.

We want to make more of the Series 1 eicosanoids, but we also need to make some Series 2 eicosanoids. The good news is that we can keep these chemicals in balance through diet and that the Sugar Control Program is a primary way to accomplish this.

Fig. 10.1: Eicosanoid Functions

Series 1	Series 2
dilates blood vessels	constricts blood vessels
strengthens immune system	weakens immune system
reduces inflammation	creates inflammation
relieves pain	increases pain
increases oxygen	decreases oxygen
increases endurance	decreases endurance
prevents blood clotting	promotes blood clotting
dilates bronchial tubes	constricts bronchial tubes
fights cancer cell growth	supports cancer cell growth

Eicosanoids are made from the essential fatty acid linoleic acid, which (except in a very low-fat diet) is plentiful from the good fats and oils we've mentioned (on p. 51 and in the chapter on fats) and from fats in food. But in order for linoleic acid to get into the cell pathway, it needs an enzyme to carry it in. This enzyme is called *delta 6 desaturase*, and it must be working up to speed.

To process enough linoleic acid and activate or speed up this gatekeeper enzyme, we need at least 30 percent of our diet as protein. But what would slow it down? Aging, stress, disease, trans fatty acids, alpha linolenic acid (ALA) and a high carbohydrate diet.

It looks like the only factors we can control here are protein intake and avoidance of carbohydrates as in the Sugar Control Program. We also need to avoid ALA; and the trans fatty acids found in margarine, in most cooked unsaturated oils and in many processed foods containing "partially" hydrogenated fats and oils. The remarkable thing is that if we control these foods, aging, stress and disease are minimized as well.

Alpha Linolenic Acid (ALA) and Eicosanoids

ALA suppresses the production of eicosanoids in the body. In this way, it acts like aspirin. While aspirin blocks the production of bad eicosanoids, thus relieving your headache or cramps, it also blocks the production of good eicosanoids. Aspirin and ALA just blocks all eicosanoid function; they can't tell the difference between the eicosanoid that is causing your headache and the eicosanoid that could cure it.

Therefore, limit your intake of oils containing ALA (alpha linolenic acid). These oils are canola, soybean, cottonseed, and black currant oil. Flax seed oil, especially, contains very high amounts of ALA and, like aspirin, blocks eicosanoid production. I can hear you screaming now that these oils contain omega-3 fatty acids and have great health benefits. But if you follow the Sugar Control Program and stimulate the production of Series 1 eicosanoids, you probably won't need these benefits from these omega-3 fatty acids. There are so many other ways to get the benefits without the side effects. These oils can be used in small amounts. You might think about using only one dose of one kind per day.

In addition, olive oil, which is monounsaturated (like canola oil) and is very good for your health, does not contain alpha linolenic acid (ALA) at all. Sesame seed oil does not contain as much monounsaturated oil as olive oil, but it is also free of ALA. That might be another choice if you really hate olive oil.

The Eicosanoid Switch—Delta 5 Desaturase

So, we have limited ALA in our diets. We are getting enough linoleic acid and eating enough protein. What's the next step?

Once enough linoleic acid has entered the eicosanoid pathway in the cell, there is an enzyme switch, like a railroad switch which determines which track the train will take. Will it take the track of making "good" eicosanoids or the track of "bad" eicosanoids?

The switch is a different enzyme called *delta 5 desaturase*. If there is more delta 5 activity, the linoleic acid will be switched onto the less desirable track of Series 2 production. If the delta-5 enzyme is inhibited (if there is less of it), that will switch the process to the Series 1, "good" track, of eicosanoid production.

The final *Jeopardy* answer is "A Hormone That Activates Delta 5 Desaturase." And the winning question is: "What is insulin?"

Insulin is the hormone the pancreas secretes to help the body normalize blood sugar. The pancreas produces insulin in response to ingestion of sugars and refined and starchy carbohydrates. The more insulin in the blood, the more likely your body will make the Series 2 eicosanoids—the bad guys.

A primary goal of the Sugar Control Program is to inhibit insulin production and stimulate glucagon (the opposing hormone to insulin). Glucagon slows delta 5 desaturase and thus promotes the production of the Series 1 "good" eicosanoids.

The high-carbohydrate diets that have been so heavily promoted in the U.S. in the last two decades actually promote the production of "bad" Series 2 eicosanoids. That probably explains the deteriorating health we have seen in the U.S. and all those dietary "paradoxes" I mentioned in Chapter 2.

Another nutrient that inhibits delta 5 desaturase is EPA (eicosapentaenoic acid), found in North Sea fish oils. This is an omega-3 fatty acid that, like glucagon, also inhibits the alpha 5 desaturase enzyme to favor production of good eicosanoids.

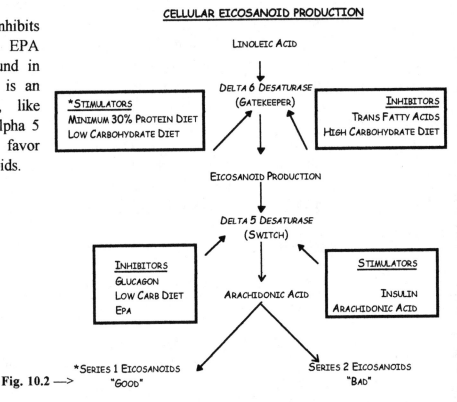

CELLULAR EICOSANOID PRODUCTION

LINOLEIC ACID

DELTA 6 DESATURASE (GATEKEEPER)

*STIMULATORS
MINIMUM 30% PROTEIN DIET
LOW CARBOHYDRATE DIET

INHIBITORS
TRANS FATTY ACIDS
HIGH CARBOHYDRATE DIET

EICOSANOID PRODUCTION

DELTA 5 DESATURASE (SWITCH)

INHIBITORS
GLUCAGON
LOW CARB DIET
EPA

STIMULATORS
INSULIN
ARACHIDONIC ACID

ARACHIDONIC ACID

*SERIES 1 EICOSANOIDS "GOOD"

SERIES 2 EICOSANOIDS "BAD"

Fig. 10.2 —>

*INDICATES PREFERRED PATHWAY

Arachidonic Acid (AA)

There is one more wrinkle in this scenario. Arachidonic acid helps produce some of the Series 2 eicosanoids. It is an essential fatty acid, so we need to have some. Too much, however, can be destructive and is deadly to lab rats. More insulin in the blood stimulates production of more arachidonic acid in the eicosanoid pathway, while glucagon inhibits AA production. The Sugar Control Program limits insulin and raises glucagon.

Dietary AA, however, also increases Series 2. It is found in the fat of red meats, in organ meats, and in egg yolks. Is this a familiar list? These are the very foods the anti-cholesterol gang has been on at us about for years. It's just that cholesterol isn't the problem—arachidonic acid is.

Eggs and meats are only a problem if you are sensitive to arachidonic acid! like the lab rats who normally would never have any dietary arachidonic acid.

Symptoms of AA sensitivity are chronic fatigue, poor sleeping habits, difficulty awakening, grogginess on awakening, brittle hair and nails, constipation, dry flaking skin and chronic minor rashes—even after you've been on Sugar Control for awhile.

If you have these problems, Drs. Michael and Mary Dan Eades[31] recommend, that you trim off all the visible fat when preparing beef. That in itself eliminates 35 percent of the

---

[31] Protein Power, p. 86.

arachidonic acid. Marinating beef in wine and olive oil for 24 hours removes most of the arachidonic acid in the meat and replaces some of it with the healthful olive oil. Discard the marinade and grill the beef. Grilling gets rid of even more arachidonic acid.

Another way to limit arachidonic acid in red meat is to eat free-range cows and game instead of commercially grown beef. The natural food for cattle is grass, not grain. Grain-feeding—which is the commercial way of feeding cattle—causes the cattle to convert the starchy carbohydrates in the grain into more fat and arachidonic acid. This is the same insulin problem that humans have in relation to arachidonic acid: The more starch we eat, the more insulin we produce to process the starch, the more arachidonic acid we make.

Range-fed animals and game have much less fat and very little arachidonic acid. They also have EPA DHA levels equivalent to North Sea fish. Commercial growers are starting to look at this situation now that we understand the relationship between our health and the type of feeds that are given to the animals that we eat. They are at least experimenting with feeds that could produce better quality, more healthful meats.

If you eat eggs—and to my mind, they are a perfect food—but are sensitive to arachidonic acid, then take some fish oil to counteract the effect of the egg yolk. Personally I feel that the egg-white-only solution (or the one egg yolk to three egg whites solution) promoted by low-cholesterol diets is addled. Egg white is the only animal protein that is incomplete and it is not that healthful or tasty a food on its own.

What To Do

Fig 10.3: To Stimulate Good Eicosanoid Production

♦ Get enough linoleic acid from good quality dietary fats.
♦ Eat at least 30 percent of your diet as protein to process the linoleic acid
♦ Follow the Sugar Control Program, or eat a diet of primarily animal foods, fresh fruits and vegetables, whole-grain rice and good quality fats. Eat grains sprouted.
♦ Use butter, ghee, or olive oil for cooking.
♦ Avoid trans fatty acids such as margarine and hydrogenated fats. Read labels. Do not cook with unsaturated oils.
♦ Avoid alpha linolenic acid (ALA) in canola, black currant, soy and flax seed oils.

Remember: To stimulate "good" eicosanoid production, reducing your level of insulin production should be all you'll need to do. If you do that by following the Sugar Control Program, you can eat all the red meat and egg yolks you want. A few people are sensitive to arachidonic acid. If you have been on Sugar Control for a few weeks and you still suffer from chronic fatigue, poor sleeping habits or insomnia, grogginess on awakening or difficulty awakening, thin brittle hair and nails, constipation, dry, flaky, chalky skin, and rashes, you may have AA sensitivity—especially if your cholesterol is still high. If so, follow the recommendations in Figure 10.4, below.

Fig 10.4: To Eliminate Arachidonic Acid from Your Diet

◆ Trim all visible fat from red meat.
◆ Marinate and grill beef (p. 101).
◆ Eat free-range meat or game.
◆ Limit egg yolks, or
◆ Supplement your diet with North Sea fish oil to complement egg yolks.

P.S. I heard a report very recently about a study with omega-3 and omega-6 oils and breast cancers. The omega-3's (as in fish liver oils) reduced tumor size drastically and rapidly, while the omega-6's supported tumor growth. This seems to support several of the comments throughout this book about the ALA content of various oils and unsaturated fats.

When we eat these fatty acids, we need to convert EPA and omega 6 to DHA. People who are ill frequently have problems with this conversion. That's why I generally recommend marine oils and DHA from algae rather than flax seed oil, for example.

❖ ⌘ ❖

CHAPTER 11—THE SUGAR CONTROL PROGRAM

Why, What, How, and What If?

❖ ⌘ ❖

This chapter arises out of the questions and misunderstandings and quirky behaviors I have experienced with patients over and over again. In this chapter, I will go through the Sugar Control Program piece by piece explaining the reasoning behind the instructions and what the instructions mean and do not mean.

There is an instruction in the Program that says: "When in doubt, leave it out!" On the one extreme, people call from a restaurant and ask if they can have halibut. The Program sheet says fish. Does that include halibut, too?

On the other extreme there is Sarah, who was still not improving after weeks on the program. She kept assuring me she was on the Program. Finally, I asked, "Okay, Sarah, what exactly did you eat for breakfast?" Sarah replied that she'd had two boiled eggs, a slice of sprouted bread and "**my** frozen yogurt. You said I could have yogurt."

Well, that was true. I did tell Sarah she could have yogurt. But I meant plain, unflavored yogurt with live cultures in it. Sarah interpreted that to mean anything with yogurt in it.

When someone attaches a possessive pronoun to an item of food, especially processed food, you know that there's a problem. After all, it's not as if Sarah herself raised the cow, milked it, incubated the milk with yogurt culture overnight, and then put it in an ice cream maker with sugar and sweetened fruit preserves.

She just went out and bought a quart of frozen yogurt—one of those foods that starts out actually being healthy when it's made from good quality ingredients and is then corrupted and co-opted with sugar, artificial colors and flavors, chemical stabilizers and preservatives, and advertised as though it will grant you a long and healthy life. There's nothing about it to keep you healthy. And nothing to make it "my" frozen yogurt. Except possibly the addictive behavior that made Sarah fend off her children, spouse and grandchildren if they wanted some too. "No! No! It's my frozen yogurt! Get your own!"

It never once crossed Sarah's conscious mind to ask about frozen yogurt, which contains all kinds of things that are on the No-No list of the Program. Addictive behavior is fed by the addiction. The Sugar Control Program is designed to free you from food addictions.

(continued on p 107)

SUGAR CONTROL PROGRAM

PERMITTED FOODS

PROTEIN (unlimited)

Red Meat (Beef, Venison, Buffalo)—AT LEAST 9 OZ. PER WEEK (in one
    serving or three 3-ounce servings)
Lamb is a white meat for most Americans. It is red meat for Arabs,
    Australians, and New Zealanders.
Game
Pork
Organ Meats (Liver, Sweetbreads, Brains, etc.)
Fish (a must for Scandinavians), Shellfish
Poultry, Fowl (Chicken, Turkey, Duck, Pheasant, Cornish Hen, etc.)
Eggs
Whole Milk, Cheese, Cottage Cheese, Plain Yogurt

FRESH VEGETABLES

Greens—Unlimited   Yellow—Small Portions
Canned—Okay (No Sugar Added)   Fresh Juice*

FRUITS (unlimited)

Fresh   Fresh Juice*
Canned Okay (No Sugar Or Syrup)

BEVERAGES

Coffee/Tea (Decaf Only), 1-3 Cups/Day, No Sweetener
Herbal Teas
Milk—(only if there is no skin, allergy, or weight problem)

WATER—MANDATORY!!!—1 Quart Per 50 Lbs Body Weight Per Day
[A 100-Pound Person Needs 8 Glasses Per Day; A 200-Pound Person
Needs 16 Glasses Per Day.]

---

*Juices labeled "Unsweetened" and "No Sugar Added" may contain added sugar or artificial
  sweeteners.. There is no longer any way to be sure.

SNACKS (unlimited)

Raw Cashews   Raw Brazil Nuts
Coconut (Fresh From Tree Only)   Yellow/White Aged Cheese

NO-NO'S

Sugar	Equal (NutraSweet)	Saccharin
Sweet 'N Low	Sorbitol	Chewing Gum
Soda Pop	Molasses	Honey
Rice Syrup	Maple Syrup	Carob
Wheat Products	Grain Products	Cereals
Seeds	Lentils	Dried Peas, Legumes
White Rice	Rice Crackers	White Starch
Arrowroot Powder	Cornstarch	Potato Starch
Cauliflower	Potatoes	Yams
Parsnips	Rutabagas	Corn
Fruit Spreads	Fruit Concentrates	Frozen Yogurt
Ice Cream	Margarine	Crisco, Spry
Mixed Drinks	Alcoholic Beverages	Beer And Wine
Soy Milk	Rice Dream	Frozen Foods
MSG	Salt (Dextrose Added)	Candy
Nut Butters	Aspartame	Mayonnaise
Candy	Cookies, Cake	Beets

OKAY

Vinegar*   Sprouted Seeds, Grains, and Lentils
Herbs and Spices   Cooked Wine in Prepared Foods
Butter   Soups Made Of Permitted Ingredients
Mustard (no sugar)   Marine Oils
                                                        Mayonnaise (p. 157)

Cold-Pressed Vegetable Oils (Olive, Sesame, Walnut, Rice Bran Are Best). One Tablespoon or More Per Day.

---

*Some vinegars contain sugar. Read labels carefully. True balsamic vinegar, for example, is aged in wood, generally comes from Modena, Italy, and is quite expensive. Many imitations can be found, some coming from Modena. They are cheaper and contain sugar.

WHEN IN DOUBT, LEAVE IT OUT!! Call Your Doctor And Ask !
(See the detailed Food Lists starting on pp. 216)

SPECIAL INSTRUCTIONS

1. You must eat some protein every two hours of your waking day.

2. The only bread permitted: 2 slices of 100% sprouted bread (flourless) or plain Essene bread per day (available at better health food stores). Bread must be 100% sprouts—no flour. Honey or sweetener is okay in this bread.

3. The only grain permitted: roasted whole-grain rice (unlimited amounts). The recipe (p. 199): Wash whole-grain rice. Toast in a dry skillet, over medium heat until golden brown or tan. Keep stirring. If kernels pop, lower the heat. Cool and store, or cook immediately. Bring liquid to boil (1 C rice to 3 C water) in covered saucepan. Add browned rice to boiling water. Simmer in covered saucepan on very low heat, 45 minutes, stirring 1-2 times. Home-made broth may replace some or all of water. Herbs may be used for flavor. This method makes your body use the rice as protein, not starch. The rice stimulates only appropriate amounts of insulin. Use rice for breakfast, hot or cold (with fresh fruit and berries, and plain yogurt), instead of cereal. Replace pasta in salads and hot dishes with rice, use in stir-fry recipes, mixed with vegetables and meat, etc.

4. When your body is ready, the doctor will add more foods to your program and test to be sure you can tolerate them.

This low-stress food program combined with your TBM treatments allows your body to rest and heal itself. The more often your sugar-control mechanism is adjusted during the first two weeks, the more quickly you will heal and the sooner you will experience renewed energy and freedom from sugar and junk food cravings.

Enjoy!! You are back on the road to good health.

(continued from page 103)

Why Is Protein So Important on this Program?

The object of this Program is to restore your body's ability to process carbohydrates. In order to do that, you need to inhibit the production of insulin (which is out of control) by eating only protein, good-quality fats and high-fiber, low-starch carbohydrates. Carbohydrates make quick energy, but the energy is short-lived. Protein produces slow steady longer-lasting energy. This sustained level of energy also eliminates sugar and carbohydrate cravings. In studies, subjects ate a high-protein breakfast. Their blood sugar rose slowly to about 120 mg/dL and then stayed in that range for 6 hours. Other subjects ate a high-carbohydrate breakfast. Their blood sugar rose rapidly and then fell rapidly and quickly. The protein-eaters felt better and more energetic throughout the day.

In the beginning phases of the program, we recommend that you eat some protein at every feeding. This permits the liver to rest and repair its communication lines to the pancreas and adrenals. It is easy to eat protein at meals, but people are usually perplexed by pick-me-up snacks. Good snacks might be: 1-2 oz of cold chicken with carrot sticks, left-overs from a meal, cold rice with fresh fruit and cashew nuts, an apple and 1-2 ounces of hard cheese, a slice of roast beef. See the menus (p. 205) for more ideas.

Why Do I Need To Eat Red Meat?

Red meat (and fresh coconut) contain a special form of the amino acid methionine, essential to optimal health. This methionine determines not only how much sugar and protein the liver can process, but also how well the liver can communicate with the pancreas and adrenal glands. Many foods contain methionine, but according to Dr. John C. Thie,[32] the special methionine in red meat catalyzes the methionine in other foods. You supply your liver with enough of this methionine by eating a minimum of nine ounces of red meat per week. This red meat ration can be divided up into 2 or 3 servings, or it can be eaten at one serving. More than nine ounces per week is fine (especially if you have type O blood), but not less.

If you are switching from a vegetarian life style or have not eaten red meat for a long time, it may take your body a week or so to start making enough of the right digestive juices to process the meat properly. Start with small servings and give yourself a chance to readapt. You may need to supplement hydrochloric acid or protease enzymes for awhile.

Can't I Get Methionine in a Pill?

The methionine in most nutritional supplements is not the same kind as found in red meat. There is a supplement source of methionine available from John C. Thie's

---

[32] Dr. Thie was a biochemist, who specialized in nutrition. He was also the father of the founder of Touch for Health.

company TPCS.[33] It's called Verufakt. However, the supplement also contains ox bile, and I find many vegetarians will not use it.

The other source of methionine is from freshly picked (less than 24 hours) coconut meat. You need a half of a coconut a day to meet your methionine needs.

But Isn't Red Meat Bad for Me?

Yes and no. Our meat supply is tainted by agri-business processing. Cattle raised on grain instead of grass have more fat. Hormones and antibiotics used in the cattle industry aren't that good for you. But most Americans are descended from meat-eaters and require meat in their diets to assure health. So take antioxidant supplements with your meat and follow the directions for defatting and marinating beef on p. 101.

Because of the levels of fat, synthetic hormones, and chemical residues found in the meat of grain-fed cattle, I recommend locating organic sources of beef, wild game or bison (see p. 222 for some sources). Range-fed and wild animals are far healthier to eat than grain-fed animals. This also applies to wild fish as opposed to farm-raised fish.

Trying to replace our animal protein needs with vegetable protein to avoid the concentration of pollutants in the food chain just does not seem to be a good trade off in health, at this point. But take antioxidants with your processed animal food.

One of the objections that vegetarians make about eating animal foods is that it brings about an acidic state in the body. We don't actually know whether this objection is valid, since many people have existed very healthfully on high-protein diets of good quality foods. And the relative pH of your diet is a minor factor in determining body pH. However, if you eat your animal foods with plenty of vegetables, especially the dark leafy greens and zucchini, the possible acidity will be easily neutralized. And those vegetables, plus the cruciferous ones, offer a plentiful supply of fiber and antioxidants.

Won't a High-Protein Diet Lead to Osteoporosis?

Again, I have to stress that the Sugar Control Program is not necessarily a high-protein diet. The amount of protein you eat depends on your needs and desires. However, vegetarians and high-carbohydrate advocates claim that a high-protein diet promotes bone loss in women after menopause.

There is much archeological, anthropological and experimental evidence that it is actually sugar and refined carbohydrates that interfere with calcium metabolism.[34] The

---

[33] TPCS Distributors, 3857 Birch St., 313, Newport Beach CA 92660. Phone orders: (714) 760-0772 or (818) 792-8000

archeological evidence is that the bones of Paleolithic hunter-gather man were larger and healthier than the bones of farmer man. And in Weston Price's worldwide anthropological research (p. 135), many native groups who began eating western refined foods went from being very healthy to having calcium problems (including osteoporosis) in many systems of the body. These conditions had been unknown to them before.

Effects of Refined Grains on Post-Menopausal Osteoporosis

Dependence on sugar and refined grains also wears out the adrenal glands, which produce hormones that regulate both blood sugar and minerals. When a woman reaches the age of menopause, her ovaries stop producing estrogen. At that point, the adrenal glands should kick in with estradiol, a substance like estrogen, which protects the bones. But the adrenal glands of a sugarholic are too tired to produce enough hormone—hence post-menopausal osteoporosis, hot flashes, irritability, vaginal dryness, etc.

Healthy indigenous women on their traditional whole-food diets do not suffer menopausal symptoms. Menopause is not an estrogen-deficiency disease as portrayed by the American medical community. But menopausal dysfunctions do occur after years of eating sugar and refined foods.

Nevertheless, I Want To Be a Vegetarian

Vegetarians have often come to me for help with their sugar-control problems. I have written at length in this book about the reasons why vegetarianism is not the healthiest plan for most westerner's with disorders of carbohydrate metabolism. But I'd like to offer a few responses to the reasons vegetarians most commonly give for not eating meat..

"I don't want to harm other living creatures." In some cultures, when people eat meat, they look upon the meat as a gift from God, a way of sharing communion with God and His creatures, or of thanking the animal for sharing its life-force. The Hawaiians, who believe that the souls of their deceased family members enter into the clan's animal (fish, for example), are not vegetarians. But they ask permission, and wait for a sign, before they kill an animal for food. And, personally, I experience plants as living creatures too.

"I want to avoid toxic pollutants in the food supply, which become more and more concentrated the higher up the food chain you eat." It's true: The higher up the food chain you eat, the more concentrated the poisons can become. But a vegetarian diet when you are not suited to it won't make you healthier either. Take your antioxidants and fight for clean food.

---

[34] There is also a lot of evidence that carbonated and phosphated diet and regular soda pops have a lot to do with osteoporosis (and skin cancer).

"I believe that it's just healthier to be a vegetarian." Everything that I've read that is reliable, and my clinical experience with patients, does not bear out vegetarianism as being healthier for non-vegetarian blood groups. Some things associated with vegetarian life styles that have been studied may make people healthier, such as living in harmony, daily prayer or meditation practices, avoiding medical doctors and avoiding prescription drugs. These can be practiced by meat-eaters as well.

The conclusions that scientists draw from studies are not necessarily accurate. Sometimes, they are looking at the hole and not the doughnut, as it were. For example, in the 70's a long-term follow-up study was done of Nazi concentration-camp survivors. The evidence was that they lived longer and were healthier than the general population. The conclusion the scientists drew was that systematic starvation is better for human health. It may be. I don't know. But neither do they, because they failed to take into account the fact that concentration-camp **survivors** are a specially self-selected group of very constitutionally strong people who survived. If they looked at the people who died, I don't think they would have come up with the same conclusion.

I used to believe that vegetarianism was better and I tried it for two years, using whole foods, protein combining, a lot of raw foods. By the end of the first year, I was much worse off than I had been, but I kept trying. Finally, I had to give up and admit that my body was too primitive for a vegan domesticated food diet.

We have a tendency to see what we already believe in. A round-earther, seeing a ship disappearing over the horizon believes that he can't see the ship anymore, because the earth is round. A flat-earther sees the ship disappear over the horizon and believes that it has fallen off the edge of the earth into hell.

My brother says that the sun is larger on the horizon, because you believe it will be.

"I believe that eating meat prevents one from achieving true spirituality." The idea that the highest states of meditation can only be achieved on a vegetarian diet is true for the Hindu masters, not for westerners. The Hindu masters said that eating meat put a fiber in the nerve synapses allowing for excitation of the synapses. This would prevent man from reaching the highest state of yoga meditation. But westerners are adapted to eating meat and meat is not an impediment for us.

"I can't stand the sight or smell of meat." Revulsion at the sight or smell of meat in a westerner is usually a symptom of major nutritional imbalances and deficiencies, especially of vitamin B6, folic acid, magnesium and zinc—and/or of emotional trauma.

Assuming that we are talking about Caucasians and many African-Americans with types O, A and AB blood, humans probably need to have varying amounts of animal food in the diet, ranging from small amounts of animal food to two-thirds of the diet as animal food.

Some vegetarians tell me that they get their protein from lettuce. While vegetables do contain protein in the cell wall and nucleus, this is not available to human digestion unless you keep termites in your stomach, or like a cow, have four stomachs and chew your cud.

While I still believe that vegetarianism is not as healthful a diet for natural meat-eaters (and most Americans are) as a diet that supplies animal protein is, it is possible to be vegetarian and be reasonably healthy. But I've also seen very little responsible vegetarianism lately.

The high-carbohydrate/low-fat diet and the notion that vegetarianism is idealistically a superior diet have become excuses for American sugarholics to eat junk-food. They believe, erroneously, that they are following a healthy heart-smart diet plan.

Sugar Control and Vegetarianism

It is possible to follow the Sugar Control Program and heathfully remain vegetarian in the tropics and subtropics where fresh coconut is available. You would have to eat the meat of half a coconut a day to get your methionine ration. And the coconut must be picked that day. Buying it in the supermarket in New York City three weeks after it was picked is not the same thing. By then protein in the coconut has converted to starch and sugar.

Besides coconut, the other vegetable source of this special methionine is Verufakt, from TPCS. It could replace red meat. However, it is expensive and it does contain ox bile and duodenum—animal products.

One vegetarian TBM doctor suggests combining kasha (buckwheat groats) and millet in a 2:1 ratio. He says three ounces a day, cooked, will also supply the methionine needed. I don't know if this is true, but I offer you the information.

But Won't My Cholesterol Go Sky High If I Eat Red Meat and Eggs?

Time and time again, I have seen patients' lab values for cholesterol, blood lipids and triglycerides fall into optimal ranges after just a few weeks on the Sugar Control Program. Read the section on cholesterol, starting on p. 29. High cholesterol is not a valid risk marker for heart disease, but it is evidence of carbohydrate metabolism problems. Normal serum cholesterol at age 25 should be 220 (not 200).

Your body needs about 3000 mg of cholesterol per day. A diet high in animal fat provides only about 800 mg. If you do not eat enough dietary cholesterol, your liver has to make it, because cholesterol is essential to health. When men keep their cholesterol levels below 200, they may need Viagra.

The only area where there may be a problem with nine ounces of red meat a week and egg yolks are in those few people who are sensitive to arachidonic acid. Refer back to page 100 to see whether you fall into that category and what to do about it.

Why Do I Need To Eat Every Two Hours?

If you have ever built a campfire or had a fireplace in your home, you will know that once you get the fire going, you need to add a log every so often to keep the fire burning at an even rate. There is a fire in your body that burns fuel to produce energy, and you need to keep feeding it every two hours in the first weeks of the diet.

In order to keep the blood sugar from fluctuating, it is best to eat frequently. If you wait to eat until "the bottom falls out," you will be sorry. You will force your adrenal glands to react in a panic and will propel yourself into that fight or flight state, where you have no control over what you eat. Your body will want sugar or simple carbohydrates and you'll feel bad until you get your blood sugar back up.

One of the major goals of this Program is to prevent the roller coaster cycle of blood-sugar stress from occurring. Allow your body to rest and recover, so that it will not overreact to carbohydrates. This is also a training diet to sensitize you to your own energy cycles and needs.

Caroline, a very hypoglycemic friend of mine, was coming to my NYC high-rise apartment for dinner one night. I lived in an apartment complex in one of two buildings on my street that were identical except for location. She had visited me many times. But she hadn't eaten anything since lunch, and it was then 6:30 P.M. The cab dropped her off on the street and, in her low-blood-sugar state, she went into the wrong building. She rang the bell of 15K and an unpleasant—as fate would have it—medical doctor answered the door. Caroline could not figure out what was wrong. And the gentleman would not help her. They wrangled back and forth for a while. Finally she managed to get to my apartment at 7:15 (45 minutes later). She was pale, trembling, and in tears. I gave her a container of cottage cheese to eat and a spoon to eat it with, and sat her down in a chair. Half an hour later she had recovered and could laugh at the incident. But these are typical symptoms for a hypoglycemic Confusion, disorientation, poor decision-making, tears (or aggression), followed by the world becoming normal again after s/he has eaten.

You can divide up your meals any way that you want. You can have breakfast, lunch and dinner, and snacks in between. You can have 6 or 7 smaller meals. **But at each feeding, have some protein**. Usually in the first few weeks of the program, a hunger alarm will go off. Pay attention to it and eat. Some people have to eat every hour and a half for the first week of the Program.

But Won't I Gain Weight If I Eat So Much?

The majority of people with carbohydrate metabolism problems tend toward obesity, have been out of control around food for years, and may have been bingeing and dieting for years. If you fall into this category, you will worry that eating often and in unlimited amounts will make you gain more weight.

And that is true—unless you go on a low-carbohydrate program. If you are overweight, your tendency will be to lose weight, naturally.

Enjoy yourself! My clinical and personal experience with this program is that if you are overweight, you will lose weight. Especially if you eat. Patients come in having lost 20-30 pounds in a couple of months. They are amazed, because they feel like they have been stuffing themselves. If you restrict your calorie and fat intake, the strategy will backfire. This program helps to normalize the metabolism. Eat!

If you eat the good foods on this Program and you are overweight, you will probably lose weight. If you are underweight, you will probably gain weight. And if you are just right, you will stay just right.

Can I Combine The Sugar Control Program with My Weight Loss Diet?

NO! Don't try to combine this program with other diets. It will defeat the purpose of the Program. It won't work—you won't lose weight, you won't get better, you probably won't be able to stick to the program, and you certainly won't feel well.

Do NOT try to limit your fat intake below 30 percent. Do not worry about fat intake. Fat is, amazingly enough, fairly self-regulating. Having some fat in your meal makes it more satisfying. A hundred calories of fat will prevent you from eating 500 calories of unsatisfying carbohydrate. Do, however, choose high-quality fats (see Chapter 5).

A number of years ago, before we knew about the connection between calorie restriction and metabolic rate, a friend of mine asked me for advice. She had a problem—if she ate more than 700 calories a day, she gained weight. What could be wrong? My friend weighed 103 pounds and literally ate a handful of lettuce leaves for lunch. I asked her how much weight she would gain. Nine pounds. Do you gain any more than that? No.

I told her that it seemed that 112 pounds was her normal weight and if she was willing to weigh 112, she'd be able to eat normally. She had to make a choice between normal weight and semi-starvation. She chose 103 pounds and semi-starvation.

Dieting and calorie restriction make people fat in a number of ways. This has been proven so many times that I am always amazed these days when there is yet another miracle pill on the market that controls appetite. These miracles steal your hard-earned money up front, then rob you of your health, and later of your self-esteem when you fail yet again. Possibly the worst weight-loss scam I have ever heard of was the one where the "diet" pills contained tape-worm eggs. You were certainly cured of obesity, but then how to cure yourself of the cure?

Do not try to limit your calories. It's counterproductive. When you lose weight by calorie restriction, you lose muscle mass. Muscle weighs more than fat, so the weight loss in poundage is impressive on the scale. However, muscle also burns more calories than fat, so your metabolism slows down and your body—recognizing a famine—adapts to very efficient calorie use. It makes a few calories go a long, long way.

It is interesting to note that whether a dieter is on a 1500-calorie weight-loss diet or on a liquid diet like Optifast, which is usually about 900 calories, s/he loses the same 1-2 pounds per week (after the first week's initial water loss).

When you try to resume the calorie intake that would previously have maintained your lower weight, you find yourself gaining again, because of the lowered metabolic rate and the famine state.

Experiments have been done with laboratory mice. They took two groups of mice of normal weight, feeding on regular Mouse Chow. Then they dieted one group by feeding them reduced fat (lite) Mouse Chow. The dieting mice lost a few ounces. The dieting mice were then returned to their original diet which used to maintain them at their normal weight. What was expected was that the mice would regain the weight to the normal level and stay there. What happened was that the mice regained the weight and then gained 10 percent more. As far as I know the mice had no neuroses that made them gain more weight, but they did lose muscle mass in dieting and their metabolisms slowed down. After dieting they needed less food to maintain their normal weight.

Stop dieting! Enjoy life on the Sugar Control Program and feel energetic and healthy. You will probably lose weight as a by-product. What a concept! Eating will actually stimulate your metabolism to burn more energy. And now we understand why the history of most veteran dieters is to lose weight by some kind of restrictive diet, regain the weight and then 10 percent more. They repeat this process over and over and over. Weight loss is relatively easy—especially in comparison with the task of keeping it off at a lowered metabolic rate.

Many people who tend to be overweight are of a pancreatic endocrine type. Their distant ancestors probably lived in areas of famine or sparse food and seasonal fluctuations in available food, and so their bodies adapted to storing as much energy as possible and using every available calorie as efficiently as possible to survive the inevitable famine. Calorie restriction is just another kind of famine and pancreatic-type bodies adapt immediately to famine conditions to store as much fat as possible.

In order to protect the muscle mass of your body on a weight-loss diet, you need to eat about 2/3 of a gram of protein for every pound of lean muscle tissue you have. Muscle tissue is made of protein. But it doesn't seem to hurt, in terms of weight loss, if you eat more protein than that.

For those overweight people who fall into the 60 percent of Americans who do poorly on high-carbohydrate diets, losing weight and keeping it off means a low-carbohydrate life style, because that's how their bodies function best. If you lose weight on a low-carbohydrate program and then go back to high carbohydrates, you will gain the weight back. This doesn't mean that you can never again have a dessert, but that you have to learn to choose wisely.

Does Sugar Control Work Like High-Protein Diets?

The Sugar Control Program is not necessarily a high-protein program. It is tailored to fit the individual. The Program emphasizes frequent feeding, eating every two hours, and including some protein at each feeding. You could do that and still eat no more than 12-16 ounces of protein a day. Even the classic Weight Watchers diet offered women 12 ounces of protein a day.

You can combine your protein with plenty of low-starch vegetables and some fruit, with sprouted bread and rice pilaf. This would not be particularly high-protein, nor would it produce ketosis (p.14).

Or, on the other hand, you can work the program more like one of the high-protein diets, as long as you:

- ♦ Eat nine ounces of red meat per week.
- ♦ Eat every two hours of your waking day.
- ♦ Include some protein in every feeding.
- ♦ Drink a quart of water per 50 pounds of body weight per day.
- ♦ Eliminate all sweeteners, natural and artificial.
- ♦ Eliminate or severely restrict caffeine (and nicotine, if possible).

There are several good high protein diets: Atkins', Protein Power, Carbohydrate Addict's, and possibly The Zone. The primary goal of all these programs is weight loss. The primary goal of Sugar Control is health gain. For overweight Sugar-Control-Program followers, weight loss usually comes as a by-product.

What are the contradictions between Sugar Control and the other programs? We don't permit artificial sweeteners, because they will blow out the sugar control mechanisms of the body even faster than sugar will. Dr. Robert Atkins, in his newsletter, has started to back off of artificial sweeteners because they are so unhealthy, especially aspartame. However, he recently recommended the herb stevia. In TBM, we find stevia just as disruptive to sugar control as the other sweeteners. The Eades (*Protein Power*) don't recommend artificial sweeteners on the basis of possible long-term side effects.

The Carbohydrate Addict's Diet (CAD) promotes a life style where you eat extremely low carbohydrates all of the time, except one hour a day, when you can eat anything you want. The contention is that if you have your one-hour eat-anything meals at least 24-hours apart, the body will adapt to non-insulin production and so it won't produce very much at the carbohydrate meal. That may work for weight loss (if—you can stop after an hour!), but it doesn't work for sugar control and it seems very stressful to me. So, I don't see any way to combine CAD with Sugar Control.

On the Atkins' Diet, if you calculated that your carbohydrate tolerance was 40 grams a day, you could eat anything you wanted to make up the 40 grams. Again, that includes foods that would blow your sugar control mechanism.

This approach allows people to make unhealthy food choices. For example, a half cup of potato salad and a raspberry pop-tart would equal about 33 carbohydrate grams. That leaves only 7 carbohydrate grams for more nutritious carbohydrates. And so, you would be deprived of the alkalinizing vegetables and fruit that could provide you with essential fiber, vitamins, minerals and the all-important antioxidants.

But Shouldn't I Still Limit the Fat in My Diet?

A mistake that Sugar Control Programmers most frequently make is severely limiting their fat intake, because of the fear of fat and cholesterol that has been drummed into Americans for the last 20 years or so.

When people limit their fat intake, they find themselves cranky, unsatisfied, and bored with their meals. And it is so unnecessary. It is also counterproductive. People who have problems handling carbohydrates turn the carbohydrates they eat into fat. They can't use the carbohydrates for energy, and so they are tired all the time. These people need fat calories for energy.

I tried the low-fat diet myself. I'm a really good dieter. I followed the program to the letter and, within a month, had gained five pounds. The only days I lost any weight were days when I ate more fat than was allowed on the program.

One friend of mine was advised to have by-pass surgery about ten years ago. I convinced him that it was an unnecessary and silly procedure and that he could regain his health with good nutrition, nutritional supplements, relaxation and exercise. He is in his mid-seventies now. He has done a great job with nutritional supplements, exercise and relaxation techniques.

But he got hold of Dean Ornish's *Reversing Heart Disease*. While there is a great deal of good information in the book, the diet is the high-carbohydrate/low-fat wonder. I called my friend one night to see how he was doing. He was gleefully eating a whole fat-free sugar-filled raspberry coffee cake (allowable on that program) and feeling smug, because he thought he was having his cake and eating it too. Since going on this diet, he has gained 40 pounds and he can't control his food cravings.

This is a pill-popping culture and the nutritional supplements my friend is taking have counteracted a lot of the dietary problems, but it's the wrong way around. If he were on the healthy low-carbohydrate diet, he would not need to spend so much money on nutritional supplements, he would lose the 40 pounds that are making him so uncomfortable, and he probably would not need that calcium-channel blocker that he still depends on, anymore.

So have some Sugar Control Mayonnaise (p. 157) on that tuna salad; have some crumbled bleu cheese with home-made vinaigrette dressing (p. 155) on that salad; enjoy a great steak. Your triglyceride and cholesterol levels will probably drop to normal for the first time in years. You will be satisfied with what you are eating. Your cravings will disappear. And you will probably lose weight if you need to.

How Important Are Vegetables?

I can't emphasize strongly enough how important dark leafy green and cruciferous (broccoli, cabbage, kale, chard) vegetables are to your health. They provide vitamins, minerals, fiber and antioxidants. Most vegetables are virtually unlimited on the program. Do avoid root vegetables and white vegetables, because of the relatively high starch content (see the Food Lists, p. 216). But eat plenty of vegetables, especially the dark leafy greens, broccoli, and zucchini. They are alkaline and will balance the acidity of animal protein. The antioxidants in them will also combat any detoxification effects you might have from weight loss and sugar, caffeine and nicotine withdrawal. Antioxidants are also youthening and fight degenerative diseases.

Frozen Foods—No-No

Frozen vegetables used to be high on my list of good ways to get vegetables, because they are picked ripe and flash-frozen. While freezing does something irreparable to the taste and texture of vegetables, it does not harm the nutrition. Unfortunately, frozen vegetables and fruits now contain added sugar. Packagers are permitted to add sugar so that if the product defrosts before it reaches the consumer, it will still retain its color. The packagers are not required to put this information on the label. And it does not affect the calorie count, because, per gram, vegetables and sugar have the same number of calories.

What Are Yellow Vegetables?

Yellow vegetables include cooked tomatoes, cooked carrots and winter squash (acorn, butternut, pumpkin, and spaghetti) and should be limited to half-cup portions, 3-4 times a week. No ketchup—it really is not a vegetable and it's loaded with sugars.

Can I Really Eat All the Fruit I Want on This Program?

Technically on this Program, fresh fruit is unlimited. However, in my clinical experience, patients with the worst sugar dependency switch from junk food sugars and artificial sweeteners to fruit, fruit and more fruit! Even though it's natural sugar with all the fiber, it's still too much of a sugar load. I recommend that fruit portions be limited to between 2-4 whole fruits per day, and that fruit always be eaten with protein foods during the body's initial healing and retraining period.

The same problem of added sugar in frozen vegetables occurs with frozen fruit, so stick to fresh. Canned (which of necessity, also means cooked) water-packed fruit (no syrup, no sugar) is acceptable as far as sugar control is concerned. It is, however, not particularly nutritious. At a restaurant or a catered meal at a meeting, it will do in a pinch.

Avoid dried fruits—they are concentrated sugar. If you must use them, replump them by soaking in water—and then use only 1-3, depending on how large and sweet they are.

And What About Fruit Juice?

Fresh fruit juice is listed on the Program as being unlimited. Personally, I believe fruit juice should be very restricted. It is basically the sugar and water of the fruit with little or no fiber. It takes eight whole apples to make a glass of apple juice—that's a lot of sugar.

Even when juice is labeled "100% juice," "no sugar added," or "unsweetened," processors are allowed to add sugar or aspartame. If apple juice is defined by the USDA as having, say, 25 percent sugar content, and grower Jones's apples only supply 20 percent sugar, grower Jones or the packager is permitted to add refined sugar to bring the sweetness up to the 25 percent level. This added sugar does not have to be listed on the label, because the juice is no sweeter than allowed. There is no longer any way that you can tell. So drink fresh juice if you are drinking juice.

A recent report of *The Journal of the American College of Nutrition* links too much fruit-juice consumption in children with digestive problems, diarrhea, gas and bloating, failure to thrive, chronic congestion, obesity and lowered immunity. *Pediatrics* (1/97) reported another study on children's height. Both the two- and five-year-olds in the study who drank more than twelve ounces of juice per day were 1.1 inches and 1.8 inches shorter respectively than their non-juice-swilling peers. It is unknown whether the lack of growth is directly due to the juice or whether it was due to choosing empty juice calories over protein and vegetable foods. In addition, I don't know what they defined as fruit juice. Was it fresh? Was it whole? Was sugar added? Did they use concentrate? Was it pasteurized? What percentage of the liquid had to be juice? Some fruit drinks only contain 10 percent juice—people mistake them for juice.

The powers-that-be also recommend that children drink pasteurized juice to prevent *E.coli* infections. This does away with the only good reason for drinking juice—live enzymes. Enzymes in juice are destroyed by pasteurization.

Drink water. I only recommend fresh raw fruit and vegetable juices for medicinal purposes. And once in awhile, as a refresher, fruit juice can be mixed 50/50 with seltzer water or club soda.

What About Fruit Juice Concentrates?

Fruit juice concentrates are used to "naturally" sweeten jams, for example. They are on the No-No list. They are just a concentrated sugar masquerading as health food. Essentially they are not quite totally refined fructose. When using packaged products, read the labels very carefully. Any word ending in "-ose" (glucose, fructose, dextrose, maltose, etc.) means refined sugar. These sweeteners, corn syrup solids, invert corn syrup, malt, monosodium glutamate (MSG), and fruit juice concentrates, are also sugar or affect the body as though they were sugar.

But Isn't It Okay To Use Artificial Sweeteners?

Artificial sweeteners of all types are not well-tolerated by people with sugar-control problems. I have seen hypoglycemics have low-blood-sugar attacks while the stuff was still in their mouths.

All artificial sweeteners on the market today, including Equal and NutraSweet, contain sugars. Along with the herb stevia, they all make the carbohydrate-intolerant person produce insulin. In addition, aspartame, officially approved by the FDA as safe, has been proven over and over to cause symptoms including memory loss, irritability, depression, tinnitus, flicker vertigo, flicker-induced seizures, gradual loss of vision and brain tumors. Over 600 pilots have reported symptoms in the cockpit due to aspartame, including *grand mal* seizures. Aspartame is the leading cause of new seizures in children. It is implicated in macular degeneration and other causes of blindness. I have read that one preliminary study funded by Monsanto showed possible birth defects—so Monsanto cut off funding and terminated the study. Aspartame is made of aspartic acid, phenylalanine and methanol. The excess glutamate and aspartate slowly destroy nerve cells. Seventy-five percent of brain cells in an area are destroyed before any overt symptoms are noticed.

Aspartame has been prohibited in soft drinks in Arizona. When soda is stored above 90 degrees (as it often is in Arizona), the chemicals in aspartame begin to disintegrate and the methanol reconverts to its wood alcohol state. Wood alcohol is poisonous to humans. Aspartame also breaks down to formaldehyde, and formic acid (the chemical that makes insect bites inflame).

Aspartame can be found in instant breakfasts, breath mints, cereals, sugar-free chewing gum, cocoa mixes, coffee beverages, frozen desserts, fruit drinks, laxatives, multivitamins, chewable vitamins, milk drinks, pharmaceuticals, soft drinks, sweeteners, instant tea and coffee, topping mixes, wine coolers, yogurt, toothpaste, and in many other products you may not think about.

Why are we feeding this to our children?

The side effects of aspartame use are playing out exactly as opponents predicted, when it was first approved by the FDA. In spite of this, the FDA continues to say that it is safe.

What About Sugar-Free Chewing Gum?

I don't recommend it. Chemicals can absorb into the system while still in the mouth.

Several years ago, I had a patient, Mr. Smith, who was taking Diabinase for adult-onset diabetes. The reason he came to see me was that he was suffering from a neuritis of a cranial nerve, a nerve that comes directly from the brain to the face. Mr. Smith had lost the muscle control of his right eyelid. The eyelid was drooping and he couldn't open his eye voluntarily, and his cheek on that side was sagging. The neurologists had told him that his condition would either clear up by itself in two years, or that it was permanent. They didn't know and, in either case, there was nothing they could do. Thank the Lord!

As part of Mr. Smith's treatment program, he received sugar control TBM adjustments and followed the Sugar Control Program. His wife came with him to each visit, so that she was sure she understood all of the directions. After a month, I still could not get his TBM sugar-control neuromuscular reflex test to stay strong. One day, when I looked at him, I noticed he was chewing gum. And I realized that he was always chewing gum. It was a sugar-free gum sweetened with aspartame.

I made him remove it and promise never to chew it again. (For bad breath after meals, chew on that parsley garnish. The chlorophyll will freshen your mouth immediately—and give you some vitamin A.) After that, his sugar stabilized. His condition cleared up within two months. He was able to control his eyelid again and the muscles in the sagging cheek regained their tone.

With the help of his medical doctor, we were able to wean him off his oral diabetic drug, with blood sugar tests near normal. His blood pressure came down, as did his cholesterol and triglyceride levels. He returned for a six-month check-up. Since his previous visit, he had remained on the basic Sugar Control Program with the addition of some potatoes and whole seeds and nuts. His fasting blood sugar was in the high-normal range at 104 and his wide blood-sugar fluctuations in response to eating had calmed down considerably.

Don't Chew Gum!

I can avoid gum easily, because I used to have a ballet mistress who would make you wear your gum on your nose, if she caught you chewing in class. At age twelve, that was enough mortification for me. Aside from the sugar or artificial sweeteners which are absorbed into your system under the tongue, gum is a stick of chemicals.

Gum forces your stomach to produce a little hydrochloric acid (HCl) continuously. Chewing motions are the beginning of your body's digestive processes. So, your body thinks there is food coming, although there isn't, and it gets ready. This can mean there will be too little hydrochloric acid available when you actually eat food. HCl begins the process of chemically digesting protein in the stomach. So chewing gum exposes you to unwanted chemicals to which you may have sensitivities, and it disrupts normal digestion.

A last word about gum: If you are chewing it, you are not drinking the water you need.

What Should I Do If I Am Allergic to a Food That's Permitted on the Program?

Don't eat it. With the exception of red meat and water, just because a food is on the "yes" lists, doesn't mean you have to eat it. If you have known food allergies or if green peppers give you gas, avoid such foods until your TBM practitioner fixes your allergies and your digestion.

One of the reasons the Sugar Control Program works so well is that it eliminates most of the foods to which people are allergic or sensitive: gluten (wheat, rye, barley), soy, corn, peanuts, chocolate, sugar, and artificial sweeteners.

There are five underlying sensitivities: sugar, mercury-silver dental fillings, mercury, bees and bee pollen. The Sugar Control Program takes care of the sugar allergy. When the other four substances are harmonized to your body by your TBM practitioner, 80 percent of your allergies will disappear. Then s/he can harmonize the few things that may be left—as long as you stay off sugar.

If you persist in eating sugar, each allergy will have to be harmonized individually.

What About Milk and Dairy Products?

There may be some foods that you eat everyday that you are allergic to and don't know it. These foods don't give you hives. Instead symptoms may show up as chronic post-nasal drip, acne, migraines and other chronic conditions. One category of food that fits this description, but is still on the Sugar Control Program, is milk and dairy products.

I frequently recommend that patients with chronic sinusitis, asthma, lung congestion, skin conditions, and migraines avoid dairy products for 3-5 months. There are many reasons.

1. Many people are allergic to milk protein.
2. No mammal, besides humans, naturally drinks milk after it is weaned.
3. Except for humans, all mammals drink only the milk of their own species.
4. Cows' milk was created by nature to grow little calves into big cows.
5. After infancy, many people naturally lose the enzyme that digests milk sugar (lactose intolerance).
6. Milk is a food that makes the human body produce mucus. So when recovering from a cold (or chronic mucous conditions), it's useful to avoid milk products (and wheat) until the congestion clears up.
7. Homogenized, pasteurized milk is a mediocre, over-processed product. It often also contains residues of unwanted chemicals, hormones and antibiotics.

Milk, like wheat, is an allergy that I can harmonize with TBM allergy treatments. However, even after the allergy has been cleared, some people just do not do well on these foods, probably because they are better adapted to a pre-agricultural diet.

Several years ago, *The Wall Street Journal* hired an independent lab to test supermarket-purchased milk samples. All over the country, they found residues of the antibiotic chloramphenicol in the milk. Because chloramphenicol is illegal to use in dairy cattle, the Department of Agriculture, when testing milk for antibiotic residues, did not test for chloramphenicol. So farmers were using it to avoid detection.

Raw certified milk can be a healthful product if you tolerate it well, but in many parts of the country, it is very difficult to get and may be illegal to sell. Years ago milk was a dirty, germ-filled product that carried diseases like scarlet fever. So, instead of cleaning up the dairy industry, the government decided on pasteurization. Pasteurization cooks the milk instead of cleaning it. This kills the live enzymes and changes the structure of the calcium to make it less digestible.

An old farmer I know in Vermont has kept dairy cattle for over 50 years. He complains bitterly about pasteurization. He is a small farmer and cannot afford the equipment. So he has to sell his milk to a processor. The processor collects milk from many small farmers. There is a minimum standard of milk production which they all have to follow. My friend's standards are much higher. But what good does it do? His milk gets thrown into the same vat with lower quality milk products. He has no financial incentive to make a quality product, nor the incentive of the pride that would come from having his name on the label. Homogenization also denatures the fat in the product and makes it unhealthy.

Your TBM doctor can determine whether or not you can use milk or other dairy products. People who only have lactose intolerance can usually digest yogurt (because the acidophilus culture has predigested the lactose) and other cultured milk products as well as butter. The process of making yogurt is a low-heat pasteurization method, but dairies still use high-heat pasteurized milk to make yogurt in the U.S.

If you are able to eat hard cheese, I recommend buying European cheese. In Europe, cheese-making is still an art. They use better quality milk.

What Can I Drink?

The Sugar Control Program helps people with a wide range of sugar control problems, from minor to very serious. People with a minor problem can probably have a cup of coffee or tea a day and still recover (assuming they are not adding the caffeine to a nicotine habit). People with more serious problems should limit their coffee and tea intake to three or fewer cups of decaf per day. The decaffeination process does not remove all the caffeine. Use products that are naturally decaffeinated. Avoid products processed with alcohol or formaldehyde.

If your doctor tells you that you have a 100 percent sugar problem, no caffeine is permitted at all.

Pure fruit juice cut half and half with plain seltzer water, club soda or sparkling water may be a refreshing pick-me-up. Check the bottle before buying, Flavored seltzers and the New York Seltzer brand may contain natural or artificial sweeteners, which are NOT on the Program. Quinine also contains sugar.

Milk is okay if you are not allergic to it. Check with your TBM doctor. Whole raw certified organic milk would be best, if you can get it.

Herbal teas are fine and some are pleasant enough that they taste good without sweeteners. Avoid maté, kava-kava or ma huang in herbal teas or products.

Drink water! If you are drinking liquid foods, you are probably not drinking water.

You Mean I Have To Drink Three Quarts of Water a Day?

I'll drown. I hate water. I'll be getting up all night to go to the bathroom. I drink tea and soda and juice. Doesn't that count?

Drink water. Your body is 66-75 percent water, the solvent in which the solid matter of your body floats. Please go back and reread Chapter 8 on water.

We lose a lot of body water through perspiration and urination, and let's not mention tears. That water loss needs to be replaced. What's left needs to be flushed out. That means we need 2/3 of an ounce of water per pound of body weight daily. That translates to a quart of water for 50 pounds of body weight per day.

To help with the concept of drinking enough water, it may be useful to get a quart or liter container. A 100-pound person would drink only two of those a day, a 150-pound person would drink three. Easy! Right?

Carbohydrate metabolism problems and dehydration are the cause of almost all chronic degenerative diseases. You may not have one of these diseases now, but if you are reading this book, you are probably well on your way. Take control of your health now.

Alcohol, Caffeine, Nicotine and Drugs (Prescription and Recreational)

You mean I can't have a glass of wine with dinner? A beer while watching the game? While wine and distilled liquors have no carbohydrates, the alcohol has a stress effect on the adrenal glands. And, if you remember, while the pancreas has the effect of lowering blood sugar when it is too high, the adrenal glands have the job of raising the blood sugar when it is too low. Beer has both alcohol and carbohydrates.

Any substance that kicks the adrenal glands (in other words, an upper of any kind) or sedates them (a downer) will affect blood sugar levels at the time and will slow or stop any progress you may be making. Most substances that begin by stimulating will end by sedating after the high wears off. Substance use and abuse will keep you on the blood sugar roller coaster.

Talk to your TBM doctor about any help s/he can give you not only in quitting these substances, but also in minimizing withdrawal and detoxification symptoms.

While we are on this subject, there are a number of natural products that kick the adrenal glands. Stimulating herbs found in teas and other products include maté, ma huang and kava-kava. Blue-green algae from Klamath Lake, sold under various brands, seems to do the same thing for a lot of people. While they may make you feel good in the short term, all of these products should be avoided by people with carbohydrate metabolism problems, because of their long-term stress on the adrenal glands.

Be aware that cough medications usually contain sugar or aspartame and lots of alcohol. Nyquil is about 40 percent alcohol. And Excedrin contains caffeine.

I think we all know by this time that smoking is not healthful nor are drugs of any variety. Wine and beer, however, in moderation can be quite good for you. If you enjoy them, you probably will be able to use these products again in moderation once your sugar control mechanism has stabilized.

I Hate Cauliflower Anyway—

But I thought it was good for me: Why can't I eat it? Cauliflower is good for you in general, but it has white starch as do white potatoes and other root vegetables. Until your blood sugar stabilizes, avoid foods containing white starch.

Can I Eat Rice Crackers?

You are permitted unlimited amounts of short, medium, or long, whole-grain rice prepared exactly as outlined in the diet (p. 106). In the Recipe section of the book, you will find many recipes using this kind of rice. Pan-toasting the dry rice, before boiling or steaming it, transforms the rice so that your body uses it as a protein. Your pancreas secretes only essential insulin to deal with the rice.

NO other kinds of rice or rice products are permitted on the diet, because they all act as sugar and cause insulin release. Avoid rice as served in most restaurants (including Japanese and Chinese). It will be processed, refined rice. Avoid, too, wild rice, rice crackers and cakes, rice noodles, puffed rice, Rice Krispies, rice syrup, Rice-A-Roni, Rice Dream, and arborio rice.

What Kinds of Snacks Can I Eat on This Program?

See the recipes and menus (p. 205) sections for snack ideas. The only kinds of nuts included in this program are RAW, uncooked, unheated, unroasted cashews and Brazil nuts, because they are metabolized primarily as protein. If you can make raw cashew nut butter in your blender, grinder, Champion juicer or food processor, you can eat it. However, if you find cashew butter at a gourmet or health food store, it will probably be made from roasted cashews. When the cashews are roasted, your body uses them as sugar. No! Peanut butter is not permitted on this program. It's a question patients ask me over and over—I don't know why, since peanuts, which are legumes, are not on the program either. And commercial peanut butter is loaded with sugar (frequently not listed on label).

If you tolerate dairy products, aged cheeses are great snacks.

Coconut meat can be eaten only if it has been picked fresh from the tree that day. If you have access to fresh coconut, you can eat it as a source of methionine. You need the meat of half a coconut per day to provide the necessary methionine. Fresh whole coconut is a very healthy food. It has been demonstrated to protect against skin cancers and is being used by AIDS patients to boost their immune systems—with very good results. However, after 24 hours, it turns into sugar and is a No-No.

Why Is Only Sprouted Bread Permitted on the Program?

Wheat berries from which wheat flour is ground are grass seeds. Seeds are a storehouse of starch ready to grow a new plant. When the plant begins to sprout, it transforms the starch to protein. So while flour ground from seed is a carbohydrate product, ground-up sprouts are a protein product that does not stimulate insulin release when you eat it.

In addition, many people with sugar-handling problems don't tolerate grains well and have sensitivities to gluten flours. I find that these people can usually eat the sprouted breads without reacting.

Two slices a day of sprouted bread are permitted. There are several breads, available in good health food stores, that are made of 100 percent sprouted grains (without milled flour). These breads usually contain some sweetener, but it has been used up by the yeast and usually poses no problem. There is also a macrobiotic rice bread permitted on the program, but it tastes like sawdust and I have never found anyone who liked it.

But the Government and "Real" Doctors (RD's) Say . . .

It occurs to me, writing this chapter, that most of the questions that perplex and worry patients going onto the Sugar Control Program come from misinformation and propaganda about health and food. The problem is that this misinformation comes from their doctors, family, friends and the media. It's like passing along a false rumor—soon everyone believes it. And some people even get to believe they actually saw it happen.

I warn you now: this section is a soapbox in Union Square. You can skip it if you want to, but—

I always say that when governmental agencies and manufacturers are advising you on health issues, watch the money. A 1996 study of the FDA showed that 37 of 49 top officials who left the FDA went to work for drug companies they had regulated. Over 150 FDA officials owned stock in the drug companies they were assigned to manage.

Their words come down to you via press releases and conferences, newspaper and news media articles. But they also come masked in sit-coms, TV commercials, dramas, movies, even novels. Some of the people who bring you these messages have simply been convinced by the party line and don't question it. They really have your best interests at heart. But others have vested interests.

The popular media are under the control of the American Medical Association and related groups, which are very powerful. But they are just labor unions, whose main goal is to protect the livelihood of their members. The AMA, itself, was formed in 1847 for the express purpose of putting a successful group of health-care practitioners out of business.

Personally, I have no objection to MD's having their say, even though most medical doctors only had about five minutes of nutrition training in medical school. What I object to is that anyone else who wants a say is treated as a lunatic or a quack. And some AMA spokesperson must get equal time—as though it were a political debate. But when it is the established church of medicine[35]—speaking in the person of Tim Johnson or Bob Arnot, for instance—no dissenting opinion is required.

My favorite commercial depicts this whole situation. It's a Rice Krispies (no you can't eat them on the Sugar Control Program!) ad from a few years ago. The scene opens in the kitchen. A young man is pouring himself a bowl of Rice Krispies, when his mother enters. She says something like, Oh, son, it's your first day of vacation from medical school, and I wanted to make you a nutritious breakfast of hot oatmeal.

The son says, I'm an almost-doctor now, Mom, and I know best. Rice Krispies is fortified with eight vitamins and minerals and has more nutrition than your natural whole grain oats. And if you really want an expert opinion, ask them— And Snap, Crackle and Pop jump right off the box to give you the True Word from the True Authorities.

A few years ago, the actor Richard Chamberlain was involved in a projected TV series in which he played a Caucasian medical doctor who had been raised by Hawaiian foster parents. Chamberlain was interested in portraying, to a general audience, traditional Hawaiian healing techniques in a positive light alongside established medical procedures. But the sponsors of the show put their collective feet down. The only way Chamberlain could get the show on the air was to clean it up. He did not have to clean up violence or language, only the depiction of traditional healing methods as valid alongside western medicine.

The TV series *Northern Exposure* did accomplish Chamberlain's mission a few years later with many story lines showing shamanism, chiropractic, environmental allergies and nutrition in a positive light, with Dr. Fleishman, M.D., tut, tut, butting-in along the way.

---

[35] To quote Robert Mendelson, M.D., from *Confessions of a Medical Heretic.*

The most open place to look for health news today is on the Internet, and—I'm sorry to have to say it—often in the back pages of *The Inquirer*. Even so, you have to pick and choose and test things out. The health product industry is big business as well—that's why established medicine really is getting involved with alternative treatments now. And where there's money, there's fraud and misrepresentation of one sort or another.

You are the best authority on your own health. Not I. Not anyone else. Among the questions I frequently ask new patients are: What was going on in your life when this problem started? What do you think began your health problems?

In my experience, you always know the truth about yourself. You just have to trust yourself. Because no doctor has been willing to really listen to them before, patients say things to me that begin, "You'll probably think I'm crazy, but after my gall bladder surgery—" "Since my mother died—" "I've been afraid to tell anyone this, but—" And they are always right on.

How Can I Make These Changes in My Life?

Plan for success. There are many snack ideas in the Menus section, p. 205, of this book. It is a good idea, especially in the beginning, to have snacks ready to eat before the hunger alarm goes off. Cook enough at mealtimes, so there are plenty of leftovers—cold meats and chicken. Eat fresh vegetables, tuna salad, fruit and cashew nuts, fruit and cottage cheese or plain yogurt (add your own fresh fruit).

It's also a good idea to keep cold cooked rice on hand to use in recipes and salads. Another helpful behavior is to make parts of meals beforehand, say after dinner. When making salad, I will prepare enough lettuce and some other ingredients for several meals at a time. Store the extra dry in a plastic bag in the frig. Squeeze the air out of the bag, before closing it.

Many people complain that it's too difficult to snack at work. In my opinion, if you can go to the bathroom, you can snack. Hard-boiled eggs travel well; so do nuts, apples, and cheese. Carry a small insulated bag with an ice-pack to keep meat and other foods cold (or hot food hot with a heat pack). Use your imagination. But do eat. You may have to set a timer, enlist the aid of a secretary or friend to support and remind you, keep the food in plain sight, so you remember to eat it, when you are very busy.

How Can I Stick to the Program When I Eat Out?

If you are going to a party or out to dinner, snack before you go. Do not arrive at a party or restaurant hungry. (I know—your mother said you would ruin your appetite, but she's been wrong before.) It is not easy to wait for your shrimp cocktail, avocado, roasted peppers, or cheese plate appetizer when you are hungry and there are bread and rolls on the table tempting you. If you have already snacked, your blood sugar is level, you are in control and can leave the bread alone. Push the bread away from you, out of your line of sight. Make it smaller and darker and imagine that the waiter dropped it on the floor and then just picked it back up and served it anyway, after spitting on it. Engage in interesting conversation with your meal companions. Drink water.

Pick a restaurant that has selections that you can eat and that you enjoy. Call ahead and let them know what you need; discuss options and order ahead. The shrimp cocktail could be on the table waiting for you. Forget about good manners. The same with a party—call the hostess and let her know that your doctor has put you on a special program. Discuss her menu, and let her know what you need. If necessary, offer to bring some things that you know you can eat.

Protein is becoming popular again, and it is getting easier to find "legal" sugar control dishes. I recently stayed at the Savoy Hotel, a bed and breakfast in Kansas City MO, and the breakfast menu contained items like omelets (of course), but also medallions of beef, lamb, caviar and smoked salmon, asparagus, avocado, vegetables. I had to ask for a fruit plate, but they brought me a beautiful plate of mixed fresh berries (raspberry, blueberry, strawberry and blackberry). I had a beef satay without sauce in a Vietnamese restaurant in the City Market. And in a Chinese restaurant, a chef's special soup made of a clear broth containing vegetables, shrimp and chicken thickened with egg white. No MSG or cornstarch.

Last month, I went on my first cruise and everyone warned me about the food: How much there was, how good it was and how many desserts there were. One of my dinner partners, Lotty, was a diabetic. She kept refusing foods that the waiter kept tempting her with and he kept bringing more foods. Finally, I realized what the problem was and told the waiter. He immediately shifted gears and made it his business to bring her only things that she could eat. So I did the same for myself. And there was plenty of gourmet food on the menu that was on the Sugar Control Program. But I must admit that fortunately I was never awake for the midnight dessert buffet.

It takes only about three weeks of behaving in a different way to change a habit. I hope I have given you lots of ideas for new behaviors to play with that will help you change from your old eating habits to new Sugar Control habits that will support you in optimum health, energy and joy.

❖⌘❖

CHAPTER 12—WHAT TO EXPECT

❖⌘❖

What To Expect When Starting the Sugar Control Program

Detoxification

If you are working with a TBM practitioner, you should have very little discomfort when starting the Program. The TBM treatments will probably prevent you from experiencing much in the way of detoxification symptoms, although your body will be getting rid of garbage that it has been storing and could not get rid of before.

The liver is the toxic waste disposal site of the body. The Sugar Control Program sets up optimal conditions for liver function and detoxification by providing high amounts of complete protein and moderate amounts of high-quality fat, while limiting carbohydrate. Most other programs that are used for detox, such as fasting and vegetarian regimes, actually reduce the liver's ability to detoxify at the very time when the body is intensely trying to get rid of stored toxins. This creates unnecessary symptoms.

If you are on the Program without the help and supervision of a TBM practitioner, you may experience one to four days of food cravings, fatigue, vague body aches and headache. These are not signs of the flu; they are signs of detoxification. Acknowledge the cravings. Recognize the healing signs. And find ways to distract yourself:

> Take a nap, a bath and/or sauna. Go for a nature walk. Listen to music. Exercise. Dance. Amuse yourself with a hobby. Read a novel. Eat something satisfying and on the Program.

If you are experiencing detoxification, a plain water enema may help to clear the poisons from your system more rapidly. Resist the cravings and stick to the Program. If you give in to that Snickers bar, it will take another four days to get it out of your system (that's why allergy rotation diets allow you to have a food one day out of four), by which time you will have committed another Snicker's bar offense. If you continue in this way, you'll never really be on the Program and you'll never experience the benefits.

Cravings and hunger are often misplaced thirst. Drink a glass a water and the craving will probably disappear. Resist them now, or you will prolong the discomfort. Remember— this Program is not forever. Once you experience how much better you feel, you can choose your old life style if you want to get sick again. Or you can make the choices that support wellness.

Increased Sensitivity

After the first four or five days of following the Sugar Control Program, you will have cleared your system of many sugars and other foods to which you didn't realize you were sensitive. If you then try to eat those foods (say you don't resist the cravings), you may have a massive negative reaction. Headache, fatigue, irritability, and diarrhea are the most common symptoms.

You may have been having negative reactions to these foods before, but the reactions were so embedded in general unwellness that you never noticed that they were related to your diet. When your system clears and you're feeling better, your negative reactions to these foods become much more noticeable.

I went to a smoking cessation clinic once to support a friend who was quitting. It was a 14-day program, with daily sessions. The participants quit smoking cold-turkey at the first meeting. After not smoking for 4 days, they came to the next meeting with their favorite brand of cigarettes unopened and their favorite method of lighting cigarettes in working order. During the meeting, they each chain-smoked two of their favorite cigarettes. However, they were not permitted to inhale. (Smokers usually draw the smoke rapidly into the throat where there are few nerve endings.) These people had to hold the smoke in their mouths, which are rich in nerve endings, and then blow it out.

By the middle of the first cigarette, participants were nauseated, throwing up, breaking out in hives. Their eyes were red and watering and their noses were running. In fact, they were having all of the allergic reactions they had experienced the first time they smoked— and had not experienced since then. Many people who can not quit smoking easily are not only addicted to nicotine, but are also allergic to smoking. They smoke as a "fight or flight" reaction: The biocomputer's plea is, "Get me a cigarette fast—or you'll feel bad!"

Many of these detox, withdrawal, and allergy symptoms can be handled by TBM, but since smoking is such a multifactorial problem, I recommend a group smoking cessation, behavior modification, and/or hypnosis program along with TBM and combination homeopathic remedies that deal with the allergy and/or the habit.

Since nicotine is a drug that kicks the adrenal glands and affects your body's sugar control mechanisms, it would be a better choice to become a non-smoker. And a great time to quit is when you are on Sugar Control, because you are eating often and can thus satisfy the oral fixation without gaining weight.

Candidiasis and Other Secondary Infections

Your body is the solar system to a host of microorganisms. When you are healthy, peace reigns. But when your system gets out of balance, interplanetary wars begin. The normal gut is home to the microorganisms (flora) *Lactobacillus*, *E. coli*, and *Candida albicans* in about equal amounts. The *Lactobacilli* help you digest your food. The *E. coli* are gram negative[36] bacteria, and do you no harm. The candida are a fungal colony. Scientists thought they did neither harm nor good. However, Dr. Stephen Paul, a biochemist, found contrary evidence while experimenting to increase cottage cheese production. He found that the *Lactobacilli*—which help produce the curds in cottage cheese, yogurt, sour cream and buttermilk—worked more efficiently when candida were present—so they may play a synergistic role in human digestion after all.

The cause of secondary overgrowth infections, like candidiasis, is disruption of the normal intestinal flora by broad-spectrum antibiotics, such as penicillin, tetracycline and Septra, which only kill gram-positive bacteria. But when you take a broad-spectrum antibiotic, it kills not only the bacteria involved in your disease, but also all the gram-positive bacteria in your body, including the *Lactobacilli* in your gut. *E.coli* are gram-negative bacteria and candida are fungi—so neither of them is affected by the antibiotic.

With the *Lactobacilli* gone, however, the *E. coli* and candida multiply to fill the vacuum. *E. coli* breed true and cause no problem, but candida are greedy and reproduce so rapidly they mutate into a more complicated life form called mold. In this form, they eventually punch holes in the intestinal wall and translocate to other parts of the body. Symptoms of polysystemic chronic candidiasis are the same ones listed on page 17. Vaginal yeast infections usually occur only when the vaginal environment changes due to birth control pill or antibiotic use, diet, etc. Then the environment becomes very hospitable to growing all kinds of germs. If candida are introduced to this environment, they will thrive.

If you have candidiasis, parasites, or other secondary infections, you have experienced Herksheimer reactions. The life cycle of each generation of candida is about 10 days. Then there is a massive die off. While your body tries to clean up this mess, you feel like death warmed over. All your symptoms flare up—the Herksheimer reaction. During the healing process, the reactions may seem stronger compared to how much better you feel otherwise. It is not a sign of a relapse. If you are being treated by a TBM doctor, you may have only one noticeable reaction. If you are following the Program without a TBM doctor, you will probably experience these reactions more often and more intensely.

TBM treatments enable the body to rebalance itself and cure the candidiasis. Without TBM, control can be effected through diet and supplementation. MD's prescribe antifungal drugs like Nystatin. All the patients I have seen who used Nystatin, experienced control of their condition, but not cure. There may be some drug cures; I don't know. The patients I see who took drugs previously failed with them. If they had been cured, they would not be in my office.

---

[36] Gram negative and gram positive are simply terms that refer to the dyes scientists use to prepare microscope slides to study these microorganisms.

Aside from antibiotics, candidiasis can be brought on by steroid use (cortisone, Prednisone), allergy shots, diets high in refined foods, endocrine imbalance, pregnancy, and digestive system dysfunction. One helpful purpose that candidiasis and parasites serve is to help control a heavy-metal body burden, like lead or mercury toxicity, by living off the waste products. So heavy-metal toxicity may have to be dealt with as well. Again TBM has specific treatments for all of this.

High-quality *Lactobacillus acidophilus* and *bifidus* cultures will help restore normal intestinal bacteria, and probiotic supplements containing fructo-oligosaccharides (FOS) will help normal bacteria re-establish themselves more quickly. FOS sounds like something to avoid on Sugar Control, but it is indigestible to humans. Another aid to re-establishing normal gut flora is butyric acid. And glutamine will help heal the gut lining.

The brush border lining the small intestine produces secretory IgA and is vitally important to immune system function. It is a first line of immune defense for all internal organs. The brush border is directly damaged in candidiasis, and is under attack from many quarters on a daily basis, including from a diet high in refined sugars and flours. Everyone should take acidophilus and FOS regularly to keep the gut and the brush border healthy by maintaining a normal balance of intestinal flora.

Other nutritional products useful in killing off candidiasis include:

Caprylic acid—broad-spectrum anti-germicidal	Deodorized garlic—enhances immune function
Grapefruit seed extract—broad-spectrum germicidal	Pau d'arco
ADP (oil of oregano)—broad-spectrum anti-germicidal	Immune system complexes (contain vitamins, minerals and glandulars)
	Antioxidants

Homeopathic combination products have also been designed to treat candidiasis. During the anti-germicidal phase of treatment of candida, parasites and systemic subclinical foci of infection, other kinds of nutritional supplements should not be used, because they will feed the microorganisms. Wait for the recovery phase.

Until I began practicing TBM, I used these kinds of products, with restrictive diets to control candida. The results were good, but they took a long time to achieve. And they were never as good as the TBM results are (and with a bare minimum of supplements).

Increased Appetite

Many patients report that in the first weeks of the Program, they are ravenously hungry. A hunger alarm goes off every two hours or so. Please obey the alarm. It goes off in response to blood sugar drops. You may feel weak or faint, or like your motor is idling too fast. Don't worry about it. This will subside after awhile, and as your blood sugar mechanisms normalize, you may only want to eat every three or four hours.

As you continue to follow the Sugar Control Program, you will probably experience a harmonious increase in energy, improved concentration and intelligence, and better sleep. Another thing that patients report after they get the sugar out of their systems, usually toward the end of the first week, is that they are starting to taste food again and it is enjoyable and delicious. Sugar is a mask to make foods palatable even when they are low-quality. Along with iodized, sugarized salt, sugar seems to glut the taste buds on the tongue so that almost all you can taste is sugar and salt. As the palette clears, the taste of real food emerges. And the taste of real food is a sensual experience, to be savored and enjoyed.

Reintroducing Carbohydrate Foods

After your blood sugar neuromuscular reflex tests have been strong for two weeks straight, your TBM doctor will tell you that it's time to start reintroducing more carbohydrate foods. There are two ways to do this. The first way: If you only had a minor problem to begin with, the doctor may recommend that the night before your next visit, you eat a junk meal of the foods you've missed most. The doctor will perform the blood sugar tests. If they are strong, you can go on to the next step. However, if the junk meal blows out the sugar tests, you have to go back on the basic Program for at least two weeks. Add back whole foods as in Step 1, below.

The second way to reintroduce carbohydrate foods is for those people for whom it is much too stressful to eat a junk meal—people who are also suffering from chronic candidiasis, multiple chemical sensitivities, environmental allergies, chronic fatigue syndrome, etc. If they eat a junk meal, it can take them weeks to recover. So, in these cases, when the sugar control test has been strong for two to three weeks, I test for which foods they can begin to reintroduce. I suggest adding only one or two per meal so that if there is an allergic or toxic reaction, we will know what caused it. I generally start patients with the root vegetables, whole seeds, raw nuts, and sprouted cooked beans and lentils. If this is successful, then a few weeks later, I test for whole-grain pasta, and a few weeks after that for whole-grain bread.

For either category, there are three levels of foods to add back over time:

1. Whole foods: cauliflower, potatoes, yams, fresh corn, beets; seeds (e.g., sesame, sunflower, pumpkin); lentils and dried beans; whole—not milled—grains (steel cut oats, wheat berries, rye, corn, millet); and raw nuts.
2. Whole-grain pasta;
3. Whole-grain bread.

The Sugar Control Program, with the healthy foods you've added, can be your new normal diet. Feeling good, having plenty of energy, being able to savor the delicious tastes of whole food can become your new normal life.

❖ ⌘ ❖

CHAPTER 13—WHAT IS A "NORMAL" DIET ANYWAY?

❖ ⌘ ❖

Remember the joke about the patient with the broken arm? "Doctor, will I be able to play the piano after you remove the cast?" The doctor says, "Of course." And the patient says, "That's funny—I could never play the piano before."

"When will I be able to eat normally again?" Sugar Control patients frequently ask. If you mean by normally, the junk-food or high-carbohydrate, refined food program that threw your body out of balance in the first place, you can do it at any time. But know that eating "normally" will make you sick again. So, let's take some time to look at what normal means when we're talking about a healthy diet.

Native Diets Produce Supreme Good Health

As a nation, we in the U.S. tend to think that we are very healthy. We have access to modern drugs and high-tech medicine, and more and more people live past 100 years. But in spite of all our advantages, we rank only 20th in the world for life expectancy[37]. For the first time since the U.S. has kept longevity statistics (about 100 years), we dropped three places this year in spite of the $949 billion we spent on "health" care. Yet, if we look at many low-tech aboriginal or indigenous groups before their contact with western civilization, we find evidence of supreme good health, with none of the degenerative diseases we suffer today. When these people died young, it was usually due to accident or epidemic.

Dr. Weston Price, a Canadian dentist and the author of several dental textbooks, noticed that the condition of a person's teeth reflected his/ her overall health. He also noticed that the teeth of the children of many of his patients were not as healthy as their parents'. And he was intrigued by anthropological reports of great health among aboriginal groups. Price was able visit a number of these groups in the 1930's when they were coming into contact with western civilization. He observed the health of natives beginning to eat modern foods such as sugar and white flour. And he was able to compare their health with that of nearby tribal or culture members who still followed their native diets.

Dr. Price was able to study a number of tribes and cultures: In Europe, the Swiss of the Loetschental Valley and the Gaelics of the Outer Hebrides Islands; In North America, Eskimos, Native Americans of British Columbia and the Yukon, as well as Seminoles, and

---

[37] Bruce Miller, M.D. *The Nutrition Guarantee.*

the remains of Pre-Columbian groups; In the South Pacific, Melanesians and Polynesians; In Africa, 30 tribes, including the Masai. Price's photographs show very healthy people who ate only their traditional diets. When these adults began eating western food, with its sugars, and milled flours, they suddenly began suffering from calcium-based diseases, which had been unknown to them before, including dental cavities, dental abscesses, osteoporosis, osteoarthritis, and atherosclerosis. They also began developing TB and cancer, for the first time, and became susceptible to other "foreign" diseases.

The first-generation adults depicted in Price's photos have broad smiles with straight, even teeth and no cavities. Where the adults began eating refined food before pregnancy, their offspring had high dental arches and cavities. The children's mouths are full of crooked and overcrowded teeth with no room for wisdom teeth. Sound familiar?

Price learned that when an Eskimo eating western food became ill with TB or cancer, western medicine could not help. But if the Eskimo returned to his native diet, he usually recovered.

Overall, Price's work showed that the people who were almost 100 percent resistant to dental disease were the hunter-gatherers-fishermen. Those eating natural-food whole-grain diets were healthy but their health was inferior to that of the hunter-gatherer. People eating only some western foods mixed with the traditional diet began to suffer dental problems and those abandoning their native diet altogether were the least healthy.

A few years ago, Pocahantas's early life received a major Disney treatment. But, did you know that after Pocahantas married John Rolfe, she moved to London with him? On a British diet, she was dead within two years at age 23. First, she developed TB, then en route home to Virginia, she contracted smallpox and died. Of course, you won't find a connection made in the history books between western food and her death.

Another change we are seeing today is among the Japanese. Living in their own culture, the Japanese have a low incidence of heart disease. However, within a generation of moving to the U.S. and adopting a western diet, their heart disease rate matches that of the European U.S. population.

Raw Versus Cooked

Price-Pottenger and the Cats

Weston Price later teamed up with Dr. Francis Pottenger in California. Pottenger was the son of a doctor who founded a TB sanitarium. One treatment at the sanitarium was to feed patients raw adrenal gland. There were no lab tests to measure the strength of the glandular tissue and hormones in each new shipment. So, in order to assay the potency of the adrenal glands, they used cats. They removed a cat's adrenal glands and then tested to see how much raw adrenal gland from a particular shipment, the cat had to eat to stay alive. That told them the potency of the gland and how much of it patients had to eat.

The cats were generally fed on cooked meat and glandular scraps from the kitchen. Dr. Pottenger noticed some health patterns among the cats and, with Weston Price, set out to study the cats' health. Price and Pottenger performed a series of raw versus cooked food experiments over a 10-year period. The cats were divided into groups. Each group lived in a separate large open pen. The diet of each group was different. In the first experiment, one group of cats was fed raw meat and the other cooked meat. In later experiments, there were four groups: raw meat, raw milk, cooked meat, cooked milk.

They started with a first generation of healthy cats. The health of the second generation depended on the type of food on which its parents had been raised. (The animals were not permitted to cross-breed among food groups).[38]

The raw-meat cats remained healthy through all the generations Price and Pottenger studied. The other cats suffered infertility, impotence, more still births, more kittens in a litter, more kittens with six toes and spinal as well as other deformities, role-reversals between the genders and other behavioral anomalies. A surprising finding was that the ability of a cat to jump from a height and land gracefully on all fours was also impaired in successive generations on the cooked food diets. In none of the various experiments they did, was a fourth generation of cooked-food cats ever reproduced. All of the third generation animals died before they could reproduce.

Over the years, Price and Pottenger also discovered accidentally that the diet of the animal being eaten—whether it was the flesh or its milk—greatly affected the nutritional status and health of the cats. Free-range grass-fed cows provided more nutritious meat and milk.

Although cats must eat meat to survive, while humans can survive on a wide variety of foods, these cat studies still raise some interesting issues. There are strong indications that these issues apply to human nutrition as well. The studies present very convincing evidence that cats should eat what they are genetically suited to eat—raw meat—to be healthiest and fully functional. They also demonstrated that the diet of the animal being eaten was a major factor to the health of the cat eating it. And finally, the studies present strong evidence that raw foods provide nutrition that is lost when food is cooked.

The Kouchakoff[39] Study

This is a provocative study of the effect of raw, cooked and processed food on human blood. Dr. Paul Kouchakoff, a Swiss researcher, reported in 1930 the findings of his

---

[38] In this age of high-tech gene manipulation, this brings up the very interesting question of the effects of pre-conception nutrition on birth defects in human offspring. Medicine already accepts the connection between pre-conception folic acid and neural tube defects (spina bifida).

[39] "Reprint 101." The Lee Foundation for Nutritional Research. Milwaukee, WI 53201. Also "Second Opinion." 7100 Peachtree-Dunwoody Rd., Atlanta GA 30328. Vol VI, No. 2, 2/96.

experiments on digestive leucocytosis. Digestive leucocytosis is the production of white blood cells in response to eating. White blood cells are usually produced by the body when it is fighting off disease or foreign invaders. In 1930, white cell production after eating (digestive leukocytosis) was considered a normal response to eating. Even though a natural process like eating healthy foods should not provoke an immune response

Kouchakoff, however, discovered that this response only occurred when the person ate cooked or processed foods. It did not occur with natural unheated foods. Whether cooked or not, the reaction was strongest with processed foods (enriched, refined, extracted, pasteurized, homogenized, sterilized, condensed—whatever).

Kouchakoff found that each food had a critical temperature, below which it would not provoke digestive leucocytosis. (Most of these temperatures were around 190 degrees.) Water was 191 degrees, 21 degrees less than the boiling point of distilled water. Milk—191. So pasteurized milk which is flash-heated to 500 degrees is a culprit, while yogurt—if it can be made from raw milk pasteurized by scalding to only 150 degrees—is friendly.

In addition, he found that one way to prevent leukocytosis was to chew food thoroughly. [It constantly amazes me how much better our health would be if we simply chewed our food and drank enough water.] Kouchakoff also found no immune reaction when people ate a cooked food along with some raw food of the same kind. As far as I know, the Kouchakoff experiment has not been repeated, and it should be.

Based on this study, I recommend searing a steak well on the outside, but leaving it pink on the inside (you need good quality meat). Cook vegetables in waterless cookware. With this method, a tablespoon or two of water is heated to boiling, producing steam. A vent on the pot is closed and the heat is turned off. The vegetable cooks in the steam and slight pressure for about 10 minutes. It comes out sweet and delicious but not overheated. Eat some of the raw vegetable with the cooked.

The Paleolithic Connection

There is no one diet that is healthful for everyone. It is the scope of another book to talk about individual diets. But I believe that the best way to find the healthiest diet for an individual is to study his or her blood type and dominant and recessive endocrine types. These attributes are genetically determined. Our bodies are still like those of cave-dwellers. About 98 percent of the human digestive system evolved before we began farming, when we were hunter-gatherers-fishermen. Everyone's blood type back then was type O and about 50 percent of Americans are still type O. Type O's are omnivorous and require a lot of protein.

There are seven endocrine glands: gonads, pituitary, pineal, thymus, thyroid, pancreas, and adrenals. In most people, one or two of the glands are constitutionally stronger, while others are predictably weaker. For example, the strong gonadal type has a weak liver and pineal, and matures young, at age 9-11. S/he is short and plump, because the growth in height stops at puberty. Gonadal types are the salt of the earth, Adam and Eve. Their blood type is O. They require red meat and a lot of protein, fish, liver, eggs; as well as greens; and sunlight exposure. Richard and Laura Power, both Ph.D.'s, have researched and pioneered *The 8 Endocrine Biotypes*,[40] combining endocrine types with blood types. In the Powers' system, your normal healthy diet is determined by the dominant gland(s) and your nutritional supplements by the recessive gland(s).

In the bibliography, you will find citations for Bieler's, *Food Is Your Best Medicine;* Price-Pottenger; *The Paleolithic Diet;* and *Dr. Abravanel's Body Type Diet.* A recent book is Peter D'Adamo's *Eat Right For Your Type.* D'Adamo's basic concept of blood types is right as far as it goes, especially about type O, but I find the Powers' information more reliable on the other blood types and more useful with the endocrine typing. Ann Louise Gittleman wrote *Your Body Knows Best*, which combines blood-typing information with ancestry and metabolic factors, and while I do recommend the book, I feel ethnic ancestry may be too recent to be the most useful guide.

A Paleolithic Patient

Gail is a very tall, thin woman, in her late 40's, with type O blood. Her predominant endocrine type is thymus with recessive liver. She came in with many life-long problems, including eczema. She responded very well to the Sugar Control Program, TBM allergy treatments, homeopathic *silacea* followed by *sulphur*, and nutritional supplements..

Based on her blood and endocrine typing, her best diet is meat, liver, and low-starch vegetables, with some fruit, berries, seeds and nuts, and arranged as four smaller meals a day. Fish, poultry, and eggs are also acceptable. She had discovered this by herself, before I began studying blood groupings and endocrine typing. So she was happy to follow the diet plan I prescribed for her after the Sugar Control Program.

When Gail first came for treatment, she was allergic to grains. I harmonized her body to grains with TBM. Although she was no longer allergic and didn't have eczematous outbreaks, grain just didn't support her in terms of energy and clear-headedness. So she didn't bother to eat them. Modern grains, especially wheat, are hybridized to have a much higher gluten content than native grains do. Gluten is poorly tolerated by many people. It causes a wide range of symptoms, from mild sinusitis to serious celiac disease.

---

[40] Richard Power, Ph.D. and Laura Power, Ph.D. The Nutrition Clinic, Inc., 5413 W. Cedar Lane, 102C, Bethesda MD, 20814. U.S.A. Phone: 301-493-4800.

A year or so after the break-up of the Soviet Union, Gail was traveling to Russia for a two-week stay. Although she was looking forward to the trip, she was anxious about staying healthy while on the trip. Russia was undergoing severe food shortages and the kind of foods she needed were unavailable there. Gail could not bring enough food with her for two weeks, and even if she could, she was not comfortable eating foods in front of her hosts that were unavailable to them. She would probably have ended up giving her food to them. She did actually bring food with her on the trip to give to her hosts.

We have noticed in TBM that the body-mind connection can accept sugary foods for medicinal purposes without going out of balance, so I suggested to Gail that since this was a survival situation she was going into—a state of famine—she could make an agreement with herself. She would ask her mind take care of her body during this period of time when she had to eat what was available, and would promise to begin eating for health again as soon as she came home. She did this and had a great trip with no ill effects. The mind-body-mind connection can produce amazing results if you let it.

You probably already have a pretty good idea of what foods support you and what foods let you down. Personally, I have type O blood. I'm the kind of person who does very well on a high-beef, high-protein diet with seafood, eggs, liver, leafy green vegetables and some fruit and rice. I do not tolerate grains or dairy well. Of course, I love pasta and cheeses, but they don't love me. They make me groggy and tired, give me post-nasal drip, and interfere both with my concentration and my weight.

Every patient I have put on an endocrine-typing program has experienced great health benefits on his or her program.

One of the strengths of mankind is its ability to adapt to change (if given time) in order to survive. However, if the food supply is suddenly changed by war, weather or economics, like the dislocation in Cuba after the break-up of the Soviet Union, then people become ill with both vague symptoms, like headaches and fatigue, and also with frank nutritional deficiency syndromes. But if the change in the food supply is gradual, as with the steady growth of processed foods in the American diet since World War II, people adapt and do not develop these symptoms. This does not mean that people are healthy, only that they are surviving. In many ways, a lot of us have probably been living on such a diet of deprivation most of our lives and survived. But if you are reading this book, you are probably not as healthy as you can be or want to be.

A Guide to Healthful Eating

The chart on the next page outlines some rules for choosing the highest-quality foods in terms of health, which usually also means flavor. When I was a teen-ager, I thought Uncle Ben's Converted Rice was the best rice around. When I became interested in nutrition, I began eating whole grain rice. After about a year of that, I was having dinner at a friend's home and she served Uncle Ben's. It tasted to me like sawdust compared to the nutty flavor of whole grain rice.

Fresh food is the best. If you have ever eaten salad, organically grown, and just picked fresh from the garden, the wonderfully delicate aromas and tastes should be enough to convince you that fresh food is better. It just seems common sense to me that as the flavors and odors disappear with age, the nutrients are changing and fading as well. And once you've eaten fish that's just been pulled out of the water, cleaned and prepared immediately, it's hard to go back even to the commercial version of fresh fish. A commercially fresh fish was caught three weeks ago, and kept on ice in the fishing boat until it got to land, where it might still be several days before the fish gets to your refrigerator, let alone your plate.

Fig 12.1: How To Choose and Prepare Healthy Foods

- Optimum: Eat fresh, organically grown, local foods.
- Second best: Eat frozen, organically grown animal and produce foods.
- Eat foods in as natural and unprocessed a state as possible.
- Avoid sugars (white, any -ose like dextrose, corn syrup, malt), concentrated natural sweeteners, and artificial sweeteners.
- Avoid foods with hidden sugar like commercial ketchup, mayonnaise, peanut butter, salad dressings, soups, etc,
- Avoid refined "enriched" flours and over-processed foods.
- Protein and vegetables should be raw or cooked below 190 degrees F to preserve enzymes.
- Grains should be whole, soaked, and sprouted before cooking, or sprouts can be eaten raw.
- Dried beans and lentils should be soaked and sprouted before cooking. Sprouts can be eaten raw.
- Sprout seeds before eating them, raw or cooked.
- Eat raw seeds and nuts.
- Use stable fats (butter, olive oil, ghee) for sauté and baking.
- Use cold-pressed unsaturated oils (rice bran, almond, walnut, sesame; also olive oil) for salads and non-cooking uses.
- Avoid margarine and other hydrogenated or heat-processed fats and oils. Avoid deep-fat fried foods.
- Each day, drink 1 quart of filtered or distilled water per 50 lbs. of body weight.
- For seasoning, use herbs and spices, sea salt or Celtic salt.

If the best choices of foods are not available to you, at least shop the outside ring of the supermarket: produce, fresh meat, fish, poultry, and dairy products. Don't bother to go down the aisles, except to get toilet paper.

If you have been successfully following the Sugar Control Program, you are probably feeling great. You are sold on your state of balanced energy and on the sensual experience good healthful food can be. You no longer want to give the food that's good for you to Mikey—because he'll eat anything. But let's face it, if you are reading this book, you were probably raised on junk food as I was. And there will be times when a hot fudge sundae looks really good. I usually find that when people have eaten well for about three months, they can occasionally indulge in such refined and sugary foods and maintain their balance and health.

But the Sugar Control Program has given you the opportunity to learn to be in tune with what's right for you. If you are craving that hot fudge sundae, your body is probably out of balance—and that craving is a stress symptom Get to your TBM doctor to get your body retuned.

If you just think it might be fun to have some, you probably can. But stay tuned, because three bites may be all you want. Your inner voice will tell you—if you are listening. And the Sugar Control Program has cleared the lines of communication so you can listen and know whether a food message is coming from the short-term fight or flight survival mechanism or whether it is coming from a balanced and harmonious state of well-being. And act accordingly.

CHAPTER 14—CONCLUSION

It is my hope that in writing this book, I have been able to help you be successful in following the Sugar Control Program. And I hope that following the Sugar Control Program has changed your life for the better as it has done for me and so many of my patients.

If you have any comments (in either praise or constructive criticism), please let me know. The praise we may want to quote to help other people choose the Sugar Control Program and this book. The criticism we will evaluate and use.

I am planning a follow-up volume of more recipes. If you come up with any and are willing to share them with others, I'll include them in the book and give you the credit—kind of a *Chicken Soup for the Sugar Control Soul*.

I have tried to make this book more chatty and practical than technical and scientific, so I have not supported all the references. But you should be able to track down further information from the footnotes and bibliography. The Internet is also a great source for a lot of this information.

If you are looking for a TBM doctor, contact the TBM office:
Phone: 1-435-652-4340
FAX: 1-435-652-4339
email: health@TBMseminars.com
Address: 1140 East Fort Pierce, #27
            St. George, Utah 84796

You can contact me at:

P.O. Box 963
Greensburg PA 15601
Phone: 1-724-832-7459
FAX: 1-724-838-7638
email: jacpal@earthlink.net

COOKBOOK

TABLE OF CONTENTS—RECIPES AND MENUS

MENUS, ETC.

APPETIZERS AND SNACKS

DIPS AND SPREADS

ANCHOVY CHEESE BALLS

12 oz cream cheese
3 T butter
2 anchovies, minced
2 T grated onion
2 tsp chopped capers

3/5 tsp paprika
1 finely chopped Brazil nut
2 drops Tabasco
sea salt to taste

Let cheese stand in packages unrefrigerated for about an hour. Work the cheese until smooth. This can be done by hand, with an electric mixer or food processor, etc. Work the remaining ingredients in so the cheese is smooth and well blended. Shape into small balls. Serve with cocktail toothpicks. Or shape into small patties and serve on "Melba" Toast, p. 199.

AVOCADO

1 avocado
1/4 onion, finely chopped

1/4 C chopped sweet pepper
herbal or vegetable seasoning

Mash avocado with onion, pepper, and seasoning. Spread into recesses of celery stalks and serve.

BAGNA CAUDA

1/2 C butter
1/2 C olive oil
8 mashed anchovy fillets

2 cloves pressed garlic
fresh ground black pepper to taste

Mix all ingredients, except pepper, in a heavy fondue pot (or a deep heavy saucepan over an at-the-table source of cooking heat: electric hotplate has least fumes). Heat and simmer about 5 minutes. Stir occasionally. Add pepper. Dip bite-sized vegetables into the warm mixture. Use long fondue forks or wooden skewers. Vegetables should be thinly sliced, seeded. Good choices include: carrots, broccoli, fennel, endive, celery, artichoke hearts, cherry tomatoes, green or red peppers, zucchini.

CAVIAR DIP

1/2 C whipping cream
2-3 T caviar
1-2 T finely chopped onion

3 sliced hard-boiled eggs, p 195
12 "Melba" Rounds, p.199

Whip the cream. Fold in the caviar and onion. Serve on a dish surrounded by egg slices and "Melba" rounds.

CLAM DIP

1 C minced clams
3 oz cream cheese
1 T lemon juice
2 drops Tabasco

1/4 tsp prepared mustard
sea salt to taste
1 T onion juice
1/4 C whipping cream

Drain the clams. Soften the cream cheese at room temperature. Mix all ingredients well. Serve with "Melba" Toast, p.199, or crudités.

DILLED CHEESE SPREAD

8 oz pkg cream [cottage] cheese
8 oz sour cream
1 T tarragon vinegar
1 T finely chopped green onions

1 T parsley, minced or crushed
1/2 tsp dried dillweed
freshly ground black pepper
parsley sprig to garnish

Blend cheese, sour cream and vinegar in food processor, blender or with hand blender, until smooth. Combine all ingredients, except garnish, with the cheese mixture in a bowl. Cover and chill. Garnish with parsley before serving.

HERBED CREAM CHEESE

12 oz cream cheese
2 T chopped chives
1T chopped parsley

1 tsp thyme
1 tsp chervil
fresh ground black pepper

Soften cream cheese at room temperature. Add herbs and spices. Work cheese until smooth and all spices blended well. Serve with crudités, on "Melba" Toast, p. 199, in omelets, etc.

PEPPER/ONION CHEESE

1 8 oz pkg cream [cottage] cheese
4 diced radishes
2 T diced green pepper

1/4 finely chopped onion
1 minced garlic clove
1 tsp parsley or dill

Blend all ingredients by hand or in food processor.

SMOKED SALMON CREAM CHEESE

12 oz cream cheese
3 oz smoked salmon, chopped

1 tsp chopped chives or onion

Soften cream cheese to room temperature. Blend ingredients well. Serve on "Melba" Toast, p 199; mix into Omelets, p. 196.

SOUR CREAM DIP

2 C cultured sour cream
2 T chopped parsley
2 T chopped chives (or onion)

1/4 tsp curry powder
sea salt to taste
1/4 tsp paprika
[1-2 T horseradish]

Blend all ingredients together until smooth and well mixed.

STUFFED GRAPE LEAVES

1/2 C olive oil
1 lb lean ground beef/lamb
freshly ground black pepper
1/2 C finely chopped onion
1/4 tsp sea salt
1 tsp dried dill weed

2 T Brazil nuts, chopped to size of
pine nuts
1/2 C pan-toasted raw Rice, p.199
1-3/4 C water
1 16-oz jar grape leaves
3 T lemon juice

Heat 1/3 C olive oil in a large skillet. Put meat in skillet to brown. Mix with pepper and 1/2 C finely chopped onion. Keep stirring and turning, till meat is no longer pink. About 10 minutes. Add nuts, pan-browned rice and 3/4 C water. Bring to boil. Lower heat. Cover and simmer about 20 minutes till water is absorbed. Turn meat mixture into a bowl and set meat aside to cool for about 30 minutes.

Separate grape leaves and rinse well in cold water to remove salt. Dry well on paper or cloth towels. Save imperfect leaves for layering evenly in the bottom of the skillet. To stuff: lay a leaf, shiny side down on a flat surface. Put 1 T of meat mixture in the center of the leaf. Fold two opposite sides of the leaf over the filling. Roll the leaf from the narrow end up loosely (rice needs room to expand) to make a package. Fill the skillet with closely fitted layers of leaf packages. Mix 3 T lemon juice, 2 T olive oil and 1 C cold water. Pour over the layers of leaf packages in the skillet. Weight down with a dinner plate. Bring to a boil. Lower heat to simmer. Simmer covered until liquid is absorbed about 30 minutes. Serve hot or cold. Makes 40.

GUACAMOLE

1 avocado, peeled and chopped
1/3 C onion, chopped
1 tomato, chopped
1/2 cucumber, peeled and chopped
1/2 tsp paprika

1/4 tsp salt
1 jalapeño pepper, minced
1/8 tsp hot dried chili pepper
1 T sour cream
1 T chopped parsley

Chop together avocado, onion, tomato, and cucumber in bowl. Season with paprika, salt and peppers. Add sour cream and parsley. Refrigerate. Serve on cucumber slices, tomato slices and celery sticks.

AVOCADOS STUFFED WITH SHRIMPS OR SCALLOPS

12 oz bay scallops or tiny shrimp
1/3 C fresh lime juice
1-1/2 tsp dried oregano
1 T fresh minced cilantro

1/2 C olive oil
sea salt
freshly ground black pepper
3 large ripe avocados
[minced chili serrano]

Put the shrimp or scallops in a bowl and add lime juice, oregano, cilantro and oil. Season and let stand for 15-20 minutes. Mixture will become opaque.

Slice all the way around each avocado to split it in half the long way. When you have sliced all the way around, hold the avocado sideways with the bottom half held firmly. Twist the top half on the bottom half and they will separate easily. With the tip of a sharp knife, stab the pit and remove it. Scoop out the pulp in little balls, preserving the shells. Mix the balls of pulp with the shrimp or scallops. Fill the shells with the mixture. [Top with minced chili serrano.]

SHRIMP COCKTAIL

5-6 large shrimp/serving
Salsa, p. 161

sprigs parsley or cilantro
lemon wedges

Follow recipe for boiled shrimp, p. 177. Chill shrimp in their shells. Peel and devein before serving. Fill cocktail glasses to half with salsa. Hang shrimp over the edges of the glass. Top with a sprig of parsley or cilantro and a lemon wedge.

CHOPPED LIVER

a liver and heart from chicken
   or turkey
1/2 chopped onion
1 clove garlic pressed

2 tsps olive oil
1 Hard Boiled egg, p.195
1/4 tsp sea salt
freshly ground black pepper

Schmaltz (rendered chicken fat) is the traditional fat used in this recipe. Sauté liver, heart and onions in the olive oil in a skillet over medium heat, about 10 minutes. Turn mixture into a wooden chopping bowl and chop with hand chopper. Blend well. For a finer consistency, put everything into a food processor bowl and process from 20 seconds to a minute, depending a desired consistency. You may want to add a little oil to improve the consistency. Season with salt and pepper. Serve as an appetizer for roast chicken dinner or as an entree for lunch. Serve with carrot and celery sticks.

CHOPPED LIVER II

2 onions chopped
2 T olive oil
1 lb chicken or calf's liver
3 cloves garlic pressed

6 Hard Boiled eggs, p.195
1 tsp sea salt
freshly ground pepper to taste

Heat skillet to hot. Add oil and heat. Sauté onions in oil for a minute. Add liver. Sauté together till liver is cooked about 10 minutes over medium heat. For chicken livers, stir and turn frequently to cook all sides. For calf's liver, turn over a few times. After about 5 minutes add the garlic.

When the liver is cooked, turn all ingredients into a wooden chopping bowl and chop and blend by hand, adding oil if necessary.

For food processing, cut up calves liver into smaller pieces. Put all ingredients in the food bowl. Process to desired consistency. Season with salt and pepper.

Mound in a serving bowl. Garnish with black pitted olives and pimento strips. Serve with crudités or "Melba" Toast, p. 199.

NOTES

DRESSINGS AND SAUCES

VINAIGRETTE DRESSINGS

The general ratio of oil to vinegar (lemon or lime juice) in a vinaigrette dressing is 3-4 parts oil: 1 part vinegar (lemon/lime). For 1 C of dressing—3/4 C oil:1/4 C vinegar.

VINEGAR: Cider, wine, tarragon, balsamic (sugar free). Save malt vinegar for cleaning.
OILS: Extra-virgin olive, walnut, sunflower, canola, rice bran, corn, sesame seed. Oil should be cold processed. Commercial brands are made with high heat and are not recommended for health reasons. Cook with olive or peanut oil. Use other oils for non-cooking purposes such as salad dressings, mayonnaise. etc.

Cold-pressed (or processed) oils should be refrigerated to prevent them from becoming rancid. (Smell the oil to be sure.) Some oils will harden in the refrigerator. When you want to use them, either take them out of refrigerator 1/2 an hour before use, or run the sealed bottle under hot water until enough softens for use. Then return to refrigerator.

FRENCH DRESSING

1/2 tsp sea salt
1/4 tsp freshly ground black pepper
1/4 C vinegar or lemon juice

1/2 tsp dry mustard
3/4 C olive or walnut oil

In blender, cruet or jar, add first 4 ingredients and blend well. Add oil a little bit at a time, shaking or blending between each addition. Use immediately, or refrigerate and store in a covered jar. Bring to room temperature before using and shake well.

HERBED FRENCH DRESSING

1/2 C French Dressing, p. 155, (made
    with tarragon vinegar)
1/4 tsp each of dried basil, thyme, sweet
    marjoram and chervil

1/4 tsp sea salt
1/8 tsp freshly ground black pepper
1/2 tsp dry mustard

Herbs should only be added when dressing is to be used within 24 hours or they become unpleasantly strong. Place tarragon vinegar French dressing in a blender jar or other lidded jar. Add the remaining ingredients and blend or shake well.

CREAMY VINAIGRETTE

3 parts olive oil
1 part vinegar
1 minced shallot
1 clove garlic minced

1/2 tsp prepared mustard
fresh ground black pepper to taste
1/4 C chopped parsley or coriander
1/3 C water

Use blender, hand mixer, etc., for best results. Blend oil and vinegar with minced garlic, and minced shallot. Add powdered mustard, pepper and parsley. Continue blending. Very gradually, add water until desired "creaminess" is reached. The proportions of ingredients can be varied depending on use. Use as salad dressing, over hot vegetables, rice, rice salads, etc.

HORSERADISH DRESSING

1/2 C French Dressing, p. 155

1 heaping T horseradish

Beat horseradish into French dressing.

AVOCADO DRESSING

1/2 C French Dressing, p. 155   1/2 ripe avocado, peeled & pitted

Mash the avocado and gradually add the dressing. Beat or process until smooth. Serve on sliced tomatoes or other crudités.

ROQUEFORT OR BLUE CHEESE FRENCH DRESSING

1/2 C French Dressing, p. 155   2T crumbled Roquefort or blue cheese

Beat the cheese into the dressing. Or just put the cheese on the salad and pour dressing over it.

"ITALIAN" DRESSING

1/4 C white wine vinegar   1/4 tsp dill (or fennel)
2 garlic cloves, sliced   3/4 C olive oil
1/2 tsp dried oregano   1 T lemon juice
1/4 tsp dried basil

Mix the first 5 ingredients and let stand 1 hour. Blend the oil and lemon juice. Then strain the mixture into the oil/lemon juice. Chill. Shake well before using.

HERB DRESSING

2/3 C apple cider vinegar   2 tsp vegetable salt
juice of 2 lemons   1/4 tsp cayenne (or 1 tsp white) pepper
21/4 C sesame oil   1/3 C parsley or coriander
1 stalk celery   1 tsp thyme
1 bell pepper   1 tsp paprika

Blend in a blender or food processor to make about 3 C of dressing. Serve over garden salad, other salads, steamed vegetables or rice.

WATERCRESS DRESSING

2 T lemon juice   1/2 tsp sea salt
1 T tarragon vinegar   1/4 tsp black pepper
1/2 C olive oil   2 C watercress (or young spinach) leaves

Combine first 5 ingredients in a jar or food processor bowl. Add watercress, chopped finely, and stir, or pulse 1-2 times very briefly. Or combine all ingredients in blender jar and blend on high.

PARSLEY-GARLIC DRESSING

1 clove garlic, halved   1/4 tsp sage
1/2 tsp parsley (or coriander)   black pepper
1/4 tsp rosemary   3/4 C olive or walnut oil
1/2 tsp thyme   1/4 C wine or balsamic (sugar free) vinegar

Combine ingredients in a cruet or jar. Shake well before each use. After 24 hours, remove garlic and herbs. Experiment with other seasonings: Tarragon, black pepper, and garlic.

MUSTARD VINAIGRETTE

8 T oil (olive, safflower, etc.)
1 T vinegar or lemon juice
1 tsp Dijon mustard

1/2 tsp black pepper
[1/2 tsp salt]

Mix all ingredients to taste. Mix dressing with tossed salad. (Sprinkle with crumbled blue cheese.)

GARLIC SAUCE

4 garlic cloves
2 egg yolks
1/8 tsp sea salt

1 C olive oil
1/2 tsp cold water
1 tsp lemon juice

Mince garlic, beat in yolks and salt. Then very slowly, beating constantly, add olive oil by droplets. As the sauce thickens, beat in the cold water and the lemon juice. This process is similar to that of making Mayonnaise, p 157. Read those instructions carefully. If the sauce doesn't thicken, follow the directions for Rebinding Mayonnaise. Serve over fish, boiled beef (cold boiled potatoes after you have completed basic Sugar Control).

ROQUEFORT SOUR CREAM DRESSING

3-4 T Roquefort or blue cheese
1 T wine vinegar

1 T chives (or onions)
1 C cultured sour cream

Combine ingredients by hand, blender or food processor. For a lower calorie version, try it with plain yogurt.

YOGURT DRESSING

1 C plain yogurt
2 T lemon juice
1/4 to 1/2 tsp dry mustard
1 tsp finely chopped or grated onion

1/4 tsp salt
1/2 to 1 tsp paprika
1 minced clove garlic

Mix ingredients together well. Serve over green salad. Also excellent as a sauce for baked fish.

YOGURT MINT SAUCE

1 C plain yogurt
1 T fresh mint, minced (1 tsp, dried)
1 T minced green onion

2 drops Tabasco sauce
fresh ground pepper

Combine ingredients in a small bowl. If desired, chill 30 minutes before serving. Serve over Burger/Bison Kebabs, p 20.

MAYONNAISE

3 egg yolks
1 T+ wine vinegar or lemon juice
1/2 tsp salt

1/4 tsp dry mustard
11/2 to 21/4 C oil
2 T boiling water

Have all ingredients and tools at room temperature. Warm gently if necessary. Add egg yolks to 3 qt bowl. Beat yolks until thick and sticky with large wire whip or with electric mixer, 1-2 minutes. Add vinegar or lemon juice, salt and mustard. Beat 30 seconds.

Begin adding the oil drop by drop (use a teaspoon, if necessary), beating constantly until sauce has thickened. About 2 stokes per second is adequate. You can switch hands, directions, etc. But don't stop beating. Watch the oil. Stop adding oil every 15 seconds to check the mixture. If this is not done right, the mixture can separate. After the sauce thickens to the texture of heavy cream, relax! Beat in the rest of oil 1-2 tablespoons at a time.

If the sauce becomes too thick, it will be stiff. Beat in a few drops of vinegar or lemon juice. Continue adding oil. Use fresh. Extra sauce can be refrigerated and will keep for about a week.

To prevent curdling, beat boiling water into sauce. Season to taste.

TO REBIND MAYONNAISE

In preparing mayonnaise, if you follow the rules, the sauce should not separate.

1. Use ingredients at room temperature.
2. Thoroughly warm and dry the bowl before adding ingredients.
3. Follow proportion of 3/4 C oil : 1 egg yolk.
4. When using refrigerated mayonnaise, do not mix it until it has warmed to room temperature.

Mayonnaise has turned when it refuses to thicken during preparation, or when the oil begins to separate—after a few days refrigeration—and the sauce curdles.

In either case, warm a mixing bowl in hot water and dry. Add 1 teaspoon of prepared mustard and 1 tablespoon of the sauce. Beat with a wire whip for several seconds until they bind and thicken. Beat in the rest of the mayonnaise by teaspoons. Be careful to add the sauce and thoroughly mix a little at a time especially at the beginning.

BLENDER OR PROCESSOR MAYONNAISE

1 whole egg	1/4 tsp dry mustard
1 T vinegar or lemon juice	1/4 tsp pepper
1/4 to 1/2 tsp salt	1 to 11/2 C oil (olive, safflower, etc.)

Whole egg mayonnaise is a lighter sauce than the hand-made egg yolk kind. Break the egg into the blender jar or processor bowl (metal blade in place). Add mustard, salt, pepper and lemon juice or vinegar. Blend 30 seconds until foamy (or process 2-3 seconds). Gradually add oil a few drops at a time until about 1/2 C has been added. When mayonnaise has thickened, you can add remaining oil more quickly. If it becomes too thick, add a few drops of lemon juice or vinegar. Taste for seasonings and correct as desired.

If the blender sauce should begin to separate, pour the mixture into a clean blender jar. Blend 2 tablespoons of turned sauce with **1 tsp prepared mustard** for a few seconds. Blend the rest of the sauce in by teaspoons. For the food processor variety, use a clean bowl with the steel blade, add **2 eggs yolks** and process. Pour the separated mixture through the feed tube very slowly.

If your blender jar does not have a feed hole in the cover, keep the lid partially on. Otherwise, you will have mayonnaise all over the cabinets and walls. Mayonnaise should last for a week to 10 days in the refrigerator. Makes 11/4 to 13/4 C.

ANCHOVY MAYONNAISE (BLENDER OR FOOD PROCESSOR)

8 anchovy fillets
1 egg
2 T lemon juice

1 T vinegar
3/4 tsp pepper
1-1/2 C oil

Put anchovies, egg, lemon juice, vinegar and black pepper into food processor bowl or blender jar. Process 2-3 seconds or blend for 30 seconds. Very gradually a few drops at a time, add oil through feeder tube or lid until mixture thickens (about 1/2 C oil used). Then you can add oil a little faster.

MAYONNAISE AUX FINES HERBES

3-4 T fresh minced green herbs (e.g. chervil, tarragon, basil, chives, parsley, oregano)
1-1/2 C Mayonnaise, p 157.

Use the herbs fresh for immediate use. If sauce is to be stored, blanch the herbs before adding to mayonnaise. Drop into boiling water for 1 minute. Drain, refresh with cold water. Dry with a towel. Mince. Stir into mayonnaise. Use for hors d'oeuvre, eggs, fish, meat.

GREEN MAYONNAISE

1-1/2 C Mayonnaise, p. 157
7-8 spinach leaves
1/3 C parsley leaves
2 T chopped shallots or green onions

1 T fresh tarragon (1/2 T dried tarragon)
2 tsps dried dill
[2 T fresh chervil]

Boil 1 C water in a saucepan. Add spinach and shallots or onions. Boil 2 minutes. Then blanch the rest of the ingredients for 1 minute more. Strain. Refresh herbs with cold running water. Dry with a towel.

If you are making mayonnaise in blender or processor, add them when the sauce has thickened. Herbs will be puréed. If you are adding herbs to hand-made mayonnaise, chop them first or purée in blender or force through a sieve. Then mix into the finished mayonnaise.

Excellent for hors d'oeuvres, eggs, fish or meat.

GREEN GODDESS MAYONNAISE

1 C Mayonnaise, p. 157
1 garlic clove, minced
3 minced anchovy fillets
1/3 C chives or green onion, minced
1/4 C parsley (or coriander) chopped

1-1/2T lemon juice
1-1/2 T tarragon vinegar
1/4 tsp sea salt
fresh ground black pepper to taste
1/2 C cultured sour cream

Combine all ingredients and mix well by hand or in food processor. Serve over fish or shellfish, on vegetable salads or crudités.

ROQUEFORT CREAM MAYONNAISE

1/2 C Heavy Whipped Cream, p. 203
2 T Roquefort or blue cheese

1 C Mayonnaise, p. 157

Crumble the cheese. Fold the whipped cream and cheese into the mayonnaise. Serve over tossed salad or green salad.

CHANTILLY MAYONNAISE

1 C Mayonnaise, p. 157   1 C Whipped Cream, p 203

Shortly before serving, blend whipped cream into mayonnaise. Serve with fruit salad.

BLENDER HOLLANDAISE SAUCE

3 egg yolks   1/8 tsp pepper
2 T lemon juice   1 stick of butter (4 oz)
1/4 tsp salt

Place egg yolks, lemon juice, salt and pepper in blender jar. Cut the butter into small pieces and heat in a small saucepan until the butter foams. Cover the blender jar and blend contents on high for 2 seconds. Uncover. Still blending on high, immediately start pouring in the butter in small droplets. If your blender lid does not have a hole for adding ingredients during blending, try to keep the lid part way on. But you may need to cover yourself with a towel. When 2/3 of the butter has been added, the sauce should look like a thick cream. Leave the milky residue in the saucepan. Correct seasonings.

Hollandaise is delicious over poached eggs, asparagus, broccoli, and fish dishes.

You can only make 4 oz of sauce at a time in a blender without clogging the works. An egg yolk, however, could absorb 8 oz of butter. To double the recipe, pour the sauce into a saucepan or bowl and, with a wire whisk, beat in an additional 1/2 C of melted butter, added in a stream of droplets.

Stir in a mixture of minced parsley, chives and tarragon to use with poached eggs.

Puréed artichoke hearts, asparagus tips, or cooked shellfish (2 tsps) can be stirred into hollandaise. Use on Eggs Benedict, p.195.

BÉARNAISE SAUCE

1/4 C white wine   1/4 tsp dried crushed chervil
2 T tarragon vinegar   1 sprig minced parsley
2 T finely chopped shallots or onion   3 beaten egg yolks
2 crushed white peppercorns   3/4 C melted butter
1/4 tsp dried crushed tarragon   sea salt and pepper

Combine all ingredients (except eggs and butter) in the top of a double boiler. Cook over direct heat until reduced by half. Strain the mixture and allow it to cool. Then, beating briskly in the top of a double boiler over (not in) hot water, add 3 beaten egg yolks, melted butter. Correct the seasonings to taste.

This is traditionally served on broiled red meat, but it also works well with other meats and fish. Serve over recipe for Swedish Meat Balls, p. 168.

BLENDER BÉARNAISE SAUCE

1/2 tsp sea salt

Prepare the Béarnaise sauce, above, up until the egg yolks. Put the mixture in the blender. Add the eggs yolks and salt. Cover the blender container. Heat to just bubbling (but do not brown) the butter. Blend the vinegar and egg mixture briefly on high. Pour the butter over the eggs in a steady stream. By the time the butter is poured in, the sauce should be finished. If not, blend on high another 5 seconds. Serve at once. If you must hold the sauce, keep it warm by placing the blender container in warm water. This is a sauce that can be frozen and reconstituted over hot water.

SAUCE NEWBURG

dry shells from 1 lb shrimp or lobster
1/2 C butter
2 T water
1 tsp finely chopped shallots or onion

1/4 C sherry
1 C cream
3 egg yolks
[1 T tomato paste]

SHRIMP/LOBSTER BUTTER: Dry the shells in a low oven (150-200 degrees) for 5 minutes. Pound in a mortar, process or blend, until they are broken up as finely as possible. In a double boiler over boiling water (the top pan should not be in the water), melt the butter. Add the ground shells and water. Simmer for 10 minutes, keeping the butter from boiling. Strain the melted butter through a cheesecloth into a bowl of ice water. Refrigerate the mixture and skim off the butter after it has hardened. This can used over the lobster or shrimp. Or as a base for:

NEWBURG SAUCE: Melt the shrimp or lobster butter in top half of a double boiler, Add the shallots or onion and cook until translucent. Add the sherry and cook about 3 minutes.

Into a C of cream beat yolks. Add the two mixtures, stirring constantly until the sauce thickens. [If desired, add tomato paste for the pink color.] Use immediately. Delicious over seafood, rice or vegetables.

PESTO

3 C fresh basil leaves (no stems)
2 large cloves garlic
1/2 C raw Brazil nuts*
3/4 C fresh chopped parsley

3/4 C fresh grated Parmesan
1/2 C olive oil
1/4 C melted butter
salt to taste

Combine everything in blender on low speed. In food processors, add whole parsley. Increase to medium speed. Work into a smooth paste. Toss with hot Rice Pilaf, p. 199.

*The traditional recipe calls for pine nuts (walnuts, pecans, almonds or mixed nuts can be used). Pesto may be made with other kinds of nuts after Sugar Control.   Serve with rice or other whole grains or, traditionally, with whole grain pasta.

SALSA

4 Prepared Tomatoes, p.185
    diced (or 4 C canned organic tomatoes)
1 medium onion, finely diced
1 clove garlic, minced
1/2 C cilantro, chopped

1 tsp dried oregano
2 tsps sea salt
[1-2 medium hot chopped green chilis]
cider vinegar or olive oil to taste

Combine all ingredients and refrigerate in a wide-mouth quart Mason jar until ready to use. Makes 1 quart. Serve over meat, poultry or eggs.

BLENDER TOMATO SAUCE

3 Prepared Tomatoes, p. 185
1 medium onion, quartered
1 green pepper, trimmed and seeded
1/3 C celery

2 T chopped parsley or coriander
                         1 tsp oregano or basil, dried
1/4 tsp sea salt
freshly ground black pepper to taste
[2 T French Dressing, p.155]

Purée tomatoes in blender or food processor. Add the rest of the ingredients and blend. Serve over Stuffed Zucchini, p. 186, or Stuffed Eggplant, p.183.

ITALIAN MEAT SAUCE

[1/3 C olive oil]
2 minced garlic cloves
1-1/2 lbs ground meat (one or combination of beef, venison, turkey, etc.)
5-6 prepared plum tomatoes, p. 185
a 6-oz can tomato paste

1/2 C Beef Broth, p. 188
1/2 tsp sea salt
fresh ground black pepper to taste
1 bay leaf
1 tsp oregano
1/2 tsp basil
[1/2 C sliced mushrooms]

[Heat oil] in large kettle or Dutch oven. Brown the meat, stirring it and turning it. Add garlic, tomatoes, tomato paste, stock, salt, pepper and herbs. Adjust seasonings to taste. Simmer sauce uncovered for about 1 hour. [In last 15 minutes, add 1/2 C sliced mushrooms.]

Serve over Rice Pilaf, p. 199, 1/2 C spaghetti squash, or after the Sugar Control Program, whole grain pasta.

MARINADES

Marinades are used both to impart flavor and to tenderize, but it is easy to overdo it. If you want to learn about them, read *Joy of Cooking*. A marinade is usually made of seasonings, sometimes oil and an acid (vinegar, wine, lemon juice). The marinating food will sit in the liquid for half an hour to over 24 hours. It is preferable to use a glass or ceramic utensil (glass baking pans work well), or stainless steel. The food should be covered with liquid or turned and basted frequently. If you choose a container that the food just fits in, it will require less marinade to cover. You should need about 1/2 C of marinade per pound of food. Soaking times vary according to size of the food:

cubed meat	2-3 hours
5-10 lb piece	overnight
leg of lamb	24 hours

VEGETABLE MARINADES

French Dressing, p 155, makes a simple marinade. If you serve a large salad at dinner and dress it in the serving bowl, you can save the remainder in the refrigerator and eat it marinated the next day.

FISH OR LAMB (SHISH KEBAB) MARINADE

2 T lemon juice
1/4 C olive oil

1/4 tsp sea salt
1/8 tsp pepper

Multiply the recipe so there is enough to baste with. Turn the meat frequently for 2-3 hours.

For a different taste, replace the above ingredients with the following ones in the olive oil:

2-3 T lime juice
fresh grated ginger to taste (1/2 tsp powder)

1-2 cloves minced garlic

LAMB OR GAME MARINADE

1 C dry red wine	1 bay leaf
1/4 C lemon juice	2 cloves crushed garlic
1/2 C olive oil	pinch nutmeg
1/2 tsp rosemary (1/4 tsp powder)	1/8 tsp allspice
sprig parsley	1/4 tsp sea salt
1/2 tsp thyme	dash of Tabasco

Combine ingredients. Marinate a leg of lamb for 24 hours, covered and refrigerated. This should cut the cooking time by 1/3.

COOKED MARINADE FOR GAME

1 C chopped celery	4 bay leaves
1 C chopped carrots	1 T thyme
1 C chopped onions	1 T basil
1/4 C olive oil	1 T whole cloves
2 qts cider vinegar	1 T allspice berries
5 C water	pinch mace
1/2 C coarsely chopped parsley	1 T crushed peppercorns
	8 cloves crushed garlic

Heat the olive oil in a 4 qt saucepan or stockpot. Sauté celery, carrots and onion until the onions are golden and translucent. Add the remaining ingredients. Bring to a boil and simmer covered for an hour. Strain and cool. Excellent for venison, mutton, rabbit, squirrel or woodchuck. Marinate 1-12 hours according to size of meat cuts. Large cuts of venison should be marinated 12-48 hours.

POULTRY MARINADE

1/4 C olive oil	1/2 tsp celery seeds
1/2 C dry white wine (lemon juice)	1/4 tsp sea salt
2 cloves crushed garlic	coarsely ground black pepper to taste
1 medium onion, chopped fine	1/4 tsp dried tarragon, thyme or rosemary

Mix the ingredients in a covered jar or bowl. Refrigerate covered until cold.

NOTES

BEEF, BISON, LAMB, GAME, VENISON

BEEF

ROAST BEEF

There are two ways to roast. Both ways require very little work. The first way is my favorite. Basically you are searing the meat on the outside. then allowing the roast to cook slowly, preserving the juices. Preheat the oven to hot, 450-500 degrees. Wipe the roast with a damp cloth. Rub it with freshly ground pepper and salt. If you have a meat thermometer, insert it in the thickest part of the roast, being careful to avoid bone in a rib roast. Place the meat on a rack in a roasting pan. Place the meat in the preheated oven. Close the door. Reduce heat to slow oven, 300 degrees. Do not baste. If possible, do not open oven door during cooking. Cook the roast until temperature is just below desired doneness (140 degrees for rare, for example). Remove from oven and set the roasting pan on the counter. Let the roast sit for 10 minutes before carving. It will continue to cook and the juices will move from the surface and settle back in the meat.

In the second method, everything remains the same, except you preheat the oven to 350 degrees and cook the roast at that temperature until done. To my taste, this produces a dryer, tougher piece of meat.

If you do not have a meat thermometer (and if you want to plan your time), here are time tables for roast beef.

STANDING RIB ROAST HIGH TEMPERATURE METHOD	STANDING RIB ROAST SLOW COOKING METHOD
Rare . . . . 16-18 minutes per pound	18-20 minutes per pound
Medium Rare . . . . . 18-20 minutes per pound	20-22 minutes per pound
Medium . . . . .20-22 minutes per pound	22-25 minutes per pound
Well Done. . . . . . . .26-30 minutes per pound	27-30 minutes per pound

A standing boneless rump or a rolled roast should require 25-30 minutes per pound.

BROILED STEAK

When broiling steak in the conventional kitchen, the best method is, I think, in the skillet. Preheat the skillet on high until a drop of water sizzles. If the skillet is hot enough, the pan should not need to be oiled. However, rubbing the pan with a little olive oil will probably give you a tastier steak and a pan that is easier to clean. If desired, sprinkle the skillet with a little sea salt and pepper. Sear the meat quickly on each side. Lower the heat to medium and cook the steak until it is done to your taste. Cooking time depends on the temperature of the skillet, thickness of the meat and your preference from just dead to burned to a crisp.

Steak can also be grilled over charcoal, gas grills, stovetop grills, and under the broiler in your oven. In the oven, place the oven rack in its highest slot, if the broiler is on top, and use a broiler pan to prevent grease fires.

ACCOMPANIMENTS: Melted butter and/or lemon juice, sea salt and/or pepper. Tabasco and freshly chopped parsley. Sliced onions and mushrooms sautéed in butter or olive oil. Dijon mustard. Horseradish. Béarnaise Sauce, p. 160.

MARINADE.   Marinating meat is a good way to tenderize inexpensive cuts and add interesting flavors and moisture, p. 162.

BEEF SUKIYAKI

2 T olive oil
3 medium onions, thinly sliced
3 stalks celery, thinly sliced
3 C spinach leaves, washed, p. 185
1 bunch scallions, 2 inch-lengths
1/2 C sliced mushrooms

1/2 C canned bamboo shoots, sliced
3/4 Beef Broth, p 188
1 lb tender beef, sliced thin
2 T Bragg's Liquid Aminos
1/4 C red wine
1/2 C mung bean sprouts

This is an excellent dinner party dish, which can be prepared at the table in an electric frying pan. In the kitchen, a heavy cast iron or other large skillet will do. Grease the pan with olive oil, heat the pan to boiling heat. Add onions, celery, spinach, scallions, mushrooms and bamboo shoots. Lay the meat over the vegetables. Add the broth, Liquid Aminos, and wine or dashi. Simmer uncovered over low to medium heat until the meat is tender and the vegetables are cooked, but still firm. Stir gently two or three times during the cooking process. Add the mung beans to pan just before serving. Serve with Rice Pilaf, p. 199.

BEEF STEW

3 lbs meat (beef, veal, venison, etc.)
   cubed for stew 2"x2" pieces
[1 T olive oil]
2 onions, sliced
2 carrots, sliced
2 stalks celery sliced
green pepper, chopped
liquid to cover (water, red wine, beef
   broth, Bragg's Liquid Aminos,
   tomato liquid or juice)

1 bay leaf
1 tsp dried thyme
1/2 tsp dried oregano
1/2 tsp dried basil
2-3 sprigs fresh parsley
1/2 tsp sea salt
freshly ground black pepper to taste
1/2 tsp rosemary or sage
[1 can Italian tomatoes, chopped, with liquid]
[3 T tomato paste]

You can purchase stewing meat already cut up, or buy chuck steak, London broil, etc., and cut it up yourself. Any combination of meats works well. The stewing process should tenderize the meat, so you can use cheaper cuts. If you chill the stew and then reheat it before serving, the fat will rise to the top and you can skim if off, if desired. The more often it is reheated, the more flavor develops.

I use a cast-iron enameled Dutch oven for stew, but any large covered heavy pot will do. This is also a good crock pot recipe. Heat the pot, [add the oil]. Sear the meat (in the oil or in a non-stick skillet) on all sides to preserve the juices. Sauté the onions in the oil or in the non-stick pan till just soft. You can also brown the carrots and celery if desired. Assemble in the stew pot, the meat and vegetables. Add the liquid in any combination desired, enough to just cover the food. While bringing to a boil, add the herbs and seasonings. This will make a delicious stew with a thin soup-quality broth.

[If a tomato taste is desired, add a can of chopped Italian plum tomatoes and liquid at the beginning of cooking.]

[For a thicker sauce, add tomato paste after 30 minutes of cooking.]

Simmer slowly, tightly covered, over low heat for 1-2 hours. Stir occasionally to prevent scorching.

POT ROAST

Use the beef stew recipe above, replacing the stew meat with 2-3 lb roast (bottom round, chuck, etc.). Simmer for 2-3 hours.

MEAT LOAF

This is one of those art works that has many, many varieties and flavors. Here is a basic program meat loaf recipe to start. The meat loaf starts with 1 lb ground meat. The meat can be beef or a mixture of beef, pork and veal. Other mixtures might include beef and ground chicken or turkey.

1 lb ground meat	1 tsp fresh lemon juice
1 egg	1 tsp sea salt
2 T chopped parsley	1/4 tsp pepper
1 T olive oil	2 T chopped onion
1 T Sprouted Bread Crumbs, p. 199	1 clove minced garlic
	1/2 C Beef Broth, p. 188

Preheat the oven to 350 degrees. Combine ingredients and blend well, shaping into a loaf. Place the loaf into a lightly greased loaf pan. Bake for 45 minutes, basting occasionally with 1/2 C Beef Broth. Serves 2-4.

If you want to double the recipe, keep it to 1 egg and increase the lemon juice to 1 T.

ADDITIONS. To stretch a meat loaf (or make it tastier), you can add finely grated or chopped vegetables. Good choices are carrot, celery, mushrooms and/or bean sprouts. For 1 lb of meat, add:

1/2 C chopped or grated vegetables	2 T Beef Broth, p. 188, cream, tomato
1/2 C Sprouted Bread Crumbs, p. 199	paste or lemon juice
1/4 C chopped Brazil nuts	

OTHER SEASONING COMBINATIONS. Mix up meat loaf with seasoning about half an hour before baking. Allow to set to give flavors a greater chance to develop. It is also possible to prepare the meat loaf and freeze it uncooked. Defrost it in the refrigerator from the night before you plan to cook it. Then pop it in the oven when you get home and by the time you have changed your clothes and prepared a salad or some vegetables, the meat loaf will be ready.

I. 2 tsps tomato paste	1 T finely diced stuffed olives
1 tsp ground anchovies	1 tsp capers
3 T sautéed mushrooms	
II. 1/4 tsp thyme	1 garlic clove, minced
1 tsp red wine	
III. 1/2 tsp thyme	1/4 tsp oregano
1/4 tsp basil	1/4 tsp sage
1/2 tsp parsley	1 T tomato paste or red wine

IV. 1/4 C crumbled Roquefort, blue cheese, or cultured sour cream
    2 T chopped chives or scallion tops
    a few drops Tabasco   1/4 tsp dry mustard

HAMBURGER

1 lb ground beef   [1 T olive oil]
[1 egg]

Shape meat into 4-5 patties. Allow 2 per serving. Heat skillet to hot. Add patties. They should sizzle. If using very lean meat, add olive oil to skillet. Heat oil before adding patties. If grilling hamburger over coals, blend meat with beaten egg to preserve the juices. Cook each side about 3 minutes over medium heat.

[1 slice of toasted sprouted bread/person] leaf lettuce
tomato slices   dill pickles

Serve over (bread) on a bed of lettuce, topped with tomato, onion, and/or Salsa, p. 161. Other combinations might be sautéed onions and mushrooms with Dijon mustard, Hollandaise Sauce, p. 160, Guacamole, p. 153. Serve with Tomato Salad, p.193.

CHILI CON CARNE

1 lb ground meat (beef, venison, buffalo, 1 tsp cumin
 chicken, turkey, pork combos)   1 bay leaf
1 C chopped onion   1/2 tsp sea salt
[1-2 T olive oil]   freshly ground black pepper
2-4 cloves minced garlic   1 can chopped Italian tomatoes with liquids
1-2 carrots diced   1 C Beef Broth, p. 188, and/or red wine
1 C chopped green peppers   2 T tomato paste
1 stalk celery, diced   [2 dried chili peppers, crumbled]
2 T chili powder

Use a Dutch oven or crockpot. Sauté chopped onions in 1 T of olive oil . Add the ground meat combination and brown throughout on medium heat. (The meat and onions can be browned without oil in a non-stick skillet and transferred to the Dutch oven.).

 Add tomatoes garlic, carrots, celery, green peppers, spices and broth and bring to a simmer over medium heat. Reduce heat to very low and simmer with lid tightly closed for 30 minutes. Stir occasionally to prevent meat from scorching and sticking to bottom of the pot. Add tomato paste, [and chili peppers]. Cook another 30 minutes. Serve over Rice Pilaf, p. 199.

CHILI WITH BEANS
(After Sugar Control Basic Program Ends)

2 C dried beans   water
1 tsp olive oil   Chili Con Carne, see above
1 tsp sea salt

Beans are easy to prepare, but require planning. Start the beans about 2 days before you make the Chili Con Carne. (Canned cooked beans are available. Make sure they have no sugar or flour additives. Home cooked beans are much more satisfying.)

 Kidney beans, pinto beans, dried lima beans, northern beans, singly or in combination, lend themselves well to chili recipes. Wash beans in a strainer and pick over them, removing dirt, stones, etc. Place beans in a large glass or ceramic bowl. (They will triple in size.) Cover with water and leave them undisturbed from overnight to eighteen hours. Check them occasionally and add water if necessary. Beans are more nutritious and easier to digest (causing less bowel gas) if they are allowed to sprout and are then slow cooked (rather than pressure cooked).

Place beans in a large heavy saucepan. Cover with additional water if needed. Add oil and salt. Bring to a boil, stirring down foam. Skim foam, if necessary. Simmer on low heat, covered, 2 hours.

Add the cooked beans to the Chili Con Carne, when you add the liquid. The liquid from the beans can be used as part of the cooking liquid for the chili. The seasonings should be doubled. Adjust to taste.

SWEDISH MEAT BALLS

1 slice sprouted bread
water, milk or stock
1-1/2 lbs meat (beef, veal, pork, liver,
    chicken, turkey, combinations)
2 eggs
1 T butter
1/4 C finely chopped onions
3 T chopped parsley

1/2 tsp sea salt
1/4 tsp paprika
1/2 tsp grated lemon rind
1 tsp lemon juice
1/4 tsp nutmeg
1/8 tsp allspice
2 T butter or olive oil
2 C Chicken or Beef Broth, p 188
fresh or dried dill

Soak the bread in water, milk or broth to cover. Have the butcher grind the meat mixture twice. Beat eggs well and add to the meat. Sauté onions in butter until golden. Add to the meat. Wring the liquid from the bread. Add the bread to the meat mixture. Add the parsley, salt, paprika, lemon rind and juice, nutmeg and allspice. Blend well and shape the meat into 1-1/2 inch balls (about 18). Heat olive oil in a heavy, covered, skillet. Add meatballs and brown. Add Beef or Chicken Broth and dill and simmer covered for about 15 minutes.

Traditionally, this is served with pan gravy, but since pan gravy requires flour, use Béarnaise Sauce, p. 160, or Hollandaise, p. 160. This is an excellent party dish. Serve over rice, in a chafing dish.

PEPPER STEAK

1 lb round or flank steak
sea salt
freshly ground black pepper
2 T olive oil
1 chopped onion
1-2 cloves minced garlic

2 diced green peppers
1 C Beef Broth, p. 188
1 C drained canned tomatoes (or 6 Prepared
    plum Tomatoes, p. 185)
1/4 C red wine

Slice the steak thinly on the bias. Add sea salt and pepper to taste. Heat the oil until hot in a large skillet. Add steak, onion and garlic and cook until the meat is brown on all sides. Add green peppers and broth. Cover and simmer over medium to low heat about 10 minutes. Add tomatoes and simmer 6-7 more minutes. Serve over Rice Pilaf, p. 199.

BURGER KEBABS

3/4 lb lean ground beef
grated peel of 1/2 lemon
1 T minced cilantro
1/4 tsp sea salt
pinch allspice

4-8 cherry tomatoes
onion slices
1 C raw rice for Rice Pilaf, p. 199
Yogurt Mint Dressing, p. 157

While rice is cooking, combine all ingredients in left column in a bowl. Blend well. Divide mixture into 4 parts. Form each part into a sausage shape. Slice onion from top to bottom about 1/2" from edge, so that you have large pieces of onion. Take a long skewer and run it through a cherry tomato, and an onion slice, then a sausage shaped kebab, repeat, and end with an onion slice and a cherry tomato. (With short wooden skewers, 1 sausage per skewer, with a cherry tomato and onion slice on each end.) Grill over ash-covered coals, on stove-top grill or broil on broiler pan 4" from heat, 5 minutes per side. Serves 2. Serve on a bed of Rice Pilaf cooked in Chicken Broth [Before serving, sprinkle with raw Brazil nuts, sliced thin and chopped.]. Cover with Yogurt Mint Sauce.

KEBAB

This is a form of cooking from the Mid-East that could (and probably does) take up whole cookbooks. Essentially, meat, poultry or even fish cubes (sea scallops, shrimp and monkfish, for example) are marinated, arranged on skewers, alternating with other ingredients (cherry tomatoes, whole mushrooms, pepper slices, onion slices) and grilled over coals or under the broiler. This is a great picnic food. The ingredients are prepared ahead of time and kept in the cooler. Arrange the skewers at the picnic. Serve over a bed of Rice Pilaf, p. 199, or shredded lettuce.

SHISH KEBAB

4-6 oz lamb per person	2-3 slices 1"x1" green or red pepper,
Lamb or Game Marinade, p.163	and onion/skewer
2 cherry tomatoes/skewer	2 whole mushrooms/skewer
	olive oil

Marinate the lamb for 2-3 hours in the marinade, wipe dry. Arrange the lamb on wooden or stainless steel skewers, alternating the pieces of meat with the vegetables. Arrange so that the amount of food on the skewer fits your grill or broiler. Grill about 3 inches from the heat source. Brush the meat frequently with olive oil, turning to brown evenly. Cook 8-10 minutes to desired degree of doneness.

VEAL

VEAL PARMIGIANA, see Chicken Parmigiana, p.173.

VEAL PICCATA

8 veal scallops, pounded thin	1 T butter
1/4 tsp sea salt	1/4 C dry white wine
freshly ground black pepper to taste	1/4 C Chicken Broth, p. 187
1 egg	juice of 1 lemon & 8 lemon wedges
2 T olive oil	[2 T chopped fresh parsley or coriander]

This recipe is cooked very quickly, so prepare all ingredients ahead of time. Slice the scallops in half the long way. Sprinkle with salt and pepper. Beat the egg on a plate and dredge the scallops in the egg. Heat 1 T of oil to hot in a large non-stick skillet. Sauté the veal quickly in one layer, fitting as many pieces in as possible at one time. Sauté about a minute on each side.

Hold the cooked veal on a warm platter while completing the rest of the dish. Heat the butter and remaining olive oil in the skillet. Return veal to skillet and cook briefly on both sides. Add the wine, chicken stock, lemon juice and any liquid that may have drained onto the warm plate. Keep turning the veal pieces to cook them evenly. When the sauce has reduced and thickened somewhat, [add fresh parsley]. Presentation: Serve at once. Arrange scallop pieces on plates with lemon wedges. Spoon sauce over the meat. Serves 4.

Serve with Asparagus, p. 161 or Tomatoes, p. 185, and Rice Pilaf, p.199.

BISON/BUFFALO

There is a growing availability of American bison (also mistakenly called buffalo). Bison is cooked similarly to beef, although it has a distinctive taste. Try it without seasonings first. Then you can replace beef in any of the recipes above with bison. Individual cuts are identical to cuts of beef. The meat, before cooking, appears darker than beef, because it is leaner and not marbled with fat. For this reason, bison cooks more quickly than beef, since the heat does not have to penetrate the fat insulation.

Most of the bison I've seen so far has been organically grown, without drugs, so it's a great choice for people with allergies to the drugs, hormones, pesticides and herbicides found in the commercial meat supply.

BISON KEBABS
see Shish Kebab, p. 169.

BISON BURGERS
see Hamburger, p. 166.

LAMB

ROAST LEG OF LAMB

5-lb leg of lamb   rosemary
garlic sliced (or 1/2 lemon)

Remove lamb from refrigerator about 1 hour before cooking. Preheat oven to hot, 450-500 degrees. Remove the papery outer covering. Rub the lamb with cut garlic or lemon. Insert slivers of garlic and rosemary under the skin using a sharp knife. Place the meat, fat side up, in an uncovered greased pan. Insert meat thermometer, being careful to avoid the bone. Put in oven. Close the oven door and immediately set oven on slow 325 degrees. I prefer lamb to be pink (about 160-165 degrees). Most Americans prefer it well done (175 degrees). Well-done lamb requires about 30 minutes/lb cooking time.

After removing the lamb from the oven, allow it to rest for 10 minutes or more before slicing. Serve with mustard or horseradish.

MARINATED LEG OF LAMB, Lamb Marinade, p. 162, covered and refrigerated for 24 hours.

LAMB CHOPS

2 loin or rib chops per person   freshly ground black pepper
sea salt   parsley

Pan broil chops less than an inch thick. Remove the outer skin from the chops. Rub the pan with a small piece of the lamb fat. Heat pan to hot. Sear the chops on each side. Turn several times during cooking. Season to taste. Serve hot. Garnish with parsley. Serve with mustard or horseradish.

EGGPLANT-LAMB CASSEROLE

2 medium eggplants, pared and diced
water
1 lb mushrooms
2 T olive oil
1/2 C chopped onion
2 cloves garlic, crushed

1 T olive oil
1/2 C chopped green pepper
2 C diced cooked lamb
1 tsp oregano
1/2 C Sprouted Bread Crumbs, p. 199
1 T butter

Use leftover leg of lamb for this recipe. Preheat the oven to 400 degrees. Cook the eggplant in boiling salted water for 15 minutes. Drain well and mash. Peel and stem the mushrooms. Simmer the stems and peelings in 2-1/2 C water for 15 minutes. Reserve mushroom liquid. Chop the mushroom caps coarsely and sauté in 2 T olive oil.

Sauté onions and garlic in 1 T olive oil until golden. Add stock drained from the mushroom stems and stir. Cook 3-4 minutes. Add eggplant, sautéed mushrooms, green pepper, lamb and oregano. Place the mixture in a buttered 2-quart casserole. Cover the mixture with crumbs and dot with butter. Bake, uncovered, 30 minutes. Serves 4.

VENISON

Venison can be prepared much like beef, the choicer cuts broiled or roasted. The tougher cuts braised, marinated or stewed. Venison is usually lean, so you may want to bard it (wrap it with bacon strips). Use Marinade for Lamb or Game, p. 163.

GAME

For other game recipes, like squirrel, rabbit, raccoon, badger, etc., I recommend *Joy of Cooking*. Just be sure to use recipes without flour or sugar or other sweeteners.

NOTES

POULTRY

ROASTED CHICKEN OR TURKEY

31/2 to 5 lb oven-roaster chicken
1 clove garlic
sprig rosemary or parsley

2 slices onion
olive oil or melted butter
chicken broth

Refrigerate bird until ready to roast. Remove giblets from body cavity. Set aside for chopped liver or stuffing. Wash bird thoroughly and pat dry. If you are not stuffing the bird, you do not have to truss it. Put garlic, onion and rosemary or parsley into body cavity. Grease the skin lightly with oil or melted butter. Place breast side up on a rack in a roasting pan. . When the bird is cooked, remove from oven and allow to rest 10 minutes, while the juices settle. Then carve. The timing is:

> 20-25 minutes per pound up to 6 lbs
> 15-20 minutes per pound from 7-16 lbs
> 13-15 minutes per pound over 16 lbs
> Add 5 minutes per pound if the bird is stuffed

Chicken or turkey is done when the internal temperature reaches 180-185 degrees, or when the juice runs clear if the thigh is pricked. If using a thermometer, place in inner thigh. Be careful to avoid the bone.

MY FAVORITE METHOD. Preheat oven to 500 degrees. Cover top side of bird with cheesecloth that has been soaked in melted butter or olive oil. Place bird in hot oven. Close the door. Turn oven setting immediately to 325 degrees (see directions for Standing Rib Roast, p.164). After the first 30 minutes of cooking, baste frequently over and under the cheesecloth with Chicken Broth, p. 187, and pan juices.

HIGH TEMPERATURE METHOD II. Put chicken into 500 degree oven uncovered. Close oven door. Turn temperature to 325 degrees. After 20 minutes, cover chicken loosely with aluminum foil. Baste with pan juices frequently.

LOW TEMPERATURE/NO WORK METHOD. Cook chicken at 325 degrees for entire cooking period. Cover either with cheesecloth, above, or aluminum foil, above. Do not baste.

Cheesecloth allows the bird to roast and develop a crispy brown skin; aluminum foil gives you a dose of aluminum with your dinner and steams the bird.

POULTRY STUFFING

giblets
1/2 C butter or olive oil
3 T chopped onion
4 C Sprouted Bread Crumbs, p. 199
1/4 C chopped parsley
1/4 C chopped celery
1 tsp crushed basil
1/4 tsp salt

1/2 tsp paprika
dash nutmeg
Chicken Broth, p. 187, melted butter or olive oil to moisten dressing lightly
2-3 eggs
11/2 C Brazil nuts
1 C sliced sautéed mushrooms

There are no set amounts of ingredients. Adjust them to your taste. There are many other ingredients that might be combined or included: chopped oysters, clams, shrimp, Rice Pilaf, p. 199, green peppers, leeks, spinach, apples. Use your imagination.

Chop giblets (liver, heart, gizzard). Melt butter or oil in a skillet. Sauté giblets with onion and mushroom. Combine all the ingredients in a large bowl.

Stuff the bird just before roasting to prevent bacterial growth. The stuffing will expand, so stuff the body cavity loosely only 3/4 full. Extra stuffing can be placed in the crop cavity. Close the openings with small poultry skewers held together with criss-crossed twine. Tie the ends of the legs together with a figure 8. Tie a string around the crop skin of the neck, leaving two long ends to tie the wings to the bird through the first joint.

VARIATIONS ON POULTRY STUFFING. Replace giblets with chopped mushrooms, and 1/4 C red wine. Use Rice Pilaf, p. 106, instead of Sprouted Bread Crumbs

BAKED CHICKEN

1 fryer, cut into parts	freshly ground black pepper
[olive oil]	1/2 tsp dried thyme
sea salt	sprig parsley
1-2 cloves garlic	2 slices onion

Preheat oven to 350 degrees. Wash chicken and pat dry. [Lightly coat skin with olive oil.] Arrange chicken in a roasting pan. Season with salt and pepper if desired. Sprinkle with crushed thyme. Place onion, garlic and parsley in the pan. Cover with aluminum foil. Bake for 1 hour, basting occasionally. During last 10 minutes of baking, uncover pan to brown skin.

ROSEMARY CHICKEN

1 fryer, cut into parts	juice of 1 lemon
[olive oil]	1/4 C wine vinegar
freshly ground black pepper	1/2 tsp paprika
1-2 sprigs fresh rosemary or	2 cloves garlic
1/2 tsp dried rosemary	2 slices onion

Prepare chicken as for baked chicken. Sprinkle chicken with pepper, rosemary and paprika. Add lemon juice, wine vinegar, onion and garlic to pan. Cover with aluminum foil. Follow cooking directions as above.

MARINATED CHICKEN

1 fryer, cut into parts	Poultry Marinade, p. 163

Prepare Poultry Marinade. Place chicken pieces in a bowl. Shake marinade well and pour over the chicken pieces. Marinate in the refrigerator about 3 hours, turning the pieces 1-2 times. Baste during cooking with any excess marinade. Cook as for baked chicken, above.

CHICKEN PARMIGIANA

1 lb chicken breast fillets	1/2 tsp thyme
1 egg	1/4 tsp basil
1 T olive oil	1/2 tsp oregano
1/2 onion, chopped	1/4 tsp sea salt
1-2 cloves garlic, minced	freshly ground black pepper
1 green pepper, seeded and chopped	Blender Tomato Sauce, p. 161
4-5 mushrooms, sliced	1/2 C Parmesan cheese

Split breasts into individual fillets. Pound with a meat mallet to break up fascia and tenderize. Beat egg on a plate. Dredge chicken fillets in the egg mixture. Heat skillet to hot. Add oil. When hot, add chicken fillets and onion. Sauté over medium heat until chicken is white and onions are translucent. About half way through this process, add garlic, green pepper and mushrooms. Sauté together until chicken is done, about 5 minutes.

Lightly grease a casserole dish with some of the olive oil. Arrange chicken and vegetables in the dish. Season with thyme, basil, oregano, salt and pepper. Cover the fillets with a layer of tomato sauce. Sprinkle with Parmesan cheese. Bake for 30 minutes.

Serve with Rice Pilaf, p. 199, and a Garden Salad, p. 192. The same recipe can be used for veal scallops parmigiana.

NOTES

SEAFOOD

FISH WITH VEGETABLES

3 lb whole fish
1/4 C oil
11/2 C chopped onion
2-4 cloves minced garlic
5-6 Prepared Plum Tomatoes, p.185
1/2 C chopped fresh parsley or coriander

1/4 C chopped fresh dill (1 T dried)
freshly ground black pepper
2 T lemon or lime juice
1 lb fresh Spinach, p. 185
1/3 C dry white wine or water

In a large skillet, heat oil and sauté onion till translucent. Add garlic, tomatoes, parsley, dill and pepper. Cook 10 minutes on medium heat, uncovered. Sprinkle fish lightly with pepper and lemon juice. Pour tomato mixture in a lightly greased 9x13x2" baking dish and place fish on top of sauce. Pour wine over the fish. Cover with foil and bake at 350 degrees for 20 minutes. Uncover and continue baking 10 minutes. Add spinach for the last 5 minutes of baking time. Arrange it in the sauce around the fish. Serves 4.

POACHED FILLETS

4 skinned flat fish fillets
3/4 C finely sliced mushrooms
1 minced shallot (or 1 T minced onion)

1 T butter
1 T chopped parsley or dill
1/2 C dry white wine

This recipe works well with fillet of sole, lemon sole, flounder, scrod, halibut. Wipe fillets with damp cloth and dry. Prepare mushrooms and shallot. Put butter in a heavy skillet and heat to sizzling. Place fillets in skillet and cover with mushroom, shallot, and parsley. Pour the wine gently into the skillet. Cover with poaching parchment paper or use the pan lid and remove occasionally to let steam escape. Simmer 10 to 15 minutes over low heat. Remove the fish to a platter and dot with butter. Continue cooking wine mixture uncovered until it is reduced in volume by half. Spoon onto fillets.

SAUTÉED FILLETS

4 flat fish fillets (see recipe above)
1 beaten egg
1 T olive oil

1/2 sliced onion
1 T chopped parsley or dill
8 lemon wedges

Rub fillets with damp cloth and dry. Dredge in beaten egg. Heat olive oil to hot in a large heavy skillet. Put fish and onions in together, sprinkle with parsley. Sauté fish 1-2 minutes on a side. Serve with lemon wedges.

BAKED SALMON FILLETS

6 oz salmon/person
plain yogurt
juice of 1 lemon
1 T chopped onion/person

1/2 tsp mustard powder
1 tsp dried dill (1 T fresh snipped)
paprika to taste
1-2 cloves garlic

Grease a baking pan in a size just big enough to hold the fish. You may want to cut the fillet in two pieces to fit. Place salmon in dish skin side down. Mix the other ingredients (except garlic) well and cover the fish with it. Add garlic cloves to pan. Cover with aluminum foil and bake in 350-degree oven 20-40 minutes depending on how thick the fish is. Salmon should be pink through and flake when done. Delicious hot or cold.

SEAFOOD STEAKS

6-8 oz steak (salmon, tuna, swordfish)   1 T Mayonnaise, p. 157
1/2 tsp dried dill/steak   lemon wedges

Sprinkle dill on top side of steak, coat lightly with mayonnaise. Place on broiler pan. Broil 2-3 minutes, 3 inches from heat source. Turn steaks, coat with dill and mayonnaise. Broil about 3 minutes. Turn heat to medium. Broil a few more minutes until done. When fish is done, it should flake easily. Cooking time depends on thickness of steaks.

SEA SCALLOPS

[1/2 C Brazil nuts, sliced fine]   1/4 C minced fresh parsley or coriander
3 shallots minced   1/8 tsp sea salt
1 minced garlic clove   fresh ground white pepper to taste
1 C dry white wine or water   11/2 lbs sea scallops
6 T butter, cut into bits

In a small saucepan, combine shallots, garlic and wine or water. Bring to a boil over high heat. Boil until the wine is reduced by half (5 minutes). Turn heat to low, add 4 T butter and whisk until it is all melted and mixed well. Stir in parsley and seasonings to taste. In a large skillet, heat the rest of the butter. When it sizzles, add the scallops. Sauté about 4 minutes over medium heat until the scallops are translucent. Place scallops on pre-heated serving dish. Pour sauce over them [and garnish with the raw Brazil nuts]. Serve at once.

CEVICHE

1 lb fresh red snapper fillets   1 C thinly sliced red onion
3/4 C fresh lime juice   1/2 tsp sea salt
3 chilis serrano, seeded and cut   fresh ground black pepper to taste
   into thin strips   2 T chopped cilantro (or 1 T dried oregano)

This is a Mexican and Central American raw fish dish. Cut the fish into narrow strips (2" x 1/4" inch). Put fish into a glass or ceramic bowl. Add the other ingredients and stir. Marinate for 10 minutes. Drain off the excess lime juice. Correct the seasonings to taste. Serve cold or at room temperature as an appetizer or main course.

Other types of fish work well here: cod or monkfish, for example, could be substituted.

SEAFOOD GUMBO

2 T olive oil   2 C Chicken Broth, p. 187
2 cloves minced garlic   1/2-3/4 tsp ground red pepper
1/2 C chopped onions   1/2 tsp each thyme and basil
1/2 C chopped green pepper   1/2 lb okra sliced in 1/4" crosswise pieces
1/2 C chopped mushrooms   3/4 lb white fish, cut into 1" pieces
5-6 Prepared Plum Tomatoes, p. 185   1/2 lb peeled, deveined shrimp
      1 C Rice Pilaf, p. 199

Heat oil in a Dutch oven or large saucepan. Sauté onions, green peppers and mushrooms until tender but still crisp. Add tomatoes with juice, garlic, broth, red pepper and herbs. Bring to a boil. Reduce heat and simmer uncovered 20-25 minutes.
   Stir in fish, shrimp and okra. Simmer until fish flakes (5-8 minutes). Serves 4.
   SERVING SUGGESTION: Pack cooked rice into 1/4 C greased measure. Unmold the rice in the center of a large soup bowl. Ladle the gumbo around the rice.

SEAFOOD RISOTTO

3 T olive oil
1 leek, chopped
1 C pan-browned rice, see Rice Pilaf,
    p. 199
21/4 C water
1 tsp minced garlic
4 oz dry white wine

8 oz clam juice (or lemon juice)
1/4 tsp ground black pepper
3/4 lb shrimp, peeled & deveined
1/2 lb sea scallops, halved crosswise
2 T chopped Italian parsley
pinch saffron (or turmeric)

In a medium saucepan, heat 2 T oil over medium heat. Sauté leek 3 minutes. Brown whole-grain rice in a dry frying pan, over medium heat until kernels are golden brown. Add to leek mixture. Add 21/4 C boiling water immediately. Cover and simmer 45 mins.

In another medium saucepan, heat 1 T oil over medium heat. Add garlic, sauté 30 seconds (do not brown). Add wine and bring to a boil. Add clam juice and pepper. Return to boil. Stir in shrimp and scallops. Cook 3 minutes, stirring occasionally, until shrimp are pink and scallops opaque. Remove seafood to a bowl with a slotted spoon. Reserve liquid.

Add saffron to 1/2 C of the reserved liquid. Add to rice while cooking. Bring back to boil, stirring constantly. Cover rice and simmer on low until done.. Taste rice for doneness. Add more water if necessary during cooking, 1/4 C at a time.

Stir in seafood and parsley. Serve immediately. Serves 4.

BOILED SHRIMP

11/2 lbs shrimp in shell
2 ribs celery, cut in 2" pieces
1 clove garlic, unpeeled
2 slices onion

juice of 1 lemon
1 bay leaf
8-12 black peppercorns
4 sprigs fresh parsley

In large saucepan, heat 2 quarts of water with all the ingredients except the shrimp. Bring to a boil. Boil 5 minutes. Add shrimp. Allow water to boil again, Remove shrimp when they turn pink (just a few minutes). Flush with cool water. Discard vegetables and herbs. If to be served cold, chill shrimp in their shells. Serve in shells and allow diners to peel and devein (it's part of the fun). Or if to be used in a recipe, shell and devein at once.

If you buy raw shelled shrimp, prepare in the same way. Remove from water as soon as they turn pink.

TUNA SALAD

1 can tuna
1 hard-boiled egg
1 tsp Dijon mustard
1/4 C Mayonnaise, p. 157

1/2 C chopped vegetables (onion, garlic,
    carrot, celery, radish, fresh parsley)
[1/2 tsp curry powder, Mrs. Dash, etc.]

Mash the egg. Put all ingredients in a bowl and mix and blend well. May be done in food processor. Chop vegetables coarse first, then add remaining ingredients to food processor and pulse 3-4 times for desired consistency.
CHICKEN OR TURKEY SALAD: replace tuna with 8 oz leftover chopped chicken or turkey.

VEGETABLES

In general, vegetables are best when locally and organically grown, picked ripe in season and served fresh. In terms of taste and nutrition, it's all downhill from there. Many areas have farmer's markets and garden markets, where you can get fully ripened produce picked that day. (Even better, grow your own, organically.) Fresh vegetables are excellent raw and can be served as crudités with a seasoned yogurt dip or cheese. In fact, the harder vegetables like broccoli, carrots, zucchini and onions can be used raw in place of bread for holding that cheese fondue. In general, smaller vegetables have more taste than larger ones.

In my opinion, the best way of cooking most vegetables is in multi-ply all stainless steel waterless cookware. The vegetables are cooked slowly with about a tablespoon of water over low heat. They turn out deliciously sweet, with their colors and nutrients intact. Next best is steaming. Place about an inch of water in a pot with a tight fitting lid. Bring to a boil. Place the vegetables in a stainless steel steam basket. Put the basket in the water. Bamboo steamers work well also. The steamers hold the food above the water in the steam. Cover tightly and cook about 5-7 minutes. You may cook vegetables of a similar size and firmness together and they will be done at the same time. If you are mixing broccoli and zucchini, either cook separately or add the zucchini after 3 minutes, so the zucchini won't be overcooked. Sauté or stir-fry are other good ways to cook vegetables to preserve taste and nutrition.

BOILED ARTICHOKE

2 large artichokes	juice of 1/2 lemon
boiling salted water	

Trim the tough outer leaves attached to the base of the artichoke. Place artichoke on its side and trim the top 1/4-1/2" with a sharp knife. Use scissors to snip off the points on the outer leaves (about 1/4"). Drop the vegetable into boiling salted water to cover. Add lemon juice.

Simmer, covered, until an outer leaf pulls off easily, about 40 minutes. Serves 2.

To eat. Pull off each leaf as you go. Dip the base end of the leaf in the sauce* and then scrape the meat off the leaf with your teeth. The point of the leaf is your handle. Put the base end of the leaf in your mouth, meaty side downward. Bite down at the center of the leaf and pull it through your teeth, scraping the meat off as you go. When you get to the thin inner leaves, cut them away. Use a spoon to scrape away the hairy choke above the heart of the artichoke. Discard leaves and hairy choke. Cut the heart into pieces. Dip them in the sauce and savor.

*SAUCES FOR ARTICHOKE: hot melted butter mixed with some lemon juice, Hollandaise, p. 160, Mayonnaise, p. 157.

STUFFED ARTICHOKE

2 medium artichokes	fresh ground black pepper
1 T olive oil	dash nutmeg
1/4 lb ground beef	pinch of oregano leaf
1 T chopped onion	2 slices fresh tomato
1 T chopped parsley (or coriander)	1 T lemon juice
1/3 C Sprouted Bread Crumbs, p. 199	1/2 tsp sea salt
1 egg, beaten	

Wash the artichoke. With a sharp knife, slice off the top third of it. Pull off the tough outer leaves around the base. Use scissors to snip off the points of the remaining outer leaves. Gently pull the center leaves apart. Put the top of the artichoke on a hard surface and press down firmly on the base. This should cause the leaves to spread farther. Turn the artichoke right side up and pull the now-exposed yellow-white leaves from the center. Sprinkle the choke and cut surfaces with lemon juice to prevent discoloration. With a soup spoon, carefully scrape and pull the fuzzy, prickly choke away from the heart. (This is important, because it has a very unpleasant taste.) Discard the choke.

Cut the stem off flush at the base, so the artichoke can stand. The stem can be peeled and cooked if desired and added to the stuffing. Tie a string around each artichoke, so that it will retain its shape while cooking. Stand the artichokes in a deep saucepan. Add a little sea salt, lemon juice and boiling water to cover. Cook, covered 20 to 30 minutes, until partly tender.

Remove with spoons or tongs from water and turn upside down to drain. Fill when partly cooled.

While artichokes are boiling, put 1/2 T oil in a skillet. Heat. Add the beef and onion. Sauté until brown. Remove from heat. Stir in parsley, Bread Crumbs (save a T of Bread Crumbs), egg, 1/4 tsp salt, pepper, nutmeg and oregano. Spoon the filling into the cooled artichoke centers. Top with a slice of tomato.

Combine olive oil with a dash of salt. Brush artichokes and tomato with the oil. Place in a shallow baking pan, or ceramic covered saucepan. Mix 1 T of Bread Crumbs with softened butter. Sprinkle onto artichokes. Fill pan with boiling water to a depth of an inch and add some lemon juice. If pan has no cover, cover with aluminum foil and bake 1 hour at 350 degrees.

Serve as an entrée with Rice Pilaf, p. 199, and a green vegetable. Serves 2.

ASPARAGUS

asparagus spears, 1/2 lb/person	kettle or Dutch oven large enough to hold
sea salt	spears horizontally
large plate	cloth napkin or dish towel

With the base end toward you, use a paring knife to peel the tough outer skin off the asparagus base. Pare from the base toward the tip. Cut deeper at the base end to expose the tender flesh beneath. If you do this, you will be able to enjoy the whole spear. Since asparagus is relatively expensive, it's worth the effort. Pare off any scales below the tip.

The French method of cooking asparagus is the best. Line up the spears and tie them together in 3-1/2" diameter bundles. Tie one string near the tip; one string near the base. Trim the bases so the spears in one bundle are all the same length.

If you are not cooking the asparagus immediately, stand the bundles up in 1/2" of cold water. Cover with a plastic bag and refrigerate.

To cook, plunge the asparagus bundles horizontally into a large kettle of rapidly boiling salted water. Return the water to the boil and simmer slowly uncovered for about 15 minutes. The asparagus is done when the paring knife pierces the base end easily. The spears should be tender and firm, not droopy.

When the asparagus is done, remove it gently from the water. Hold it for a few seconds to drain. Place the bundle on toweling. Cut and remove string. Best to serve it immediately, but the asparagus can be kept warm wrapped in the towel or cloth napkin, kept in a warm place for about 20 minutes. It will loose a little texture, but will maintain taste and color.

There are other methods of cooking asparagus that work well. For all of them, prepare the spears as above. 1.) Asparagus can be steamed standing up in a deep narrow pot, like a Pyrex pot or Corning coffee pot. Put an inch of water in the bottom of the pot and cover. Steam 5-7 minutes. 2.) After trimming, asparagus can be cut into 2" pieces lengthwise and steamed or cooked in waterless cookware (tying is unnecessary).

SERVING: Asparagus is delicious served with lemon and butter. Traditionally asparagus is served with Hollandaise Sauce, p. 160.

Asparagus is equally delicious served cold as a salad or appetizer with a Vinaigrette Dressing, p. 157. Cooked, it is an excellent addition to a salad, an omelet, a casserole, or a stir-fry dish.

ITALIAN ASPARAGUS

1 lb fresh cooked Asparagus, p 179
1 med Prepared Tomato, p. 185
2 T chopped green onions
1/8 tsp dried oregano leaves

1/8 tsp dried thyme leaves
fresh ground black pepper to taste
2 T freshly grated Parmesean cheese

While asparagus is cooking, combine all ingredients in a bowl, except the cheese. Mix well. Arrange the cooked asparagus on a serving platter. Spoon tomato mixture over asparagus, sprinkle with the cheese. Serves 4.

BEANS, GREEN, SNAP OR WAX

1 lb beans per 2-3 people

Most beans today are stringless. Look for clean, fresh-looking, firm beans. You want young beans with immature seeds and of a uniform thickness. Trim off the ends with a knife. To retain best flavor, use 1/4" thick diameter beans and leave them whole. If they are thicker, slice on the bias into 21/2" lengths. Steam beans or cook in waterless cookware for 7 minutes. Beans should be tender but slightly crunchy. Serve immediately. Toss with butter.

BEANS WITH BUTTER AND LEMON

1 lb hot Green Beans (above)
1/4 tsp sea salt
fresh ground pepper to taste

2 T softened butter, cut in pieces
1 T lemon juice
1 T minced parsley

Prepare Green Beans recipe. Put cooked beans in heavy-bottomed saucepan. Toss gently over moderate heat. Toss and shake the pan, don't stir the beans. This will evaporate the moisture in about 2 minutes. Add salt, pepper and a little butter, Keep tossing over medium heat. Add the rest of the butter gradually alternately with drops of lemon juice. Keep tossing. Serve beans immediately in a warmed vegetable dish, garnished with parsley. Serves 2-3.

BEANS IN CREAM

1 lb Green Beans, trimmed and washed
1/4 tsp sea salt
fresh ground black pepper to taste

1 T softened butter
1 T minced shallot
1/2 C whipping cream
1 T minced parsley or tarragon

Steam or waterless-cook Green Beans about 4 minutes, so they are only partly cooked. Drain. Toss beans in a heavy-bottomed saucepan or skillet over moderate heat to evaporate their moisture, about 2 minutes. Toss with salt, pepper and butter. Pour in the cream. Cover the pan. Boil slowly for 5 minutes or so, until the beans are tender. The cream should have been reduced by half. Correct the seasoning. Place in preheated vegetable dish, sprinkle with parsley or tarragon. Serve immediately.

BROCCOLI

Choose broccoli with smallest buds possible. The more purple the better. Yellowish color or open buds indicate that the broccoli is past maturity and will not be as tasty and will have a stronger odor. Broccoli cooks more rapidly and retains its color better when divided into florets about 3 inches long. Peel the thin green "bark" off the stem and stalks to reach the tender white flesh. Cut the stem into bias pieces.

Steam broccoli or cook in waterless cookware about 7 minutes after water boils.

Broccoli goes well with melted butter or Hollandaise Sauce, p. 160; or cold with Vinaigrette, p.157, as a separate vegetable course or appetizer.

BROCCOLI AND OLIVES

1 bunch Broccoli	sea salt to taste
3 T olive oil	fresh ground pepper to taste
2 clove garlic, minced	1/3 C pitted black olives, chopped
	[3 T grated Parmesan or Romano cheese]

Steam the broccoli about 5 minutes. Drain and reserve the liquid. Heat the oil in a skillet, add the garlic and sauté until lightly browned. Add the broccoli and seasonings. Cook slowly over low heat about 10 minutes. Add a little of the drained broccoli liquid (water is okay) if the pan gets too dry.

Add the olives. Heat 2 more minutes. Serve immediately, [sprinkled with cheese]. Serves 4.

BRUSSELS SPROUTS

Brussels sprouts (1/4 lb/person)

Choose firm, healthy, fresh rounded heads. Try to get them a uniform size, with bright green leaves. If they are soft, they are old, tasteless or unhealthy and will be soft and mushy when cooked. Avoid sprouts with worm holes.

Trim the base of each sprout with a small knife and cut a cross in the base for quicker cooking. Trim off yellowed or wilted leaves.

For best cooking, steam or cook in waterless cookware or steamer for 6-8 minutes after water boils.

Serve with butter. Brussels sprouts go well with roast duck, turkey, beef, pork, ham, or liver.

CARROTS

1 medium carrot/person

Choose firm, well-colored smooth carrots. Avoid carrots with hairy knobs on them. These are nematode (round worms) nests and indicate nematodes throughout the vegetable. You will not cook the vegetable at a high enough temperature to kill them.

Scrub the carrots under cold water. Do not peel. Slice the carrots into 1/8 to 1/4" slices on the diagonal. In steamer or waterless cookware, steam for 6-7 minutes, depending on the thickness of the slices. I like to cook carrots with green or wax beans, onion slices and broccoli and serve with butter.

VARIATIONS: 1.) Cut carrots as above or julienne into 2" x 1/4" long strips. Sauté in a little oil. 2.) Dice carrots and unpeeled apple (1 apple: 4 carrots) and sauté together until tender.

EGGPLANT

A whole medium eggplant is low in carbohydrates (only 6.5 carbohydrate grams), is a very satisfying vegetable and can be eaten freely as long as it is not breaded or dredged in flour. Eggplant makes a wonderful foundation food on which to build creative recipes. With a little imagination, I bet you could come up with a pizza-type recipe using only level 1 foods and eggplant as the base instead of pizza dough.

Eggplant contains a lot of water and, in unthickened recipes, should be drained. Do this by peeling, and slicing or cubing. Sprinkle with lemon juice to prevent discoloration. Then either sprinkle with kosher salt and drain in a colander; or stack slices on paper towels and weigh down with heavy a plate. Let sit for an hour to remove excess moisture. Then dry the eggplant with toweling. To prevent discoloration, cook eggplant in stainless steel, glass or ceramic. When fried or sautéed, eggplant can also absorb massive amounts of oil. This can be minimized by making sure the oil is hot before adding the eggplant.

Eggplant has male and female fruits. The male eggplant is reputed to be less bitter. The male have fewer seeds and can be identified by looking at the spot on the bottom. The round spot is male, the long spot is female. We are accustomed to seeing long eggplant with purple skin, but Chinese eggplant has beautiful white skin (which gives the vegetable its name) and is tastier. A round Italian eggplant with purple skin that lightens to pink near the stem has been coming onto the market lately and is excellent.

BROILED EGGPLANT

1 medium eggplant
2 cloves garlic, minced
1 tsp grated onion

1/4 tsp sea salt
1/4 C olive oil or melted butter

Peel the eggplant. It is not necessary to drain it. Slice eggplant into 1/2" slices crosswise. Place on a greased baking sheet and brush with oil, season with garlic, onion and salt. Save enough oil to baste eggplant twice more. Broil about 5 inches from heat source about 5 minutes, basting once with oil.

Using a pancake turner, turn eggplant slices over. Brush with remaining oil mixture. Broil about 2 minutes longer or until tender.

Serve plain or with Tomato Sauce, p. 161. Sprinkle with grated cheese, if desired.

SAUTÉED EGGPLANT

1 eggplant
1 egg, beaten
1 T chopped fresh parsley
2 T olive oil

1/2 tsp dried oregano or 1/4 tsp dried basil
1 onion sliced
1 clove garlic, minced

Peel eggplant. Drain (see Eggplant, above). Slice into 1/2" pieces crosswise. Dip in beaten egg seasoned with parsley and basil or oregano. Sauté onion and garlic until onion is translucent. When oil is hot, add eggplant slices. Sauté about 4 minutes on a side or until tender. Add oil, if needed. Serve hot. Serves 4.

EGGPLANT PARMIGIANA

1 Sautéed Eggplant recipe, p. 182
2 T olive oil
1 clove garlic, minced
1/3 C chopped onions
2-1/2 C Prepared Plum Tomatoes, p. 185

salt and black pepper to taste
1/4 tsp dried basil
1/2 C grated Parmesan cheese
1/4 C mozzarella cheese
butter

Sauté garlic and onions in 2 T olive oil in heavy skillet until onion is transparent. Add tomatoes, basil, salt and pepper. Cook, stirring occasionally for 30 minutes.

Preheat oven to 350 degrees (moderate). Alternate layers of eggplant slices, tomato mixture, and cheeses. Dot the top with butter and bake 30 minutes. Serves 2-3.

EGGPLANT CURRY

11/2 C chopped onion
2 cloves minced garlic
1 tsp turmeric
1 tsp cayenne
1 tsp cumin
1 tsp sea salt

1 medium eggplant, unpeeled, cut into 1"
    cubes and drained; see Eggplant, p.182
1 T fresh chopped coriander (parsley) leaves
2 T oil
11/2 C sweet green peas, steamed (or 1/2 C
    each chopped broccoli, diced carrot, diced
    celery, etc.)

Sauté onion, salt, turmeric, cayenne, cumin and salt in a large, heavy skillet, until onion is translucent. Add eggplant. Sauté, covering well with the spice mixture.* Cover and cook, stirring often, about 15 minutes. Eggplant cubes should be tender, but not mushy. A little additional water or oil may be added if mixture is too dry.

Add 1/2 the fresh coriander and cook 2 minutes longer. Serve immediately, topped with coriander and the vegetable(s).
*OPTIONAL: 1 large tomato, peeled and chopped (see Prepared Tomatoes, p. 185) can be added at this point.

Serve with Cucumber Raita, p. 194, and Rice Pilaf, p. 199. Serves 4.

RATATOUILLE

2 zucchini
1 small eggplant
5 ripe plum Tomatoes, Prepared, p.185
3 cloves garlic, minced
1 large onion, sliced thinly
1/4 C olive oil

1/2 C sliced black olives
2 green peppers, seeded and cut in strips
1/2 tsp dried oregano or 1/4 tsp dried basil
1/4 tsp sea salt
black, pepper, to taste
1 T capers

To prepare: Slice the zucchini. Peel and cube the eggplant. Drain for 1 hour (see Eggplant, p. 182). Prepare the tomatoes.

Use a large skillet with a cover to sauté garlic and onion in the olive oil, until onion is translucent.   Add the zucchini, eggplant cubes, olives and green pepper to the skillet. Season with basil or oregano, salt and pepper. Cover and cook slowly for an hour.

Add the tomatoes. Simmer uncovered until the mixture has thickened. Add capers during last 15 minutes of cooking.

Serve hot as a vegetable side dish, or cold as an appetizer.

STUFFED EGGPLANT

2 lb eggplant
6 oz ground meat, poultry, or shrimp
4 oz Rice Pilaf, p. 199
4 Brazil nuts, chopped
1 beaten egg
1/4 C chopped mushrooms

1 T butter, diced
1/2 C Chicken Broth, p. 187
1 tsp minced onion
1/2 tsp sea salt
1/4 tsp ground black pepper
1 T chopped parsley

Slice the top off the eggplant, right under the leafy green cap. Follow the lines of the cap to create a scalloped edge. Save the top for a lid. Scoop out the pulp, leaving a 1/2" shell. Add the pulp to a small quantity of boiling water or stock. Cook until tender and drain.

In a large bowl, combine the cooked pulp with the remainder of the ingredients. Preheat the oven to 400 degrees. Fill the shell. Cover with the leaf lid. Bake the eggplant until filling is heated about 45 mins to an hour.

ALTERNATE RECIPE: Bring a kettle of water to a boil. Drop eggplant in and boil 15 minutes covered. Remove from water. Drain and slice eggplant in half lengthwise. Carefully remove pulp, leaving a 1/2" thick shell.

Chop the eggplant pulp and add it to the stuffing ingredients above. Fill each eggplant shell half with the stuffing. Place on a greased baking pan. Brush the tops with additional oil and bake at 350 degrees, about 45 minutes.

Serve as is or top with Tomato Sauce, p 161, and grated Parmesan or Romano cheese.

MUSHROOMS

1/4 lb mushrooms/person   butter or oil

Wipe mushrooms with a damp cloth. Do not wash unless they are sandy. Trim the stems and slice, or chop. Melt butter or heat oil in skillet until hot. Toss in mushroom slices. Turn heat to medium. Stir frequently to turn while sautéing. Mushrooms are done in 2-3 minutes and will begin releasing a lot of the oil they absorbed at first.

As a garnish for steak, sauté 2-3 sliced mushrooms with 2-3 slices of onion/person.

STUFFED GREEN PEPPERS

6 large green peppers   3/4 C grated Parmesan cheese
1/4 C olive oil   2 C Rice Pilaf, p. 199
1/2 C chopped onion   3 T chopped parsley or coriander
2 cloves garlic, minced   1/4 tsp sea salt
3/4 lb ground meat (veal, beef, pork,   freshly ground black pepper
   turkey, chicken or mixture)   3/4 C Beef Broth, p. 188, or tomato juice

Trim the stem ends from the peppers and carefully remove the seeds and pith.

In a large skillet, heat the oil, add onion and garlic and sauté until the onion is transparent Add the meat, stirring until it is browned. Stir in the cheese, rice, parsley, salt, and pepper. Mix well. Set aside till the mixture is cool enough to work with. When cool, stuff the peppers with the meat mixture.

Place the stuffed peppers in a greased baking dish. Pour the broth or juice over and around them. Bake until the peppers are tender, 30-40 minutes at 350 degrees. Baste occasionally with the pan liquid, adding more liquid if necessary.

SNOW PEA PODS

Snow peas are expensive, but used as flavoring a little goes a long way. Trim the ends. They require very little cooking and are also delicious raw in salads or by themselves. Sauté for a minute or two. In sautéed dishes, add snow pea pods at the end and cook for a minute or so. In steamed vegetable medleys and wok cooking, add snow pea pods about a minute before dish is finished cooking.

SPINACH

2 lbs spinach   1 T butter
1/4 tsp sea salt

Spinach is grown in sandy soil and must be washed very well to get the grit out. Trim off the stem ends of the spinach with a sharp knife. Fill a large bowl with water. Soak the spinach in the water. Lift the spinach out of the water into a colander. Pour the water out. Repeat the process till sand is washed away. If you pour the soaking water over the spinach, you will just pour the sand back over the spinach too. Pick over the leaves, discarding the bruised ones. Cut off stems. Use a large saucepan to steam or waterless cook spinach. Pack the spinach in. It will wilt down to about 1/5 the original volume when cooked, about 4 minutes. Serves 4.

SAUTÉED SPINACH

cooked spinach, see above   1 clove garlic, minced
3 scallions   1 T butter
                                                 [2 T grated Parmesan cheese]

Cook spinach about 2 minutes. Remove spinach to a bowl and squeeze excess moisture out. If spinach is too hot, use the back of a wooden spoon. Chop spinach coarsely. Wash scallions well. Trim roots and tops of stalks. Slice in 1/4" rounds crosswise. Melt butter in skillet. Add scallions and garlic to sizzling butter. Sauté for 1 minute. Add spinach. Continue sautéing, constantly stirring over medium-low heat for 3 or minutes. [Optional: garnish with Parmesan cheese.] Serves 4.

    SOUR CREAM SPINACH: Prepare Sautéed Spinach. Then add 1/2 C sour cream, salt and pepper to taste. Stir mixture constantly 2-3 minutes. Serves 4.

    Make extra Sautéed Spinach and refrigerate to use later in an Omelet, p. 196.

TOMATOES

Tomatoes can be wonderful fruit (although we call them a vegetable) when eaten freshly picked, ripe and organically grown. In that condition, they contain vitamins A, B-complex, C, and important minerals. They usually retain much of their nutrition for 5-6 days after picking, under refrigeration. Tomatoes can be ripened upside down on a windowsill for a few days, but will never taste as good as vine-ripened ones. Unfortunately most of those fresh red tomatoes in the supermarket were grown without minerals, picked green weeks ago, ripened in transit with ethylene gas and taste like cardboard. Organically grown canned tomatoes, unsalted, are a good alternative. Commercially canned tomatoes, although possibly packed when fresh often contain salt, sugar and other chemicals. Fresh tomatoes cannot be frozen. Italian plum tomatoes are generally sweeter. Hothouse and hydroponic tomatoes available off season are usually inferior unless organically grown.

PREPARED TOMATOES

When recipes call for tomatoes, it's relatively easy to use fresh ones. Boil a pot of water. Add fresh whole tomatoes and boil for about 30 seconds. Remove with a slotted spoon or tongs. With a sharp paring knife, cut out the stem end, and from that end, peel the skin off the tomato. It will come away easily. Holding the tomato in your hand, palm down above a bowl, gently squeeze the tomato to release the seeds and some of the water (Tomatoes add thickening to recipes, so the less juice the better.). Discard the juice, skin and seeds. Chop tomatoes coarsely and add to soups, stews, sauces, etc.

ZUCCHINI

1 small zucchini/person

Zucchini is very alkalinizing and is a useful balance for the more acidic animal protein. Wash zucchini well. Trim the ends. Slice in 1/4" crosswise pieces (or julienne). Steam or waterless cook for 5 minutes. Serve with butter or lemon juice.

STUFFED ZUCCHINI

2 large zucchini
Stuffed Eggplant, p. 183, stuffing

1 clove garlic, minced or crushed
1/4 C oil
8 T Tomato Sauce, p. 161

Wash zucchini thoroughly. Do not trim the ends. Steam whole zucchini for 2 minutes. Remove from heat. Slice in half lengthwise. Scoop out meat of zucchini leaving 1/4" thick shell. Prepare stuffing for stuffed eggplant, replacing the eggplant meat with the zucchini meat.

Place the stuffed zucchini in a greased baking pan and add oil and garlic. Cover and bake at 350 degrees until tender, 40-45 minutes. Remove from pan. Garnish with heated Tomato Sauce. Serves 4.

NOTES

SOUPS

CHICKEN BROTH

1 soup chicken, 4-5 pounds	1 T dill weed
water to cover	1 tsp thyme
1 large onion with skin (for color)	1/2 tsp sage
2-5 whole cloves	1/2 tsp rosemary
1-2 stalks celery	sea salt
1-2 carrots	black pepper
1-2 sprigs parsley	1/4 tsp turmeric (for color)

[Herb bouquet: Lay out a damp piece of cheesecloth. Place parsley on it. Sprinkle with dill, thyme, rosemary, and sage. Wrap cloth around parsley and herbs. Tie with kitchen string.] Or add the herbs directly to the boiling water.

Wash chicken well and place in large kettle, Dutch oven or stock pot. Cover with water. Bring to a boil.

While water is heating, prepare vegetables. Cut ends off onion, but leave skin on for color. Stud onion with 2-5 cloves (that is, insert clove by piercing the onion flesh with the pointed end of clove). Trim ends and leaves off 1-2 celery stalks. Trim washed carrots and cut in three pieces crosswise.

Allow water to boil for a few minutes. Skim scum from surface of soup with slotted spoon or cheesecloth. Repeat several times. Then add all the vegetables and seasonings.

Cover pot. Lower heat, so soup just simmers. Simmer for 1 hour. Soup can be used at this point. Or remove chicken. Cut flesh off breast, thighs and drumsticks to use in salad or soup, etc. Return bones to pot and simmer another 1/2 hour. Remove bones and vegetables with slotted spoon and discard.

Strain soup through fine sieve, strainer or cheesecloth. Serve plain or as:

CHICKEN SOUP WITH RICE: Add 1/2 C Rice Pilaf, p.199, per bowl of soup.

CHINESE CHICKEN EGG DROP SOUP. Heat soup. Add scallion slices (cut crosswise), and a few mushroom slices. When soup is boiling, remove from heat. Break raw egg into soup, through the tines of a stainless steel fork. Stir egg with fork as egg strands harden. Serve immediately.

STORAGE AND SERVING. If hot soup is poured into canning jars and the lids secured immediately, it can be kept up to 3 weeks in unopened jars in refrigerator. Soup can also be frozen in plastic 1/2-pint containers for later use in other recipes.

When soup is refrigerated, fat congeals at top. This can be skimmed before use.

TRADITIONAL: As a main course, serve the freshly cooked hot soup. Remove the chicken and vegetables. Add fresh carrot and onion slices and simmer about 10 minutes. Add pieces of the soup chicken. Add Rice Pilaf, p. 199.

AFTER SUGAR CONTROL: Add cooked barley to chicken broth.

CHICKEN VEGETABLE SOUP

1 C Chicken Broth, p. 187	5-6 chopped mushrooms with stems
4-5 Prepared Tomatoes, p. 185	1 C diced zucchini
1 tsp dried basil	1 stalk diced celery
1 tsp paprika	3 C Chicken Broth, p. 187
1/4 tsp sea salt	1 C diced cooked chicken from Broth recipe
1 T olive oil	2 cloves minced garlic
1/2 C chopped onion	2 T Burgundy or dry red wine
2 diced carrots	freshly ground black pepper

Combine broth, tomatoes, herbs and salt in a 6 qt saucepan, stockpot, or Dutch oven. Bring to a boil and simmer for 10 minutes. Meanwhile add oil to large skillet. Bring to high heat and sauté the vegetables for 4-5 minutes. Add the vegetables, 3 more C of broth, chicken, wine and pepper and simmer uncovered for 10 more minutes. Serve hot. Serves 6-8.

WINTER SQUASH SOUP

3 C cubed winter squash   4 C Chicken Broth, p. 187
1 diced onion   Cajun seasoning, 1/4 tsp
1/2 C sliced celery

Steam whole squash for 1/2 an hour on a rack over water either on the stove in a covered pot or in the oven over a roasting pan. Remove squash, let cool enough to work with. Peel and remove seeds. Cut into 1-inch cubes. [Prepare ahead.]

Place squash, onion and celery in stock and simmer over low flame for 1/2 hour. Remove vegetables, saving soup. Mash vegetables or process lightly in food processor or blender. Return mixture to soup. Season; simmer 5-10 minutes longer.

COLD CREAM OF SORREL SOUP

1/2 lb sorrel, finely chopped   4 egg yolks
1 tsp butter   2 C light cream
5 C Chicken Broth, p. 69

Sauté the sorrel in butter until wilted. Set aside. Bring the chicken broth to a boil, while lightly beating the yolks and cream together. Combine ingredients and serve.

BEEF BROTH

4 pounds of shin beef   1 onion studded with 2-5 cloves
1 beef or veal bone   4 leeks if available or 2 extra onions
1 clove garlic   4 carrots
1 bay leaf   2 celery stalks
1 tsp thyme   [1 T sea salt]
1-2 sprigs parsley   6 quarts water

Beef broth can be made in almost the same manner as chicken broth. Place beef into water. Bring to a boil in a large kettle or stock pot. Skim the scum off the surface. While waiting for the beef to boil, prepare the vegetables. Crush the garlic clove on cutting board, using heavy end of knife blade or cleaver. Peel or not. Wash parsley. Peel and trim onion, and stud onion with cloves. Cut roots and stems off leeks. (Or trim and peel the extra onions.) Use only white part of leek. Slice lengthwise and wash grit and dirt out carefully. Peel carrots (if carrots are organic, just scrub them well). Trim celery stalks.

After skimming, add the vegetables and seasonings to the pot. Bring to boil again. Reduce heat. Cover and let simmer for 3-4 hours. If liquid cooks down too much, add more water.

If prepared a day ahead and chilled, fat can be removed easily before reheating. The soup can be served with the boiled meat and fresh vegetables and rice.

Reserve extra broth as in chicken broth recipe for other soups, etc.

BEEF VEGETABLE SOUP

6 C Beef Broth, p. 188
1 C string beans, cut in 1/2-inch lengths
2 onions thinly sliced
2 carrots, thinly sliced

3 leeks, thinly sliced
4 celery stalks, trimmed and diced
1 C green peas
1 C Rice Pilaf, p. 199

Wash vegetables. Peel and trim onions, carrots and celery. Place broth in large stockpot. Bring to a boil. Add vegetables. Cover and simmer about 20 minutes. Add cooked rice. Simmer, covered 10 more minutes. Serve hot.

Soup can be varied with different vegetables, depending on what's in season. Zucchini, tomatoes, scallions, shredded cabbage, chopped kale, spinach, Swiss chard, peppers, and mushrooms add color and flavor to soup. Most of these vegetables take less time to cook and should be added 10 minutes before completion.

PRESENTATION: Sprigs of parsley or chopped chives make an attractive garnish. Or soup can be sprinkled with Parmesan or Romano cheese (if cheese is tolerated).

AFTER SUGAR CONTROL PROGRAM: other ingredients can be added or substituted: diced potatoes, barley, cooked chickpeas, pinto or kidney beans, to name a few.

VEGETABLE BROTH

Vegetable broth can be made from any mixture of leaves and parts of vegetables that you would normally throw away: bruised lettuce leaves, potato skins, carrot tops. When preparing salads or vegetables for steaming, save the discards for 2-3 days until you have enough for soup. Experiment to find flavors you like with different combinations of vegetables and different combinations of herbs.

1 onion studded with 2 cloves
2 carrots
2 stalks celery
1-2 cloves garlic

1/2 lb spinach
3-4 sprigs parsley
kale
herb bouquet (thyme, sage, basil)

Trim onion, leaving skin on. Stud with cloves. Trim carrots and peel or scrape skin, cut in 2-inch pieces. Trim celery and remove leaves. Cut each stalk in 3 pieces. Garlic can be cooked with skin on. Wash parsley. Trim kale. For the purposes of vegetable broth, stalks can be left on spinach and kale. Carrot tops are also good broth ingredients.

Spinach usually contains a lot of sand. Trim spinach. Wash spinach by soaking in water bath. Remove the leaves by hand from the bath, setting aside. Then pour the water off. Refill container with fresh water. Repeat the washing process, removing leaves from water by hand. If you pour the water out while the spinach is still in it, the sand will be poured back over the spinach.

AFTER SUGAR CONTROL: Add whole cut up, washed potato to soup, or parsnips.

Vegetable broth (sometimes called potassium broth, when used in juice fasts) makes an excellent refreshing and restorative drink hot or cold. It will keep several days in the refrigerator. It can also be frozen for later use as a base for more complex soups, flavoring in stews, rice or other grains, etc.

BLACK BEAN SOUP (ALLOWED AFTER BASIC SUGAR CONTROL)

1 lb black (turtle) beans
1 T oil
1 medium carrot, in thin 1" slices
2 medium onions, finely chopped
2 stalks celery, finely chopped
2 minced cloves garlic

2 T finely chopped parsley
11/2 C puréed Prepared Tomatoes, p. 185
1 tsp sweet basil
1 T seasoning (Cajun, curry, Mrs. Dash or
     Vegesal)
lime (or lemon)

Pick over and wash the beans. Put in a large bowl. Coat beans with the oil to prevent foaming. Cover generously with water and let soak overnight or all day. Add water. Bring the beans to a boil and simmer very gently, covered about 11/2 hours until soft but not mushy.

Add carrots, onions, celery, garlic, parsley, tomato purée, basil and seasonings. Simmer another 1/2 hour till vegetables lose most of their crunch.

GAZPACHO

1 clove garlic, peeled
1 red onion, sliced
1 cucumber sliced, seeded
3 Prepared Tomatoes, p.185
1 green pepper, seeded
[1 T hot pepper, chopped]

1/8 tsp salt
1/8 tsp cayenne
1/4 C vinegar
1/4 C olive oil
3/4 C tomato juice
2 T lemon or lime juice

4 raw eggs* or Beef Broth, p. 188

Purée garlic, onion, cucumber, tomatoes, green pepper [hot pepper] and eggs in blender, food processor or sieve vegetables and mix well with eggs or Beef Broth. Season with salt, cayenne, vinegar, olive oil, tomato and lemon juice. Chill about 3 hours, along with olives, soup tureen and soup bowls. Gazpacho must be served ice cold. Serves 8.

GARNISH I

1 can pimento, or 3 fresh, chopped
1 chopped onion
1 chopped green pepper
1 diced cucumber

1 can ripe olives, sliced
[1 C Croutons, p.199]
[clove garlic]
[2 T olive oil]

Portion out chopped fresh tomato, cucumber, onion, green pepper and pimento in separate bowls. Pour chilled liquid into each bowl. Top with sliced olives [and/or Croutons, p. 199, sautéed in oil and garlic just before serving].

GARNISH II

4 oz shrimp and/or lump crab meat/person   6 Croutons, p. 199 / person

---

Beware of salmonella *poisoning when using raw commercial eggs. Organic, free-range eggs should not pose this problem*

SALADS

Salads are endlessly various: hot or cold, served as an appetizer after the entrée, as the entrée, they can be fruit and/or vegetable—and are never quite the same twice.

Although iceberg or head lettuce is considered a sweet delicacy in France, because—apparently—the French know how to cut and serve it, there are many more interesting-tasting **salad greens**. They may be used individually or in combination. Leaves are best torn into bite-sized pieces. Consider: Boston, Bibb or cos lettuce, romaine, ruby or green leaf, chicory, arugela, radiccio, watercress, spinach, beet tops. Field greens, such as dandelion (before flowers have set) and lamb's quarters, are also wonderful.

Salad ingredients should be washed and dried before use. The salad spinner is a great time saver for this. It is usually a plastic tub into which a basket fits. Then there is some mechanism for spinning the basket and pulling the water out by centrifugal force (which we know doesn't exist). Fill the basket with the washed shredded greens. Close the bucket and spin the basket. The old-fashioned low-tech method is to spread out a large, terry towel. Place whole lettuce leaves next to each other on the towel. Then roll the towel into a cylinder and pat gently. Unroll and repeat till all the greens are dried.

You can make enough salad for two or three days. Without dressing the salad, store the surplus in a well-closed plastic bag from which all the air has been eliminated. Do not put salad dressing on the salad until you are ready to eat it. [Unless you like vinaigrette-pickled salad. In that case, store the dressed salad in an appropriate covered container for 3-12 hours before eating the salad. This could also be last night's leftovers for lunch.]

BASIC TOSSED SALAD

salad greens (see introduction)
cucumber slices
scallions (1/8" crosswise rounds)
radish, diced

tomato slices (or cherry tomato halves)
sweet green (red or yellow) pepper, rings or diced
mushrooms, sliced

Determine amounts of ingredients by the size salad you want, the number or people eating and your taste. Toss ingredients by hand or using serving spoons till well-mixed. Serve with dressing, fresh lemon juice and black pepper, or serve without dressing. Many other ingredients can be added according to what's available and to your taste. Some suggestions are: Bermuda onion rings, shredded carrots, diced celery stalks, shredded red or green cabbage, alfalfa sprouts, sliced pitted olives, pimentos, hot Tuscan peppers.

ARMENIAN SALAD

4 large Prepared Tomatoes, p 185, cubed
2 cucumbers, diced
2 stalks celery sliced
1/2 C red onion, finely chopped
1/2 bunch chopped watercress
1/4 tsp dried thyme
(1 tsp Vegesalt)

1/4 C chopped parsley (or coriander)
pinch basil
pinch dried mint or tsp fresh
1/4 tsp tarragon
2 T extra virgin olive oil (or other cold-pressed oil)
fresh juice of 1 lemon

Prepare tomatoes, p. 185. If cucumbers are waxed to preserve them, peel. Otherwise, leave the skin on.

Combine tomatoes, cucumbers, celery, onions, watercress, thyme, parsley, basil, mint in large salad bowl. Toss. Mix lemon juice and oil well. Pour onto salad and mix well.

GARDEN SALAD

2/3 C romaine lettuce torn in pieces
1/2 C raw grated zucchini
1/2 C raw grated carrot
1/4 C alfalfa or bean sprouts

3 sliced mushrooms
4 cucumber slices
2 scoops avocado
raw cashews to taste

Whether you are serving this salad as an entree for 1 person or as side salad for 2 or more will determine your serving dish. Toss lettuce, zucchini and carrot in a large salad bowl. Garnish with the remaining ingredients. Serve with Herb Dressing, p. 156.

COLE SLAW

small head cabbage (red and/or green)
bean sprouts

French Dressing, p. 155

Remove the outer leaves and core from the cabbage. Shred or chop the remaining cabbage, preparing only what you will eat now. Use enough French Dressing to just moisten the slaw.
VARIATIONS: 1.) Use Chinese celery cabbage or bok choy 2.) Add pared, diced apple or pineapple.

GREEK SALAD

Prepare the Armenian Salad, p. 191. Sprinkle with feta cheese and sliced olives. Dress with extra virgin olive oil and lemon juice to taste. Sprinkle with fresh ground black pepper as desired.

CHEF'S SALAD

basic Tossed Salad, p. 191
sliced olives
1 hard-boiled egg/person

1/4" x 1"strips of hard cheese, ham, chicken
    and/or turkey

Prepare tossed salad as desired. Add desired quantity and choice of cheese, ham, chicken or turkey, and hard-boiled egg. Garnish with olives.

CAESAR SALAD

sea salt
1 clove garlic, peeled
1 tsp dry mustard
fresh juice of 1/2 lemon
4 T olive oil

romaine lettuce (1 large or 3 small)
1 T grated Parmesan or Romano cheese
1 can anchovies, drained
1 raw egg
1 strip well-done crumbled bacon
    or Croutons, p. 199

A large wooden salad bowl is preferred. Sprinkle the bottom with sea salt and rub with garlic slice. Add mustard and lemon juice. Stir with wooden spoon until mustard dissolves. Add the olive oil and stir blend mixture rapidly with spoon.

Wash the romaine well and dry with salad spinner or towel. Shred into bite-sized pieces. Put them in the salad bowl and sprinkle with the cheese. Add the anchovies.

Break the egg* over the salad and mix gently, but thoroughly. Sprinkle with crumbled bacon bits or with Croutons made of sprouted bread.

*Beware of salmonella poisoning using raw commercial eggs. Organic, free-range eggs should not pose this problem. I have seen recipes where the whole egg was plunged into *boiling water for 60 seconds before being used in the salad, but the center would not get hot enough with this method to kill* salmonella.

SALAD NIÇOISE

1 clove garlic
2 peeled, quartered tomatoes
1 peeled, finely chopped cucumber
1 can solid white meat tuna, broken up
French or Italian Dressing, p. 155, 156

1 hard-boiled egg, sliced
12 coarsely chopped pitted black olives
1 C Bibb or Boston lettuce, torn in pieces
1 C romaine lettuce, torn in pieces

Rub salad bowl with garlic. Add all ingredients and toss well. Toss with French or Italian Dressing.

STRAWBERRY-SPINACH SALAD

1/3 C Mayonnaise, p.157
1/4 C 100% orange juice (no sugar added)
1 tsp poppy seeds

1/2 lb fresh spinach, washed,
  trimmed and torn
2 C sliced fresh strawberries

Dressing: Combine mayonnaise, orange juice, and poppy seeds in a small bowl. Stir well. Salad: Wash spinach, p. 185, trim and tear leaves. Toss spinach and strawberries in a large bowl. Arrange on individual salad plates. Drizzle the dressing over each salad. Serves 6-8.

TOMATO SALAD

2 large tomatoes
balsamic (sugar free) vinegar
olive oil

black olives, pitted and chopped
4 T crumbled blue cheese (Roquefort)
capers

Slice tomatoes. Arrange on 4 salad plates. Drizzle 1 tsp balsamic vinegar over each serving, followed by 1 T olive oil. Sprinkle olives, blue cheese and capers.

HEARTS OF PALM SALAD

chilled canned hearts of palm
romaine leaf, washed, whole
stuffed olive slices
green or red pepper rings
chopped parsley (or coriander)

paprika
French Dressing, p 155
Blue Cheese Dressing, p 156
Mayonnaise, p 157

Cut palms into lengthwise strips. Serve over a bed of romaine lettuce. Garnish with olive and pepper rings. Sprinkle on parsley and paprika. Serve with choice of salad dressing.

COLD RICE SALAD

1 C Rice Pilaf, p. 199
1/2 C chilled cooked Broccoli (or other
  vegetables)
8 oz cubed cold chicken (or 1 can tuna)
Italian Dressing, p 156

4 oz raw cashew nuts, coarsely chopped
1 stalk celery, chopped
1/4 raw, onion, chopped
6 sliced black olives

Mix all ingredients in a bowl. Serve with Italian dressing and toss well.

RAITAS

A raita is an Indian yogurt dish usually served as a cooling accompaniment to the spiciness of curries, but it is delicious with many western foods.

CUCUMBER RAITA

1 cucumber
3 C yogurt
3/4 tsp ground cumin

1 tsp sea salt (optional)
dash cayenne pepper

Peel the cucumber and chop fine. Lightly whip the yogurt. Add the rest of the ingredients and mix well. May be chilled. (Note: if using fresh cumin, the taste is released by roasting gently on an ungreased pan under the broiler for 5 minutes. Grind with a mortar and pestle or in a spice grinder.) Serves 6.

BANANA RAITA

2 ripe bananas
3 C yogurt
dash cayenne pepper

dash cinnamon
dash cardamom
1 tsp fresh lemon juice

Purée one banana with some yogurt in a blender or food processor (or mash by hand). Chop the other banana into 1/2 inch cubes. Combine all ingredients. May be chilled. Serves 6.

CARROT RAITA

1 pint yogurt
1/2 C grated
3 tsp raisins

1 tsp sea salt
1/2 tsp cayenne pepper

Whip yogurt lightly. Wash, scrape and grate carrot. Add all ingredients to the yogurt. May be chilled. Serves 4

WATERCRESS RAITA

1 pint yogurt
1/2 C watercress leaves, chopped fine
1/3 sweet green pepper, chopped fine

1 clove garlic
1 tsp sea salt
1/4 tsp cayenne pepper

Whip yogurt lightly and add the other ingredients. Chill if desired. Serves 4.

NOTES

EGGS AND OMELETS

BOILED EGGS

Examine eggs for cracks before you bring them home. Cracked eggs put you at risk for salmonella poisoning. Also cracked eggs will break in the boiling process. Put eggs in their shells in saucepan with enough cold water to cover. Bring to a boil. Reduce heat to simmer, 3-5 minutes for medium soft-boiled eggs. For HARD-BOILED EGGS, either simmer eggs for 10 minutes; or when the water boils, put a tight-fitting lid on the saucepan, turn off the heat and let stand for 10 minutes. Plunge eggs in cold water to keep yolks from discoloring.

CODDLED EGGS

Remove eggs from refrigerator. Let stand to remove chill. Meanwhile, boil water in both the top and bottom of double boiler. Remove from heat. Drop the shelled eggs gently from a tablespoon into the upper half of the double boiler. Let stand 4-8 minutes over lower half. Do not return to heat.

POACHED EGGS

eggs   1 tsp sea salt
1 T vinegar   [butter or oil]

To a quart of boiling water, add vinegar and salt. Remove from stove. Break the eggs carefully into a saucer one at a time. Slip each egg into the hot water. Or use a greased egg poacher. Cover the pan, set over very low heat, about 5 minutes. Do not boil. Eggs are done when whites are set and a film has formed over the yolks. Remove from pan with a skimmer or slotted spoon.
SERVE: on a foundation of 100% sprouted bread toasted dry or buttered; over Hamburger, p. 166 or steak, p. 164; over broiled eggplant slice, p. 182, on sautéed Portabella mushroom; or on a bed of Rice Pilaf, p. 199.
EGGS BENEDICT Serve poached eggs over a foundation, as above (or a slice of sprouted bread toast). Put a slice of cooked Canadian bacon, or turkey breast slice over foundation, the poached eggs on top of that. Garnish with Hollandaise Sauce, p. 160.

SCRAMBLED EGGS

3 eggs   dash of pepper
1/4 tsp sea salt   1 tsp butter
1/3 C milk or water   1 T chopped fresh parsley

Beat eggs lightly. Add liquid and seasonings. Heat butter to sizzling, add eggs, lower heat to low immediately. The secret to non-stick scrambled eggs is to heat the butter until it is bubbling and just starting to turn brown, before adding the eggs. Either stir the eggs constantly until they are thick. Or, let eggs cook undisturbed until edges begin to set. Using a knife or spatula (not a rubber scraper), nudge edges gently about an inch centerward, allowing liquid egg to fill in the space at the edge. Do not break the surface of the eggs. Transfer to a heated plate (or eat right out of the pan). Garnish with parsley.

FRIED EGGS

eggs   1 tsp butter/egg

Heat butter to sizzling. Gently break eggs into sizzling butter, one at a time. Fry slowly until yolk has a thin white covering. For sunny side up, cook this way until done. For eggs-over-easy, turn eggs with pancake turner, being careful not to break them. Cook another minute or so.

DEVILED EGGS

4 hard-boiled eggs   1/8 tsp cayenne pepper
1/8 tsp sea salt   1/2 tsp prepared mustard
1 T mayonnaise   paprika
                                        [1/2 tsp curry powder, Mrs. Dash]

Remove eggs from shells carefully. Slice in half lengthwise. Remove yolks with a spoon. Mash yolks with other ingredients to form a paste. Refill hollows of egg white with the paste. Sprinkle with paprika for color. [Use other seasoning as desired.]

OMELETS

Personally, I love eggs and think that omelets are a joyous food. If you want to learn to make really good omelets, you may need a lesson from a pro. Teaching you the fine art of making omelets is not in the scope of this book. There are a number of good cookbooks that do that. Julia Child's *Mastering the Art of French Cooking*, vol. 1, has a wonderful chapter on making omelets. Omelets are great for any meal of the day.

BASIC OMELET

2-3 eggs   a grinding of black pepper
1-2 T water   1 T butter
[1/4 tsp sea salt]

Make 2-3 egg omelets individually. They are more tender than an 8-egg omelet and easier to control. They take 1-2 minutes to cook. Have the filling ready. Preheat the plates.

Break eggs into a bowl. Add [salt] and pepper. With a fork, beat eggs just enough to blend thoroughly. (If you are making several individual omelets, break all the eggs into the bowl and season. Use a ladle or cup measure to dole out uniform amounts of egg mixture to the omelet pan. Two large eggs = 6 T = about 2/5 C; three large eggs = 9 T = 3/5 C.)

Heat butter in pan over very high heat, turning the pan to coat bottom and sides with sizzling butter. When the foam has almost subsided and the butter is beginning to turn brown, the pan is hot enough to receive the eggs. Pour in the egg mixture. While sliding the pan back and forth with one hand, spread the egg mixture evenly over the pan with a fork in the other hand. In a few seconds, they will have the consistency of custard. [Add filling at this point.] Tilt the pan 45 degrees away from you. Use the back of the fork to gather the edge of the omelet nearest to you and fold it over toward the other side [covering the filling]. Hold the pan tilted over the heat 1 or 2 seconds more to brown the bottom of the omelet lightly. Do not overcook—the omelet should be soft and creamy at the center.

HERBED OMELET: When eggs are in the bowl, beat in 1 T of fresh herbs. Use your choice of chervil, parsley, chives and/or tarragon. Save some to sprinkle over the top of the finished omelet.

CHEESE: Sprinkle 1-2 T grated Swiss or Parmesan over the cooking eggs at the point indicated in the basic omelet recipe. If you sprinkle cheese over the finished omelet as well, then dot with butter and put under a hot broiler to very quickly brown the cheese.

ASPARAGUS AND CHEESE: Add 2-3 cooked Asparagus Spears, p. 179, 1 T Swiss or Parmesan cheese while omelet is cooking.

CHICKEN, MUSHROOM AND ONION: Use cubed cooked chicken, sliced mushrooms and chopped onion. Sauté briefly to heat, before starting the omelet. Add while omelet is cooking.

SHRIMP, CRAB OR LOBSTER MEAT: Dice meat, add during cooking.

SAUTÉED SPINACH, p. 185, 2-3 T of sautéed spinach. Beat into the egg mixture before cooking.

ONIONS, GREEN PEPPER, TOMATO SAUCE: Chop onions and green pepper, about 1 T of each. Add to cooking omelet, with 1 T of Tomato Sauce, p. 161. Garnish finished omelet with 1 T Tomato Sauce and Parmesan cheese. Broil quickly under very hot broiler to brown cheese.

NOTES

BREADS AND GRAINS

SPROUTED SEEDS AND LEGUMES

All kinds of seeds, grains and legumes can be sprouted as long as they are whole and raw. The seed is a packet, stored as carbohydrate energy, for the plant to draw upon until it grows roots and can feed from the soil, sun, air and water. When the sprout begins to grow, the seed converts to protein and is much more nutritious and, for humans, easier to digest. The basic principle in sprouting seeds is to keep them in a darkish place for a few days, keep them moist in such a way that the water can be changed frequently. Some natural food stores sell a three-tray plastic sprouter that is very easy to use. Canning jars also work well. Plastic lids are made to fit canning jars. The lids are pierced with different size holes for different size seeds. Or using the two-piece Mason jar lids, replace the center of the lid with cheesecloth and screw it down with the rim of the lid. Lay the jars on their sides to give more growing room to the seeds. Largish terra cotta saucers for flowerpots, lined with paper toweling are also good sprouting receptacles.

Wash the seeds. Pick over them to eliminate dirt, stones and dead seeds. Put seeds in the jar or tray with enough water to keep seeds moist. Change the water 2-3 times per day. Cover the receptacle with a dish towel for the first 2-3 days, if necessary, to simulate darkness. The sprouts will begin to grow. Harvest them when the first two leaves form. Wash away seed husks. Start a new batch every few days, so you will have successive batches to munch on.

Broccoli seeds sprouts are all the rage for health, taste, and antioxidants. Soy, mung beans and alfalfa seeds are well known. But all the cresses and mustards make delicious and tangy sprouts. Radish seeds are good, Wheat berries sprout into wheat grass. Barley, rice, chick peas, buckwheat, and dried beans may all be sprouted. When buying seeds for sprouts, look for organic, non-imported sources. All raw fruits, vegetables, herbs, etc., that are imported into this country are treated heavily with pesticides when they get to our docks. (That's why those strawberries that may cause Montezuma's revenge in Mexico usually cause no diarrhea problems when they cross the border into the U.S.)

ESSENE BREAD

wheat berries	onion, chopped fine
parsley, chopped fine	green pepper, chopped fine
celery, chopped fine	carrots, minced

Soak wheat berries in water 15 hours. Pour water off and allow wheat to sit until sprouted. Put sprouted wheat through Champion juicer, vegetable chopper, or meat grinder. Add vegetables, etc. Form into loaf or patties. Bake in the sun or warm place 70-90 degrees until firm. It may be necessary to turn these a few times so that the under side does not get sticky. Bake about 12-24 hours. The longer they set, the more the flavors go through the bread..
VARIATIONS: After the basic Sugar Control Program has ended, add caraway seeds and poppy seeds. Use raisins and dates instead of vegetables.

ESSENE FLATBREAD

This is a recipe I picked up watching TV. Unfortunately, I never got the name of its author. On the other hand, I have tried it several times without success. I'm including it here in case someone can do something with it. If you can, let me know, please.

1 C wheat berries, sprouted	1/2 tsp sea salt
water	

Sprout the wheat, p. 198. This will take 5-7 days. Put the sprouts in a food processor with the salt and enough water to make a consistency a little thicker than whipping cream. Pour out onto a cookie sheet and spread evenly. Bake for 30 hours at 150-160 degrees. You should wind up with a crisp flatbread. Cool. Break into pieces.

FRENCH TOAST

2 slices 100% sprouted bread	cinnamon powder
1 egg	nutmeg
1/4 C milk or yogurt	2 tsps butter

Beat egg with milk. Add cinnamon and a dash of nutmeg. Moisten bread with water (do not soak). Soak the moistened bread in the egg-milk mixture for 5-10 minutes. Heat skillet to hot. Melt butter till sizzling. Put bread in skillet. Turn heat to medium. Brown bread on both sides. Serve with butter.

Suggested accompaniments: cottage cheese; 2 slices bacon; fresh berries or other fruit.

CROUTONS

1-2 slices 100% sprouted bread	1-2 T melted butter

Slice off crust. Slice the bread into 1/2" wide strips. Cut the strips into 1/2" cubes. Place the cubes on a cookie sheet. Paint the tops and sides with the melted butter. Brown lightly for 5 minutes in the upper third of a 450 degree oven.

"MELBA" TOAST

Take a slice of sprouted bread. Slice it in two, so that you have two pieces of bread that look like the original but half as thick. Cut off the crusts. Slice bread into 1" squares or use a cookie cutter to make rounds or other shapes. Follow the recipe for Croutons, above. Use as a foundation for canapés. Cover with cheese, Tuna Salad, p. 177, Guacamole, p. 153, flavored cream cheese, p. 152, Chopped Liver, p. 154, etc.

SPROUTED BREAD CRUMBS

4-5 slices 100% sprouted bread

Stale bread is excellent for bread crumbs. Break bread into smaller chunks and place in blender jar or food processor bowl. Blend or process until bread is in crumbs. This can be done by hand using a hand chopper and bowl (or by a restless person while watching TV). Store excess in freezer in plastic bags. Use in stuffing, meat loaf, etc. Remember to count it in your daily bread ration.

RICE "PILAF"

1 C **whole grain** rice (long, short or medium grain)
3 C water

Wash rice in strainer. Place washed rice in dry heavy skillet over medium heat. Stir, as kernels gently toast. About 5 minutes. If kernels "pop," the heat is too high. Cool and store for later use. Or place toasted rice immediately into 3 C boiling water in heavy saucepan. [Optional: add 1/4-1/2 tsp sea salt and/or 1 T rice or malt vinegar.] Bring to a boil. Cover. Reduce heat to very low. Let simmer covered for 45 minutes. Fluff with a fork a few minutes before completion.

VARIATIONS: Chicken, beef or vegetable broth can be used in place of some or all the water for added flavor [See soup recipes, 187-188.]

Herbs and spices may be added before simmering. Some suggestions are: 1) 1/4 tsp basil, 1/2 tsp oregano and 1/2 thyme. 2) 1/8 tsp saffron or 1/4 tsp turmeric. 3) curry powder or Cajun spices (1/2 tsp or to taste).

CHINESE FRIED RICE

1/4 C olive or peanut oil
5 sliced mushrooms
3 C cooked cold Rice Pilaf, p 199
5 minced scallions

[3/4 C julienned pork, shrimp, or chicken]
3 eggs
1 T Bragg's liquid aminos
[1/4 C minced coriander leaves]

Heat oil in a heavy skillet on high. Quickly sauté mushrooms and set aside. Add more oil to skillet if needed. Turn heat to medium. To hot oil, add rice and scallions. Mix well until warmed. [Add meat.] Make a hollow well in the center of the rice mixture. Remove from heat. Break 3 eggs into well and scramble until partially cooked. Return to heat, mixing eggs and rice well. Sprinkle with Bragg's Liquid Aminos [and coriander leaves].

Add mushrooms. Serve with lightly steamed or sauteéd snow peas. Serves 4-6.

CURRIED RICE

1 T olive oil
1/4 C chopped green pepper
4-5 sliced mushrooms
1/2 C chopped onions

1 clove minced garlic
2 C cooked Rice Pilaf, p 199
1 T curry powder

Heat oil in a large (non-stick) skillet on high. Sauté pepper and mushroom for 1-2 minutes. Remove from skillet and set aside. Sauté onions, garlic and rice together over medium heat, turning often, adding oil if needed. After 2-3 minutes, add curry powder. Continue cooking over medium to low heat, stirring often. When rice mixture is hot, remove from burner. Return to heat for another minute. Serve as an accompaniment to meat, fish or chicken. **VARIATION:** As rice is heating, add 6-8 oz pre-cooked julienned chicken or beef (leftovers) to turn this into a main dish. Serves 3-4.

SPANISH RICE

1 T olive oil
1 C thinly sliced onion
2 C Prepared Tomatoes, p. 185
1/2 tsp sea salt

1-2 tsps paprika
2 seeded green peppers, chopped fine
2 minced garlic cloves
3 C water, Chicken Broth, p. 187, etc.
1 C whole grain rice, brown or white

Heat olive oil in a skillet over high heat, sauté onion until transparent, lowering heat to medium. Add Prepared Tomatoes, 1/2 tsp sea salt, 1-2 tsps paprika, green peppers and garlic. Stir frequently. In 2 qt heavy saucepan, bring 3 C liquid to a boil. Meanwhile pan-brown the rice (p. 199). When rice is browned, add it and other ingredients to the boiling liquid. Stir. Bring to a boil again. Cover. Simmer over low heat 45 minutes.
VARIATION. Sprinkle finished rice with shredded jack or cheddar cheese.
VARIATION. Mince 4 slices bacon. Sauté bacon until crisp. Remove the bacon from pan and set it aside. Sauté the above ingredients (except the rice) in the bacon drippings. Add all ingredients to the rice, including the bacon. Cook as above or steam the rice in a double boiler for an hour. Stir frequently, adding water or Broth as necessary.

BEVERAGES

FROOT SOOPS

orange	apple
grapefruit	pineapple
lemon	pear
lime	melon
banana	kiwi
grapes	other fruits in season

Peel fruits as needed. In a food processor or blender, combine a liquid fruit from the left column (e.g., orange) with one or more solid fruits (apple) in the right column. Liquefy. Experiment with mixtures to find your favorite flavors and textures. Pour into glasses and "drink" with a spoon.

VARIATION: Half fill a large tumbler with seltzer water or Perrier. Pour in froot soop and stir. [Does not count as part of your water ration.]

SMOOTHIE: Serve over shaved ice.

GRAPE KNEE-HIGH

1 C grape juice	1 banana

Blend well. Enjoy.

NOTES

DESSERTS

APPLE SAUCE

2-1/2 lb apples
1 C water
1 T lemon juice

1 cinnamon stick
3 whole cloves
pinch nutmeg

Pare the apples. Remove stem and core. Cut in quarters. Put all ingredients in a saucepan with tight-fitting lid. Bring to a boil. Reduce heat. Cover and simmer for 30 minutes. Remove whole spices and mash apple mixture or purée in blender or food processor. Serve warm or cold. Lasts several days in refrigerator.

Use in place of mint jelly or cranberry sauce with lamb or poultry, if desired.

BAKED APPLE

1 apple per person
butter
1 C boiling water

cinnamon powder
orange juice

Preheat oven to 375 degrees. Grease a shallow ceramic or glass baking dish and put about 1/4 inch of boiling water in the bottom.

Rome apples make good baking apples. Wash apples, remove stem and core to within 1/2 inch of the bottom of the apple. Put a pat of butter in the well with some cinnamon and 1/2 tsp orange juice in the well. Bake for 30 minutes until soft but not mushy.

Eat hot [with cream].

Or chill and serve with Whipped Cream, p. 203.

MANGO-PAPAYA

1 large mango
1 papaya

6 fresh apricots
[1 banana instead of apricots]

Peel the mango and papaya. Put all ingredients in blender or food processor. Blend well. This can also be frozen and eaten, especially in a Donvier ice cream maker.

RICE "DREAM"

2 C cooked Rice Pilaf, p. 199
1/2 to 1 C apple juice
1 apple, cored, chopped

3 slices water-pack or fresh pineapple
   chopped
4 Brazil nuts chopped.

Rice should be chilled. Blend rice and juice well by hand to desired moistness. Add fruit; sprinkle with nuts. Serve in sherbet dishes.

Serve with Whipped Cream, p. 203.

FRUIT AND CHEESE

apples, peaches, pears, grapes

aged cheeses (Swiss, Roquefort, cheddar, etc.)

Arrange slices of fruit and cheese on dessert plates and enjoy.

WHIPPED CREAM

Chill 1/2 pint whipping cream, the bowl and the beater. A chilled copper bowl and a balloon whip are the best tools for whipping cream. Electric equipment rarely produces a smooth light cream, but electric mixers, hand blenders, food processors and electric blenders can all be used. Follow manufacturer's directions.

LIGHTLY BEATEN CREAM: Whip slowly at first, gradually increasing the speed until the beater leaves light mounds on the surface of the cream.

STIFFLY BEATEN CREAM: Beat a little longer, until cream is stiffer and forms soft peaks. Do not beat past this point or cream will turn granular and begin to turn into butter.

Serve over fresh fruit.

NOTES

MENUS, ETC.

❖ ⌘ ❖

ABOUT MENU SUGGESTIONS

❖ ⌘ ❖

On the following pages, you will find menu suggestions for breakfast, lunch, dinner, snacks and parties, followed by restaurant and eating out strategies and tactics. The menus are simply ideas for combining recipes in this book (and the recipes are also ideas for you to be able to take other recipes and adapt them).

Portion sizes are up to you and your appetite. One purpose of the Sugar Control Program is to get your metabolism working normally. Eating is a way to do this. When you restrict calorie intake, two negative things happen: 1) You lose muscle tissue and since muscle tissue burns calories, your metabolism slows; and 2) Your body thinks famine is at hand and your pancreas gears up to store as many calories as possible as fat to draw upon later.

Be careful in combining meals that you observe the two-slice per day limit on bread. Bread includes: 100 percent sprouted bread, "Melba" toast, croutons and bread crumbs.

❖ ⌘ ❖

P.S.—WHAT'S WRONG WITH DIET SODA, ANYWAY?

❖ ⌘ ❖

It contains caffeine to kick the adrenal glands and raise the blood sugar, so it's an upper, then a downer, and it is addictive. Artificial sweeteners activate the blood-sugar control mechanisms and cause allergies and free radicals (aging). Caramel-coloring in colas causes cancer, and the soda ingredient glycol is also used in anti-freeze in car radiators. The fizz is created by phosphoric acid, which upsets both the calcium-phosphorus balance (causing osteoporosis) and the hydrochloric-acid balance (burning the lining of your stomach and interfering with digestion, thus causing bloating and gas). Carbon dioxide (a gas you breathe out to get rid of) is also used to make the fizz. Aluminum particles from the soda-can get into the soda. Aluminum is associated with Alzheimer's disease and breast cancer. High sodium content leads to edema, causing water-weight gain. Soda pop kills normal intestinal bacteria, paving the way for candidiasis.

If you leave a tooth in a glass of cola overnight—instead of under the pillow for the tooth fairy—it will have disintegrated by morning and leave nothing behind.

And if you are drinking soda, you are probably not drinking water. Santé!

MENUS

The following menus are just suggestions for sample meals. I usually find that people are most perplexed about breakfast, snacks and restaurant eating. Just remember:

1. Eat nine oz of red meat (beef, bison, venison) per week. You can eat it in one serving or 3 or 4 smaller portions.
2. Eat only 2 slices of 100 percent sprouted bread/day, so don't combine meals that go over the bread limit on the same day.

BREAKFASTS

1/2 grapefruit
2 Poached Eggs on
2 slices 100% sprouted bread
herbal tea or decaf coffee or tea

Omelet of your choice
1/2 C strawberries
1/2 banana, sliced
1/2 C Rice Pilaf
herbal tea or decaf coffee or tea

1 bowl of Rice Pilaf, (warm or cold)
mixed with 1/2 C plain yogurt,
1/2 diced apple, and
2 chopped Brazil nuts
herbal tea or decaf coffee or tea

2 medium Boiled Eggs
1 breakfast steak or hamburger
2-3 slices tomato
herbal tea or decaf coffee or tea

2 slices French Toast with butter
1 Poached Egg
1/2 C strawberries or blueberries
herbal tea or decaf coffee or tea

1-2 oz melted aged cheese on
1 slice 100% sprouted bread, with
mustard and tomato [and/or onion] slice

1 bowl Rice Pilaf
with chopped apple
herbal tea or decaf coffee or tea

4 oz chicken chopped into
bowl of Rice Pilaf with
1/4 C plain yogurt and
5-6 raw cashews
herbal tea or decaf coffee or tea

fruit plate (cantaloupe, grapes, berries,
banana slices, kiwi slices, apples,
Brazil nuts)
1/2 C cottage cheese or yogurt
1 slice 100% sprouted toast
[with butter] or 1/2 C Rice Pilaf
herbal tea or decaf coffee or tea

Eggs Benedict
cantaloupe and watermelon slices
herbal tea or decaf coffee or tea

rib-eye steak
tomato slices
herbal tea or decaf coffee or tea

LUNCHES

Chef's Salad
Creamy Vinaigrette Dressing
1/2 C Rice Pilaf

1/2 C Tuna Salad on a bed of lettuce
with 1/2 sliced avocado & tomato
wedges
1/2 C Rice Pilaf
balsamic vinegar and olive oil dressing

1-2 Hamburgers on
1 slice 100% sprouted bread
with sautéed or grilled
onions and mushrooms
Garden Salad with French Dressing

1/2 Roast Chicken or parts
Broccoli and Olives
1/2 C Rice Pilaf
Garden Salad with French Dressing

Chicken Vegetable Soup
turkey and Cole Slaw sandwich
with [mayonnaise] & mustard on the
100% sprouted bread

bowl of Gazpacho
1/2 Avocado Stuffed with Shrimp or
Scallops
Beans with Butter and Lemon
2 "Melba" Toast

Fillet of Sole
Greek Salad
1/2 C Rice Pilaf

bowl of Chili Con Carne
over Rice Pilaf
Tossed Salad
with Parsley-Garlic Dressing

Chopped Liver on
celery stalks and
2 "Melba" Toast
Salad Niçoise

Meat Loaf
Tossed Salad with dressing
Broccoli

DINNERS

rib-eye beef Steak grilled
with onions, mushrooms and
sweet red peppers
Broccoli, Zucchini, Onion medley
Curried Rice

chicken breast
Curried Rice
Cucumber Raita
Carrots and Green Beans

Shrimp, Crab or Lobster Omelet
Tossed Salad
1/2 C Rice Pilaf
Asparagus

Roast Leg of Lamb
Yogurt Mint Sauce
Broccoli and Olives
Rice Pilaf or Curry

Chinese Chicken Egg Drop Soup
stir-fried chicken breast
with onions and broccoli
chicken broth, water, white wine sauce
cashews
over Rice Pilaf

Eggplant-Lamb Casserole
Green Beans with slivered Brazil nuts
Rice Pilaf

Beef Stew
Rice Pilaf
Zucchini and Onions
1 slice 100% sprouted bread

Cold Cream of Sorrel Soup
Caesar Salad
cold Roast Chicken
1/2 C Rice Pilaf

Boiled Artichoke
with butter and lemon juice
Fish with Vegetables
Tossed Salad with Dressing
Rice Pilaf

Seafood Risotto
Zucchini and mixed vegetables

Seafood Gumbo
with Rice Pilaf
1 slice 100% sprouted bread
or "Melba" Toast

Veal Piccata
Asparagus
String Beans with pimentos
Rice Pilaf

Ratatouille
Shish Kebab
Rice Pilaf

Tossed Salad with Dressing
Baked Salmon Fillet
Green Beans, Carrots and Onion
Rice Pilaf

Chicken Vegetable Soup
Chicken Parmesan
Broccoli with slivered Brazil nuts
Rice Pilaf

Gazpacho Soup
Ceviche
Rice Pilaf
Guacamole
Green Beans

SNACKS

Avocado Stuffed with Shrimps or
Scallops

Celery ribs or other crudités with:
    Chopped Liver
    Tuna Salad
    Turkey or Chicken Salad

1-2 Deviled Eggs

1-2 oz hard aged cheese
1 apple
1/4 C raw cashews

Hard-Boiled Egg
celery and carrot sticks

2-3 oz of chicken, turkey, roast
beef, cheese, etc.

1/4-1/2 C cottage cheese
or plain yogurt
with fresh fruit

1 glass raw certified milk

1-2 oz hard Swiss, Jahrlsberg,
provolone, muenster cheese, etc.,
melted on 1 slice of 100% sprouted
bread coated with mustard and tomato
slice. Sprinkle with Vegesalt, Mrs.
Dash, etc.

handful of raw Brazil nuts or cashews
1 apple or pear
1/2 C of grapes

Shrimp Cocktail

Ceviche

small Chef's Salad

a cup of Soup (see recipes)
with 2-3 pieces "Melba" Toast

1/2 C Rice Pilaf
with 1/4 C plain yogurt
5-6 raw cashews
1/2 chopped apple

1-2 oz cheese melted on
1 slice 100% sprouted bread with
mustard and a tomato slice. Sprinkle
cheese with Mrs. Dash or other combo
spice

PARTY FARE

SIT-DOWN DINNER OR BUFFET

avgolemono soup (3 C hot Chicken Broth, p. 187, poured slowly into 2 eggs beaten with
juice of 1 lemon, add 3/4 C Rice Pilaf, p. 199. Serve immediately.)

Stuffed Grape Leaves
Cucumber and Carrot Raitas
Ratatouille
Greek Salad
Shish Kebab

Rice Pilaf or Curried Rice
Baked Apples [with Whipped Cream]
sparkling mineral water

CANAPÉ/HORS D'OEUVRE PARTY

DIPS
    Avocado
    Caviar
    Clam
    Sour Cream
crudités
"Melba" Rounds
[chips and crackers—if you can resist
eating them yourself]
Shrimp Cocktail
Chopped Liver II

Ceviche
Deviled Eggs
cheese platter
fresh fruit bowl or plate—strawberries,
blueberries, kiwi slices, banana slices,
orange sections, tangerine sections,
chopped apple, melon balls, etc.—lemon
juice to prevent browning of cut fruit
sparkling unsweetened mineral waters
Fruit Smoothies

TIPS AND TRICKS

- Plan.

- Make shopping lists from the recipes that you plan to use. Stock up on supplies of Program foods.

- Keep a supply of snacking foods on hand: cold leftover meat, chicken, turkey, tuna salad, chopped liver, hard-boiled eggs, crudités, cold leftover cooked vegetables, marinated salad, "Melba" toast, cheese, cashews, Brazil nuts, etc.

- Get rid of non-Program foods. Give them to people you don't like.

- Get the whole family on the Program. That makes it much easier to plan, cook and shop. The support will make it much easier for the person actually on the program to stay on it. And everyone else will feel better as well.

- Carry snacks and other necessary food with you when you travel. Use an insulated bag with an ice- or hot-pack if necessary.

- If you work outside the home, use after-dinner time to do advance steps on the next night's dinner.

- Cook extra food. Plan for using leftovers as snacks or in casseroles, etc. Make extra portions to freeze in serving-size containers. Freeze chicken, beef and/or vegetable broth in half-pint containers for use in recipes or to make yourself egg-drop soup for lunch.

- Salad-making can be a lot of work. You can prepare enough salad to last for two to three days. Do not dress the extra salad (unless, like me, you like marinated salad). Store in a plastic bag. Squeeze out all the air and refrigerate. Add the tomatoes later.

- Cook lots of Rice "Pilaf." Eat it hot right after cooking. Cold rice can be used in stir-fried recipes, Curried Rice, Chinese Fried Rice, or eaten cold for breakfast cereal or in "pasta" salad.

- Use a pint- or quart-sized container for drinking water. Twelve glasses of water (for a 150-pound person) is easier to drink if it's only 3 quarts.

DINING OUT?—PLANNING COUNTS!

Dining out is a fact of life in our very mobile, very busy society. If you are going to be healthy and stay healthy, you have to create strategies to deal with it effectively. Planning is the key to being in control.

There are many different kinds of eating out situations. Many of them require different strategies:

RESTAURANT EATING, FROM GOURMET TO FAST FOOD
DINNER AT A FRIEND'S, THE BOSS'S, YOUR AUNT'S
THE BIRTHDAY PARTY, THE WEDDING
THE BAR/BAS MITZVAH
RACING TO THE AIRPORT RIGHT FROM THE OFFICE
STAYING IN A HOTEL FOR A CONFERENCE WITH SET MEALS

I heard recently on *Entertainment Tonight*—the word direct from Hollywood—that protein is in for dieting and health. Thank you—it's been 20 years of carbohydrate is king with people getting sicker and sicker. But I've noticed lately that it's becoming easier to find Sugar Control meals when dining out. I was going to a Toastmasters luncheon recently. In the 10 years I've been a member, the meals at functions are always a sugarholic's delight (or nightmare). This time, I called the hotel to see what kind of special meal I could arrange. But it turned out they were serving a buffet of salad and fresh turkey and ham, deli meats, deviled eggs and cheese—all on the Sugar Control Program. I brought roast beef slices to get me through snack times and fresh fruit for dessert after lunch.

The easiest place to dine out is at a **gourmet restaurant**: Start with a shrimp cocktail, roasted peppers, an antipasto, or paté. Follow the appetizer with a salad. Most salad dressings contain sugar, so choose oil and vinegar dressing. Gourmet restaurants can supply you with balsamic (sugar free) vinegar and olive oil. A little crumbled blue cheese, fresh ground pepper and garlic and you're in business. A steak, roast chicken, sautéed or broiled fish, shrimp scampi are all good choices. Fresh fruit and aged cheese make a great dessert. Service is a by-word at good restaurants and the chef can usually cater to your needs. Veal piccata, for example, is normally made with some flour in the recipe, but it can easily be made by dredging the veal in beaten egg. The sauce will not be quite as thick. You can call ahead and discuss your requirements or just ask when you arrive.

Beware of **Chinese restaurants**. Many foods are coated with flour and sautéed or deep-fat fried. Sauces are made of soy sauce and almost always contain sugar. Avoid the rice; it is refined. When refined rice was introduced to China, only the wealthy elite could afford it—and they came down with beriberi. Cornstarch is used as a thickener for soups and sauces. Even MSG acts as sugar for people with reactive hypoglycemia. Many restaurants now serve a steamed diet menu, or you can ask the chef to cook to your specifications. Dragon and Phoenix soup, a clear broth with chicken and seafood and an egg-white thickener, is usually acceptable (leave out the cornstarch). Chicken with cashews works if they throw the cashews on at the end, so they don't actually cook them. Be careful of the sauces. Suggest chicken broth, white wine, lemon juice for sauce—no sugar, no cornstarch, no MSG. Stir-fried scallops and whole fish are good choices.

How about a place like Denny's? For breakfast, an omelet or steak-and-eggs will work (not chicken-fried). Hold the potatoes and bread. Bring your own bread if you like—most restaurants (except in NY) will toast it for you and supply butter. For lunch, a salad with chicken or fish, unbreaded, please. For dinner, roast beef and salad. Hold the vegetables—they're frozen. One time, I ordered cole slaw—which I'm not all that fond of—but it was the only thing available. One bite was enough to tell me it was full of sugar. Fresh fruit or fruit cup (no syrup) can be eaten at any meal.

At the **salad bar,** go for permitted vegetables: lettuce, spinach, green peppers, tomatoes, onions, mushrooms, grated carrot, cucumbers, broccoli, sprouts, radishes. Add hard-boiled egg and grated cheese. Use oil and vinegar or oil and lemon juice for dressing. I was having a particularly bland salad in a mid-range hotel restaurant one time. I made a tangy salad dressing by mixing 1 T oil with 2 tsp vinegar and lemon juice with fresh pepper and 1/2 tsp of prepared mustard. I mixed it on a saucer and poured it on the salad with a little Parmesan cheese.

Salad bars and buffets are not easy for many people. Have you ever seen a film where the baseball batter can't hit the ball, time after time? Then all of a sudden, here comes the baseball—moving slowly and as large as a basketball. Who could possibly miss? Try this strategy:

> THINK OF THE FOODS THAT ARE GOOD FOR YOU. VISUALIZE THEM AS BIG, VERY COLORFUL AND RIGHT IN FRONT OF YOU. THEN IMAGINE THE FOODS THAT ARE NOT ON YOUR PROGRAM. SEE THEM SMALL AND DIM AND FAR AWAY AND DOWN IN THE CORNER, WHERE YOU CAN FORGET ABOUT THEM. AND MAYBE THEY EVEN SMELL BAD.

When **traveling,** if possible, pack a small insulated food bag. I have a soft light-weight bag made of that NASA reflective material. There are a number of great bags and packs on the market. I pack hard-boiled eggs, cheese, turkey, sometimes fruit, 100 percent sprouted bread. And I include a small blue-ice pack. I pack the eggs in a Rubbermaid container. It doubles as an ice container when my blue-ice pack has lost its cool. In hotel rooms with no refrigerators, I chill the blue-ice in the ice bucket or sink for 6-8 hours, then put it in the insulated bag. I keep alternating between the blue ice and the Rubbermaid container to keep the food cool. Where there's an honor bar, I remove some things to make room for my food. I try to take enough food to fill in where meals are set and I can only eat half of what they are serving, or if I need snacks. I usually carry herbal tea bags with me as well.

The same insulated bag can brown-bag great lunches to **work**. You can bring hot or cold meals. Make enough at dinner so there are good leftovers to eat with little extra work.

On **airplanes**, people look at me enviously while they try to deal with airplane food. My favorite is to stop at a Japanese restaurant on the way to the airport and get sashimi to go with plenty of ginger and horseradish, or I brown-bag it.

Here's an outrageous **rice** recipe for hotel rooms. Pan brown the rice at home. Allow it to cool and pack it for traveling, mixed with a little sea salt and herbs, if desired. Bring a 1-pint wide-mouth Thermos along. Before bed, put 1/2 C dry rice in the Thermos, cover with 1 1/2 C boiling water (make it in the coffee maker in your room or get it from the restaurant). Turn the Thermos occasionally to make sure the rice is soaked through. In the morning, you will have warm cooked rice for breakfast. If you are at the Hampton Inn, you can get milk and fruit too at the breakfast bar to add to your rice.

For **parties**, I suggest that you eat before you go, so you arrive in control of your appetite. Think of yourself as the designated driver—in terms of eating sanely. Actually there have been instances of people arrested on DUI's. They failed the blood test, even though they were not drinking at all. However, with a little help from candidiasis, the sugar they were eating was being rapidly converted to alcohol in their systems.

Bring food offerings that are on your program to the party. Bring sparkling mineral water to drink. Call ahead and discuss your dietary requirements with the host. S/he may be serving things you can eat—or may be willing to serve them. But you need to spell everything out in detail. One of my patients who had irritable bowel syndrome was on the Sugar Control Program combined with some other restrictions. She was invited to her niece's graduation party. Her sister-in-law said there would be no problem—she was serving chicken. When my patient arrived, it turned out the chicken was broasted. My patient tried to remove the skin, but chemicals in the oil had penetrated deep into the flesh and she was ill for several days.

A good strategy for many situations is to go to the supermarket for dinner. Many markets now have salad and food bars. At the deli counter, you can often buy a rotisseried chicken, roast beef or turkey cooked at the market (as opposed to the formed packaged meat, which contains sugar, MSG and a whole range of interesting chemicals).

YES, YES FOOD LISTS

RED MEAT*

ANTELOPE	CARIBOU	OSTRICH
BEEF	ELK	REINDEER
BISON	LAMB**	VENISON
BEAR	LIVER	
BUFFALO	MOOSE	

WHITE MEAT

ALLIGATOR	KIDNEY	SWEETBREADS
BACON	LAMB**	TRIPE
BEAVER	PORK	WOODCHUCK
BRAINS, ALL KINDS	RABBIT	
FROG'S LEGS	SQUIRREL	
GOAT	SNAILS	
HAM	RATTLESNAKE	

*Unlimited amounts, but at least 9 oz red meat per week (in one serving or three 3-oz. servings, or four 2-oz. servings. More, if desired). **Lamb is considered red meat for those of Mediterranean or New Zealand heritage.

DAIRY

BUTTER	FETA	PROVOLONE
BUTTERMILK	GORGONZOLA	RICOTTA
	GOUDA	ROMANO
CHEESES	GRUYERE	ROQUEFORT
AMERICAN	HAVARTI	SMOKED CHEESES
BRIE	JACK	STILTON
BLUE CHEESE	JAHRLSBERG	SWISS
CAMEMBERT	LIMBURGER	
CHEDDAR	LORRAINE	CREAM
CHEVRE	MONTEREY JACK	MILK (cow, goat,
COLBY	MOZZARELLA	sheep)
COTTAGE	MUENSTER	SOUR CREAM
CREAM	PARMESAN	YOGURT, PLAIN
EDAM	PORT SALUT	
FARMER'S	PROCESSED CHEESE	

POULTRY

CHICKEN	DUCKLING	PHEASANT
CORNISH GAME	GOOSE	TURKEY
HEN	GROUSE	
DUCK	GUINEA FOWL	

SEAFOOD

ABALONE	HADDOCK	RED SNAPPER
AHI AHI	HAKE	SABLEFISH
ALBACORE	HALIBUT	SALMON
ALEWIFE	HERRING	SARDINES
ANCHOVY	INCONNU	SCALLOPS
BARRACUDA	JACK	SCUP
BASS	KINGFISH	SEA URCHIN
BLUEFISH	LINGCOD	SHAD
BONITO	LOBSTER	SHARK
BUFFALOFISH	LOX	SHEEPFISH
BULLHEAD, BLACK	MACKEREL	SHEEPSHEAD
BUTTERHEAD	MAHI MAHI	SHRIMP
CARP	MENHADEN	SISCOWET
CHUB	MONKFISH	SKATE
CLAMS	MULLET	SMELT
COD FISH	MUSKELUNGE	SNAPPER
CONCH	MUSSELS	SOLE
CRAB	NOVA	SPOT
CRAPPIE	OCTOPUS	SQUID
CRAYFISH	ORANGE ROUGHY	SWORDFISH
CROAKER	OYSTER	TAUTOG
DOLPHIN FISH	PERCH	TERRAPIN
DRUM	PICKEREL	TURTLE
DUCK	PIKE	TILEFISH
EEL, RAW &	POLLOCK	TOMCOD
SMOKED	PORGY	TUNA
FINNAN HADDIE	PRAWNS	WHITEFISH
FLATFISH	QUAHOG	WHITING
FLOUNDER	RAJA FISH	WRECKFISH
GROUPER	REDFISH	YELLOWTAIL

EGGS

CHICKEN	FISH ROE	SHAD ROE
CAVIAR	GOOSE	SALMON
DUCK	OSTRICH	TURKEY
	ROE	

UNLIMITED VEGETABLES

ALFALFA SPROUTS	DAIKON	PICKLES, DILL
ARTICHOKES	DANDELION	POKE GREENS
ASPARAGUS	GREENS	RADISHES
BEAN SPROUTS	FLOWERS, EDIBLE	SAUERKRAUT
BEANS, GREEN	EGGPLANT	SNOW PEAS
BEET GREENS	ENDIVE	SOUR GRASS
BIBB LETTUCE	ESCAROLE	SWISS CHARD
BOSTON LETTUCE	FENNEL	SPINACH
BOK CHOY	FIDDLEFERN	SQUASH, SUMMER
BROCCOLI	FINOCCHIO	Casserta
BRUSSELS SPROUTS	GARLIC	Chayote
CACTUS	GHERKINS	Cocozelle
CARROTS, raw	GRAPE LEAVES	Cymling
CAPERS	HERBS	Pattypan
CABBAGE	KALE	Scalloped
CELERY	KOHLRABI	Spaghetti
CHICORY	LEAF LETTUCE	Straight, Crookneck
CHILI PEPPERS	LETTUCE	Vegetable Marrows
CHINESE CABBAGE	MUSHROOMS	Zucchini
CHIVES	MUSTARD GREENS	STRING BEANS
COLLARD GREENS	NASTURTIUM, leaves	TOMATOES, raw
COMFREY LEAVES	ONIONS, raw	TRUFFLES
CORIANDER LEAVES	PARSLEY	TURNIP GREENS
COS LETTUCE	PEPPERS, green or red	WATERCRESS
CUCUMBER	PIMENTOS	WINTER MELON

MISCELLANEOUS

100% SPROUTED BREAD	WHOLE GRAIN RICE–LONG,
BRAGG'S LIQUID AMINOS	SHORT, BASMATI
MUSTARD, PREPARED	WINE, COOKED IN FOODS

LIMITED VEGETABLES

(4-6 oz portions 4-6 times per week)

		SQUASH, contd
ARTICHOKE HEART	PEAS	Des Moines
BAMBOO SHOOTS	PUMPKIN	Gold Nugget
BRUSSELS SPROUTS	RUTABAGAS	Hubbard
CARROTS, cooked	SCALLIONS	Peppercorn
CELERIAC	SQUASH (WINTER)	Table Queen
LEEKS	Acorn	Danish Turban
OKRA	Banana	Turks Turban
ONIONS, cooked	Butternut	
OYSTER PLANT	Calabaza	

FRUIT

APPLES	CRANBERRIES	ORANGES
APRICOTS	FIGS, FRESH	PAPAYA
AVOCADO	GRAPEFRUIT	PAW PAW
BANANA	GRAPES	PEACHES
BLACKBERRIES	GUAVA	PEARS
BLUEBERRIES	HONEYDEW MELON	PINEAPPLE, FRESH
BOYSENBERRIES	KIWI	PLUMS
CAIMITO	LEMONS	RASPBERRIES, RED
CANTALOUPE	LOGANBERRIES	STRAWBERRIES
CASABA MELON	MANGO	TANGERINE
CHERRIES	MUSKMELON	UGLI FRUIT
COCONUT, FRESH	NECTARINES	WATERMELON

FATS AND OILS

ALMOND OIL	EVENING PRIMROSE	RICE OIL
BUTTER	GHEE	SAFFLOWER OIL
CANOLA OIL	OLIVE OIL	SESAME SEED OIL
MARINE OILS	PEANUT OIL	WALNUT OIL

NO-NO FOOD LISTS

STARCHY VEGETABLES

ARROWROOT
BURDOCK ROOT
ARTICHOKE,
JERUSALEM
BEETS

CAULIFLOWER
CORN
CORNSTARCH
JICAMA
PARSNIPS

POTATO, WHITE
POTATO STARCH
RUTABAGA
SWEET POTATO
YAMS

SWEETENERS

ANY -OSE
CAROB
CORN SYRUP
CYCLAMATES
DEXTROSE
EQUAL
FRUIT-JUICE-
CONCENTRATE

ALL FRUIT SPREADS
FRUCTOSE
GLUCOSE
HONEY
MALT
MANNITOL
MAPLE SYRUP
MOLASSES

MSG
NUTRASWEET
RICE SYRUP
SACCHARIN
SORBITOL
SUCROSE
SUGAR
SWEET 'N LOW

SWEETENED OR REFINED FLOUR FOODS

BAGELS
BARBECUE SAUCE
BISCUITS
BREAD
BREATH MINTS
CAKE
CANDY
CEREALS
CHEWING GUM
CRACKERS

DIET SODA POP
FROZEN FOODS
ICE CREAM
KETCHUP
MAYONNAISE
NUT BUTTERS
RICE CRACKERS
RICE DREAM
MORTON'S SALT
SALAD DRESSING

SCRAPPLE
SODA POP
SOY MILK
SOY PRODUCTS
WHEAT PRODUCTS
WORCESTERSHIRE
SAUCE
YOGURT, FROZEN
YOGURT,
FLAVORED

NO-NO FOOD LIST (CONTD)

SEEDS, NUTS

ALMONDS	LENTILS	PEAS, SPLIT
AMARANTH	MILLET	RICE, REFINED
BULGUR	NORTHERN BEANS	RICE, CHINESE
BEANS, BAKED	OATMEAL	RICE, JAPANESE
BEANS, DRIED	OATS, STEELCUT	SOY, TOFU
CHICK PEAS	PINTO BEANS	TRITICALE
KIDNEY BEANS	QUINOA	

ALCOHOLIC BEVERAGES

ALES	LIQUEURS	WHISKY
BEER	MALT DRINKS	WINES
BOURBON	MIXED DRINKS	
BRANDY	SCOTCH	

METRIC CONVERSIONS OF VOLUME

250 mL replaces 1 cup

175 mL replaces 3/4 cup

160 mL replaces 2/3 cup

125 mL replaces 1/2 cup

75 mL replaces 1/3 cup

50 mL replaces 1/4 cup

25 mL replaces 2 tablespoons

15 mL replaces 1 tablespoon

5 mL replaces 1 teaspoon

2 mL replaces 1/2 teaspoon

1 mL replaces 1/4 teaspoon

SPECIAL FOODS AND INGREDIENTS

Bragg's Liquid Aminos
Live Food Products
Santa Barbara CA
805-968-1028

a soy protein product
1/2 tsp contains 275 mg protein; 50 mg
carbohydrate; 110 mg sodium; 2 calories

Food For Life Breads
29991 E Doherty St.
Corona CA 91719

100% sprouted flourless breads; great breads
contains some sweetener, but the yeast has
converted it—well tolerated—natural food
stores

Lifestream Natural Foods
9100 Van Horne Way
Richmond, BC Canada V6X 1W3

Essene bread—a heavy chewy bread, an
acquired taste, but I've acquired love it—
I love this bread—natural food stores

whole grain rice

health food and specialty stores, River Rice

MAIL ORDER SPECIALTY FOODS & APPLIANCES

Forbes Buffalo Acres
Rt. 388 & 108
New Castle PA 16101-9701
724-658-4082

prime, organic, USDA, bison meat
lower fat and calories than beef

Colman's
1-800-442-8666

organic meat

Maverick
1-800-49-RANCH

organic beef, bison, lamb

Jamar Foods
1-800-59-STEAK

natural meat, poultry and seafood
certified Belgian blue beef

Walnut Acres Organic Farms
Penns Creek PA
1-800-433-3998

rice, organic meats, seasonings, etc.

Royal Ostrich Farm
RR9 Box 43
Greensburg PA 15601
1-800-274-3263 (M-F 8-5 ET)

commercially raised ostrich
low fat, lower calories than white
meat chicken
also information & recipes

Essential Water and Air
1701 West Walnut Hill Lane
Irving TX 75038
1-800-964-4303
http://www.ewater.com

shower filters, travel-sized to whole-house
reverse osmosis water purification systems,
air filters—free-standing and central
Professional discounts available.
email: Fred@ewater.com

SPECIAL TRAINING

The TBM organization has developed a special self-help health course for lay people. It
is called Environmental Stress Management (ESM). For more information, about classes
near you, call 1-800-426-4ESM.

❖ ⌘ ❖

BIBLIOGRAPHY

❖ ⌘ ❖

Atkins, Robert C., M.D. *Dr. Atkins' Diet Revolution*. NY: Bantam Books, 1972, 1985. The original low-carbohydrate diet for weight loss has many things in common with the TBM Sugar Control Program.

_____*Dr. Atkins'* New *Diet Revolution*. NY: M. Evans & Co., 1992.

_____ and Fran Gare, M.S. *Dr. Atkins* ' New *Diet Cookbook*. NY: M. Evans & Co., 1994. Good recipe ideas, but skip the ones with artificial sweeteners.

Barnes, Broda, M.D. and Lawrence Galton. *Hypothyroidism: The Unsuspected Illness*. New York: Thomas Y. Crowell, 1976.

Batmanghelidj, F., M.D. *Your Body's Many Cries for Water*. POB 3189, Falls Church, VA: Global Health Solutions, 1992. A unique and important perspective on the importance of water to health.

Bieler, Henry G., M.D. *Food Is Your Best Medicine*. NY: Vintage Books, 1972; NY: Random House, 1965. A classic in nutrition.

Child, Julia, Simone Beck and Louisette Bertholle. *Mastering the Art of French Cooking,* NY: Alfred Knopf, 1961. Great gourmet recipes and simple instructions for even the novice chef.

_____ and Simone Beck. *Mastering the Art of French Cooking, Vol. 2*. NY: Alfred Knopf, 1970. More of the same.

Craig Claiborne. *The New York Times Cookbook*. NY: Harper & Row, 1961.

Crook, William G. *The Yeast Connection*. Jackson, TN 38301: Professional Books, POB 3494, 2nd ed, 1984. Candidiasis from the holistic medical perspective.

Davis, Adele. *Let's Eat Right To Keep Fit*. NY: Penguin Books, 1970. NY: Harcourt Brace, 1954. The mother of good nutrition books.

Diamond, John, M.D. *Behavioral Kinesiology*. New York: Harper and Row, 1979.

Dufty, William. *Sugar Blues*. NY: Warner Books, 1976. How a very sick writer kicked the sugar habit and regained his health. Very readable.

Eades, Michael R., M.D., and Mary Dan Eades, M.D. *Protein Power*. NY: Bantam, 1996. Weight-loss protein diet.

Eaton, S. Boyd, M.D., Marjorie Shostak and Melvin Konner, M.D., Ph.D. *The Paleolithic Prescription, A Program of Diet and Exercise and a Design for Living*. NY: Harper & Row, 1988.

Environmental Stress Management. Sandy, UT: ESM, 1995. Textbook available only with ESM classes. TBM adapted for lay people into a self-help health-care program. Call 1-800-426-4ESM for a class near you.

Fallon, Sally. *Nourishing Traditions*. 3368 F Governor Dr., San Diego CA 92122: Promotion Publishing, 1995. 1-800-231-1776. Excellent health-oriented book.

Pierre Franey. *Low-Calorie Gourmet*. NY: 𝕿𝖎𝖒𝖊𝖘 Books, 1984.

Fredericks, Carlton, M.D., and Herman Goodman. *Low Blood Sugar and You.*. NY: Constellation, Intl., 1969. The father of popular information about sugar and health.

Gittleman, Ann-Louise, M.S, with Templeton and Versace. *Your Body Knows Best*. NY: Pocket Books, 1996, 1997. No one diet is right for everyone.

Hawkins, David R., M.D. *Power vs Force*: The Hidden Determinants of Human Behavior. SR 2, Box 817, Sedona, AZ 86336: Veritas Publishing. A psychiatrist explores the neuromuscular reflex test and consciousness.

Rachel F. Heller, Ph.D., and Richard F. Heller, M.D. *The Carbohydrate Addict's Diet*. NY: Signet, 1993.

Lappé, Frances Moore. *Diet for a Small Planet*. NY: Ballantine Books, 1971. Revised, 1975. How to combine vegetable proteins to make complete proteins for humans.

McCully, Kilmer S., M.D. *The Homocysteine Revolution*. POB 876, New Canaan, CT 06840-0876: Keats Publishing, 1997. Phone orders 1-800-858-7014.

Miller, Bruce B., M.D. *The Nutrition Guarantee: A Complete Guide to Better Health, Disease Prevention and Treatment*. The Summit Publishing Group, 1998.

Netzer, Corinne T. *Encyclopedia of Food Values*. New York: Dell, 1992. Calorie and macronutrient counts, cholesterol, sodium and fiber.

Page, Melvin E., D.D.S., and Leon Abrams, Jr. *Your Body Is Your Best Doctor*. Price Pottenger Foundation, PO Box 2614, La Mesa CA 91943. Phone 619-574-7763. A sensible nutrition book, for a change, with information on endocrine typing and diet.

Pressman, Alan H., D.C, Ph.D., with Shiela Buff *The Complete Idiot's Guide to Vitamins and Minerals*. NY: Alpha Books, 1997. Great reference.

Price, Weston A., D.D.S. *Nutrition and Physical Degeneration*. 1939. Available from the Price Pottenger Nutrition Foundation, PO Box 2614, La Mesa CA 91943. Phone 619-574-7763. The classic study of supremely healthy isolated aboriginal populations and the devastating effect of processed foods on their health. Even more important today that in 1939.

Rombauer, Irma S. And Marian Rombauer Becker. *The Joy of Cooking*. Indianapolis: Bobbs-Merrill, 1931, 1975. Everything you wanted to know about cooking and eating. A joy to read as well as cook from.

Schmid, Ronald, N.D. *Traditional Foods Are Your Best Medicine*. Another sensible nutrition book, based on the Weston Price studies. Look to the healthiest foods of your ethnic background for clues on what is best for you to eat. Available from International Foundation for Nutrition and Health, 3963 Mission Blvd., San Diego CA 92109. (619) 488-8932.

Sears, Barry, Ph.D. *Enter the Zone*. NY: Harper Collins, 1995. The dangers of the high-carbohydrate/low-fat diets and a novel way to balance macro-nutrients.

Tannahill, Reay. *Food in History*. NY: Crown, 1988, 1973. How man's search for food has influenced history, religion and society.

Watt, Bernice K. and Annabel Merrill. *Composition of Foods*. Agriculture Handbook No. 8, Washington, D.C.: United States Department of Agriculture, 1963. Calories, macro- and micronutrient content of foods.

Williams, Roger. *Biochemical Individuality*. NY: Wiley & Sons, 1956.

_____*Nutrition in a Nutshell*. NY: Dolphin Books, 1962. A nutritional pioneer (discoverer of pantothenic acid) writes about human nutrition and biochemical individuality. Genetics determine nutritional needs.

PERIODICALS

Alternatives. Dr. David G. Williams. POB 829, Ingram TX 78025.

Alternative Medicine Review: A Journal of Clinical Therapeutics. Thorne Research, 90 Triangle Drive, Sandpoint ID 83864. 1-208-263-1337. Email: altmedrev@thorne.com; http://www.thorne.com

Health Freedom News. National Federation of Health. POB 688, Monrovia CA 91017.

Dr. Atkins' **Health Revelations**. Agora Health Publishing. 105 W. Monument St., Baltimore, MD 21201. http://www.atkinscenter.com.

Dr. Jonathan Wright's **Nutrition and Healing**. Publishers Mgt Corp. POB 84909, Phoenix AZ 85071. 1-800-528-0559.

Price-Pottenger Nutrition Foundation Journal. Price-Pottenger Nutrition Foundation, POB 2614, La Mesa CA 91943.

Search for Health. Valentine Communications Corporation. POB 11089, Naples FL 33941.

Second Opinion. William Campbell Douglass, M.D. Second Opinion Publishing, Inc. POB 467939, Atlanta GA 31146-7939.

The Townsend Letter for Doctors and Patients. Port Townsend WA. Order: 360-385-6021; FAX ORDER: 360-385-0699. Web: http://www.tldp.com.

What Doctors Don't Tell You. Lynne McTaggart, editor. 105 West Monument St., Baltimore MD 21201

AUDIO TAPES

Wieder, Sam. **Wake Up and Win: How To Stress-Proof Your Body and Ignite Your Energy**. Greensburg, PA: New Energy Dynamics, 1996. $19.95 + $3.00 shipping. (PA residents, add $1.20 sales tax). **Make checks payable to Sam Wieder**. Master Card/Visa/Discover. Mail orders: POB 963, Greensburg PA 15601. Phone: 724-832-7459, FAX 724-836-8606. Two cassette tapes, an hour and fifty minutes, of great practical and motivational health information, presented in a fun and dynamic way. Action Guide included.

INDEX TO SUGAR CONTROL BIBLE

Wake Up and Win

How to Stress-Proof Your Body and Ignite Your Energy

By Sam Wieder
(Dr. Jacqueline Paltis, Consulting Editor)

If you have trouble taking charge of your health, you've got to hear this tape program. Sam Wieder is one dynamic motivator!

Dr. Victor Frank, D.C., N.D.

Wake Up and Win will help you:

◆ **Stress-proof your body.**

◆ **Release tension now.**

◆ **Rejuvenate your mind and body in minutes.**

◆ **Eat to sustain vibrant health and energy.**

◆ **Stay alert and alive on high-stress workdays.**

◆ **Transform your overworked body into an energy machine.**

◆ **Discover the action steps you can take today to wake up your energy and win whatever you want most from life.**

About the Creator of Wake Up and Win

Sam Wieder is a professional trainer who teaches and empowers people to take charge of their lives. Certified as both an NLP Trainer and Environmental Stress Management Instructor, he has trained and motivated seminar audiences in the United States, Canada, and Europe.

I need Wake Up and Win. Please rush me this order.

(A 2-cassette, 112-miniute audio program with a 12-page action guide.)

$19.95 + $3.20 shipping (PA residents: Add $1.20 sales tax)

No. of Programs Ordered _____   Total Enclosed _____

Name _____ Address_____

City _____ State _____ Zip _____

Phone _____ Fax _____ E-mail _____

Credit Card Orders (Circle one.)   Visa   MasterCard   Discover

Account No. _____ Expiration Date _____

Signature _____

Send check or money order to: Sam Wieder * P.O. Box 963 * Greensburg PA 15601

Phone: 724-832-7459 * Fax: 724-836-8606   SCB

The Sugar Control Bible and Cookbook

The Complete Nutrition Guide to Revitalizing Your Health

By Dr. Jacqueline Paltis, D.C., N.D.

**Break the junk food habit
and make healthy eating a way of life.**

This easy-reference guide:

- Dispels the nutrition myths that may be making you sick and tired.
- Explains how the TBM Sugar Control Program helps restore your health.
- Presents a proven program to eliminate junk food cravings.
- Shows you how to easily adopt a healthier way of eating.
- Provides simple and gourmet recipes and menus.
- Includes tips for sticking to the program when traveling and eating out.
- Offers practical, ready-to use guidelines on how to eat for optimum health.

SINGLE COPY PRICE: $29.95

Sugar Control Bible and Cookbook Order Form

1-5 books--$29.95 each * 6-11 books--$24 each * 12-23 books--$21 each * 24+--$18 each
(U.S. Shipping: $5 first copy; add $1.50 for each additional copy.)
(PA residents: Add sales tax of 6% to total book order.)

No. of Books Ordered _____   Total Enclosed _____

Name _____ Address_____

City _____ State _____ Zip _____

Phone _____ Fax _____ E-mail _____

Credit Card Orders (Circle one.)   Visa   MasterCard   Discover

Account No. _____ Expiration Date _____

Signature _____

Send check to: Dr. Jacqueline Paltis * P.O.B. 963 * Greensburg PA 15601
Phone: 724-832-7459 * Fax: 724-838-7638

Wake Up and Win

How to Stress-Proof Your Body and Ignite Your Energy

By Sam Wieder
(Dr. Jacqueline Paltis, Consulting Editor)

If you have trouble taking charge of your health, you've got to hear this tape program. Sam Wieder is one dynamic motivator!

Dr. Victor Frank, D.C., N.D.

Wake Up and Win will help you:

◆ **Stress-proof your body.**

◆ **Release tension now.**

◆ **Rejuvenate your mind and body in minutes.**

◆ **Eat to sustain vibrant health and energy.**

◆ **Stay alert and alive on high-stress workdays.**

◆ **Transform your overworked body into an energy machine.**

◆ **Discover the action steps you can take today to wake up your energy and win whatever you want most from life.**

About the Creator of *Wake Up and Win*

Sam Wieder is a professional trainer who teaches and empowers people to take charge of their lives. Certified as both an NLP Trainer and Environmental Stress Management Instructor, he has trained and motivated seminar audiences in the United States, Canada, and Europe.

The Sugar Control Bible and Cookbook

The Complete Nutrition Guide to Revitalizing Your Health

By Dr. Jacqueline Paltis, D.C., N.D.

**Break the junk food habit
and make healthy eating a way of life.**

This easy-reference guide:

- Dispels the nutrition myths that may be making you sick and tired.
- Explains how the TBM Sugar Control Program helps restore your health.
- Presents a proven program to eliminate junk food cravings.
- Shows you how to easily adopt a healthier way of eating.
- Provides simple and gourmet recipes and menus.
- Includes tips for sticking to the program when traveling and eating out.
- Offers practical, ready-to use guidelines on how to eat for optimum health.

SINGLE COPY PRICE: $29.95

Sugar Control Bible and Cookbook Order Form

1-5 books--$29.95 each * 6-11 books--$24 each * 12-23 books--$21 each * 24+--$18 each
(U.S. Shipping: $5 first copy; add $1.50 for each additional copy.)
(PA residents: Add sales tax of 6% to total book order.)

No. of Books Ordered _____   Total Enclosed _____

Name _____ Address_____

City _____ State _____ Zip _____

Phone _____ Fax _____ E-mail _____

Credit Card Orders (Circle one.)   Visa   MasterCard   Discover

Account No. _____ Expiration Date _____

Signature _____

Send check to: Dr. Jacqueline Paltis * P.O.B. 963 * Greensburg PA 15601
Phone: 724-832-7459 * Fax: 724-838-7638